The Spiritual Person

The Spiritual Person

An Intellectual Biography of Watchman Nee

PAUL H B CHANG

OXFORD
UNIVERSITY PRESS

OXFORD
UNIVERSITY PRESS

Oxford University Press is a department of the University of Oxford.
It furthers the University's objective of excellence in research, scholarship,
and education by publishing worldwide. Oxford is a registered trade mark of
Oxford University Press in the UK and in certain other countries.

Published in the United States of America by Oxford University Press
198 Madison Avenue, New York, NY 10016, United States of America.

CIP data is on file at the Library of Congress

ISBN 9780197793626 (hbk.)
ISBN 9780197793633 (pbk.)

DOI: 10.1093/9780197793664.001.0001

Paperback printed by Marquis Book Printing, Canada
Hardback printed by Lightning Source, Inc., United States of America

The manufacturer's authorized representative in the EU for product safety is
Oxford University Press España S.A. of Parque Empresarial San Fernando de Henares,
Avenida de Castilla, 2 – 28830 Madrid (www.oup.es/en or product.safety@oup.com).
OUP España S.A. also acts as importer into Spain of products made by the manufacturer.

Contents

Introduction

A network of congregations quietly rings the globe, comprised of Christians meeting in homes and unassuming buildings, which, architecturally, often bear little resemblance to traditional "churches." A few outward characteristics are obvious. The local gatherings are of varying sizes, from twelve or thirteen to two or three thousand. Frequently, the members share meals together, often before or after services, which can be boisterous and participatory. Generally, no pastor, priest, or designated religious officiant presides. As the Spirit leads, different members stand to call hymns, declare verses from the Bible, give personal testimonies, or shout praises to God. But, for all their openness about their beliefs and their tireless attempts at outreach, it can be hard for outsiders to understand who these Christians are.

When asked, congregants readily and happily acknowledge their fellowship and unity with other like-minded groups from around the world. If asked for the name of their local church or the name of the church network as a whole, however, their answers can seem confusing, either generic and vague or surprisingly precise. An inquirer may be told that the church has no name, that it is simply named with the local city, or that it is the same church to which all Christians belong. A visitor may even be treated to an extemporaneous Bible study, explaining the naming customs of churches in the New Testament.

As it turns out, all of these individuals and congregations speak of familiar Christian doctrines with a similar accent. From Ethiopia to the Philippines, from Canada to Chile, visitors will hear talk of releasing the spirit, denying the self, and caring for the body of Christ. Furthermore, these Christians will also share the same implicit ecclesiology, which underlies their explanations for who they are and what they represent. The source of these teachings, as it turns out, is a Chinese Christian minister most members will respectfully refer to as "Brother Nee."

As a matter of fact, the ways in which these Christians discuss their cardinal beliefs and the unique practices that embody their faith can largely be traced to the influence and ideas of a single man, Watchman Nee (1903–1972). Nee was an unconventional Christian minister who spent nearly his entire life in China. His prolific writings and church leadership have left an impressive legacy. Nee has millions of followers within China and millions more in the rest of the world, putting him in rare company among Chinese thinkers. It is likely that Nee

The Spiritual Person. Paul H B Chang, Oxford University Press. © Oxford University Press 2026.
DOI: 10.1093/9780197793664.003.0001

has reached more international audiences than any other Chinese author besides Confucius, Laozi, and Mao Zedong. As a result, secular scholars, Christian admirers, and critics within and outside the church have repeatedly engaged with various aspects of his life and theology.

While scholars have often emphasized different aspects of Nee's thought, many of Nee's followers have also selectively engaged with his ideas according to their own tastes and motivations. Thus, it is fair to say that at least for some of Nee's followers, especially his earliest Chinese ones, he was mainly relevant as someone who pointed out the unscriptural nature of Western denominations and taught them that baptism should be conducted by immersion. Other followers, especially in the West, have considered Nee to basically be a teacher of individual, devotional piety, helping them to appreciate Christ more and, subsequently, to conduct their daily lives in a more holy, victorious manner.

Both of these alternatives represent common, incomplete understandings of Nee's work. Certainly, one of the reasons for his writing's long-lasting, broad-based appeal is its ability to be distilled into such readily accessible forms. If the fact that Nee's thoughts can be reduced to simple slogans helps to explain the breadth of his audience. It is necessary, however, to delve into his work as a whole to understand the depth of some of his followers' loyalty.

Minimal or partial interpretations of Nee's work have stood, in part, simply because there is so little consensus about whether Nee's work even has a center, much less what that center might be. Certainly, Nee wandered over a vast, heterogeneous terrain. This was to be expected, since most of his works were addressed to specific questions, persons, and situations. He also had the preacher's gift of making his topic of the moment seem crucially important or relevant, which means that, without context, a partial reading of his works might convince a reader that any one of a number of themes, ideas, or practices was Nee's central concern or hermeneutic.

There is a well-known Chinese tradition of the "sage presenting as an ordinary person" or "not allowing the real person to show" (zhenren bu louxiang). Nee certainly exemplified this aspect of his own culture. Any attempts to recreate the person at the center of Nee's story must rely heavily on the rare instances in which Nee or one of his associates was willing to talk about his personal life, history, and disposition. He said almost nothing about his personal life: for instance, his relationships with his wife and with his family. But he spoke at length about selective personal experiences in order to mine them for illustrative anecdotes, usually in the context of spiritual lessons learned, and it is possible to extrapolate from these sparse materials to create a picture of his life.

Raised in a household that was dominated by the forceful personality of his mother, Nee was alternately swept up in the great cause of national salvation and the quotidian pleasures of bourgeois life. He enjoyed fine clothes, lottery tickets, and movies. The dream he guarded most closely in his heart, however, was to gain glory in the literary sphere. Swept up in the promise and disappointment that surrounded the new Chinese cultural movements of May 4th, Nee hoped that his writings would awaken China and restore its domestic unity and international prestige. Christianity had no part in his plans for the future. In any case, the religion was rapidly and dramatically falling out of favor among educated young Chinese as a "Western religion" that was complicit with Western nationalism and imperial domination.

In a surprising turn of events, however, Nee's own mother experienced a dramatic conversion, and he, too, came to embrace Christianity. The Western religion that had been so easy to dismiss became an intensely personal and intimate affair. Casting aside his dreams of literary glory and national influence, Nee spent his days as a local preacher, working with other Christian classmates to spark a revival in his school and city. His background and training were not so easily suppressed, however, and one of the ways he distinguished himself from his fellows was in his early decision to begin a periodical. Throughout the rest of his life and career, he would be continuously engaged in some kind of literary production, and he may have gained a wider audience as a Christian than he would have as a secular commentator.

Even as a young man, barely out of his teenage years, his Chinese prose was written with an impressive eloquence and confidence. His deft but understandable biblical exegesis soon convinced hundreds and then thousands of Chinese Christians that he understood the Bible better than even the distinguished theologians and spiritual teachers from the West. As he covered topics from daily devotional practice to church administration with his unique theological perspective, his followers began to form congregations with a distinct group identity. Nee visited them, invited them to conferences, and trained their leaders personally. For almost thirty years, his personal biography and his leadership of these Chinese churches have been closely intertwined. Soon after the victory of the Chinese Communist Party (CCP), however, Nee was imprisoned as part of the Party's attempts to consolidate its control over society. He would stay in prison for the next twenty years until his death.

It is important to know these bare, biographical facts of Nee's life, but they cannot explain the mysteries of his popularity and enduring appeal. What was the relationship between Nee's life and his writings? How and why did a young, Chinese Christian with no formal theological education create such a complex theological system? And of course, what exactly did Nee teach that captivated so many varied audiences?

The main project of this book is to engage Nee's writings in their original languages and contexts to define the content of Nee's voluminous and eclectic intellectual output. In terms of genre alone, the more than sixty volumes of

Nee's collected works include magazines and newsletters, messages to general audiences, intimate trainings of trusted colleagues, long and short monographs on specific themes, translations of important foreign language materials, biblical exegeses, manuals for church organization, and various catechetical curricula. His topics were just as varied, covering a vast array of theological issues, biblical themes, and practical advice.

Furthermore, Nee was never a systematic or academic theologian. His material was always meant for living congregations and everyday Christians. His claims and terminology are not entirely consistent, and he frequently writes in a somewhat repetitive, didactic style that circles back to the same question from different angles. These repetitions may occur multiple times in the same paragraph or in different texts over many years, with variations of differing significance.

All this is to say that, like the parable of the elephant and the blind people, different people may depict Watchman Nee's writing in many ways. And yet, Nee's message was not entirely chaotic or inconsistent. After all, his followers have created a tightly knit, growing fellowship of thousands of congregations, which is more socially and ideologically cohesive than many denominations. They have also persisted in perpetuating his teachings for over seventy years since his imprisonment and fifty years since his death. Beyond these followers are millions more who may have never joined a local assembly, or any Christian church at all, but who have found Nee's words to be inspiring or important.

This book argues that Nee drew from various traditions of Christian theology to create a comprehensive theological system that proved to be attractive in the Chinese society of his day and adaptable to many other contexts and cultures. His theology made universal claims about the possibility of human transcendence and grounded these claims in concrete local communities. This potent combination of the aspirational and practical was communicated as Christian devotional literature, a popular genre aimed at a mass audience, with the shared assumption that the Bible was authoritative and a shared discourse that could be described as evangelical, Pentecostal, and charismatic.

Nee claimed that the Bible consistently taught that the human spirit (Chinese: *ling,* 靈) was distinct from the human soul (Chinese: *hun,* 魂). According to Nee, although the human soul and body had been corrupted, God had reserved the human spirit as a point of unity with the divine, allowing believers to follow the flow of the divine life, to effortlessly please God, and to experience spontaneous victory over sin. Nee depicted the endpoint of this spiritual journey as a pro-social pliability, a willingness to serve and an inability to be offended, which would help Christians to flourish in local congregations.

The church was the other major concern of Nee's theology, and it was tightly tied to his teachings on individual holiness. Nee suggested that God had biblically set the boundaries of the church to those of the city, so that each city should have only one church, under one leadership. Large cities could, of course, end up having multiple places of meeting and worship scattered throughout the city. Still, Nee placed great importance on the city limits as a practical parameter. Such limits would force all the Christians living in that city to learn how to live together peaceably and love one another. They could not form another congregation or hide behind their theoretical love for other Christians far away. Instead, Nee taught that they had to stay where God had placed them and find spiritual resources to solve any interpersonal problems.

The two aspects of Nee's theology thus depended on one another. Nee believed that observing God's restrictions for the church would force individual Christians to learn to follow Christ. Simultaneously, Nee argued that spiritual maturity would lead to more love and unity in daily Christian life, since the end goal of spirituality was the church as the body of Christ. Finally, Nee mapped these teachings onto a cosmic timeline, wherein the church's final victory would occasion Christ's second coming, with a special reward to all the faithful Christians who had achieved spiritual maturity.[1] While Nee's eschatological language appealed to certain strands of popular Protestant beliefs, his insistence that the end goal of God's plan was the church, and his repeated injunctions about the importance of ecclesial unity, reached deep into the catholic tradition.

This book traces the steps by which Nee formulated this distinct message by paying close attention to his publications. Of particular interest is the way in which Nee developed his ideas in conversation with twentieth-century Chinese society and the history of Christian thought. In service of such a project, this book joins a significant and growing group of historians, theologians, and area specialists, many of whom have explored Nee's work and who have illuminated the surprising connections between contemporary China and Christian discourses, practices, and institutions.

Watchman Nee and Modern China

The earliest and largest group of Nee scholars was most interested in his teachings for their Christian content. Their works may contain a few biographical notes to relate the general facts of Nee's life, but otherwise, they simply

---

[1] Grant Wacker sees early Pentecostal movements as being impelled by a similar combination of pragmatism and the supernatural, or transcendent. Nee did not promote charismatic gifts like speaking in tongues, but he shared the Pentecostals' mutual heritage of fundamentalist and holiness traditions. Imminent, Adventist eschatology was also a common theme between Nee and the Pentecostals. Grant Wacker, *Heaven Below: Early Pentecostals and American Culture* (Cambridge, MA: Harvard University Press, 2001).

take Nee's Christianity for granted while ignoring his Chinese context. Most of these studies have approached Nee's writings from Christian, confessional perspectives and have focused on one aspect or another of his voluminous oeuvre as if they were standard academic or theological writings produced at a university, without regard to China or Nee's particular historical context. Many of these scholarly works were completed in the 1960s, 1970s, and 1980s, when Nee's works reached what was probably their highest circulation in Europe and North America.[2]

More recently, scholars operating from more secular or ecumenical perspectives have also begun to pay closer attention to Nee, using broader frameworks of research. These have tended to see Nee as participating in larger currents of Chinese religion. Thus, historian Lian Xi has emphasized the common elements between modern Chinese Christians, including Nee, and indigenous Chinese religious traditions. In particular, Lian highlights their shared apocalyptic and millenarian themes.[3] Meanwhile, theologian Alexander Chow has suggested that Nee propounded a fundamentalist or legalistic theology, while also reflecting a particularly Chinese interest in the unity between heaven and humanity.[4]

A third group of recent scholars has similarly paid attention to Nee's Chinese context but has come to the conclusion that Nee stood almost entirely aloof from larger trends in Chinese society and history. According to historian Daniel Bays, "In 1926–1927, at the height of national political drama in the 'Nationalist revolution', Nee barely paid attention. He was busy refining some of his basic ideas, applying the fruits of extended reading in works of the mystic Jessie Penn-Lewis and, holed up in Shanghai, writing the longest book he ever wrote, *The Spiritual Man*."[5] Similarly, Sinologist and theologian Chloë Starr suggests that

---

[2] This work is voluminous and remains mostly unpublished, in the form of PhD dissertations and Master's theses. Just a few examples in alphabetical order by surname include Marc Barthélémy, "De l'anthropologie à l'éthique: la pensée de Watchman Nee" (Master's thesis, Faculté Autonome de Théologie Protestante, 1999); William Clyde Bassett, "The Formulation of a Basis for Counseling from a Christian Theory of Personality as Represented by C. S. Lewis and Watchman Nee" (EdD diss., University of Arkansas, 1976); Olivier Baudraz, "De la Sanctification selon Watchman Nee: Une analyse de son anthropologie et de sa soteriologie" (Master's thesis, La Faculté Libre de Théologie Réformée d'Aix-en-Provence, 1984); Jonathan T'ien-en Chao, "The Chinese Indigenous Church Movement, 1919–1927: A Protestant Response to the Anti-Christian Movements in Modern China" (PhD diss., University of Pennsylvania, 1986); James Mo-Oi Cheung, "The Ecclesiology of the 'Little Flock' of China Founded by Watchman Nee" (Master's thesis, Trinity Evangelical Divinity School, 1966); Norman Howard Cliff, "The Life and Theology of Watchman Nee, Including a Study of the Little Flock Movement Which He Founded" (Master's thesis, Open University, 1983). For more examples, see the chapters by me (as Zhang Hanbang), Zhou Fuchu, and Li Junhui in *Busi jiu busheng* (Taipei: Olive CCLM Press, 2011), 244–266, 360–392.

[3] Lian Xi, *Redeemed by Fire: The Rise of Popular Christianity in Modern China* (New Haven: Yale University Press, 2010).

[4] Alexander Chow, *Theosis, Sino-Christian Theology and the Second Chinese Enlightenment: Heaven and Humanity in Unity* (London: Palgrave Macmillan, 2013).

[5] Daniel Bays, *A New History of Christianity in China* (Malden, MA: Wiley-Blackwell, 2012), 132–133.

Nee's writings assume "a universal truth and universally applicable Christianity." His writings "are peppered with Chinese examples and cases, but he uses these primarily to illustrate Christian truths, rather than to determine them." She adds, "If we were to strip Ni Tuosheng's [Watchman Nee's] Chinese examples away, his point would almost always still stand," in contrast to other Chinese Christians for whom the "particular lens or narrative frame" of the Chinese "literary or philosophical traditions" and "social environment" were more directly relevant.[6]

This book acknowledges the strengths of this previous scholarship while taking a new approach. On one hand, even though Watchman Nee lived in Republican China, it is clear that he rejected appeals to both traditional and contemporary Chinese literature, philosophy, politics, and society. He was a Chinese citizen, writing Christian literature in elegant, modern Chinese, but his works fundamentally depended on "universal truth and universally applicable Christianity"—a key reason his writings have so successfully crossed cultural and linguistic boundaries for decades. On the other hand, Nee's refusal to draw from his Chinese heritage and environment was especially significant *in his Chinese context.*

In this Chinese context, Nee's life spanned a crucial stretch of modern history. Nee was born under the Qing Empire, lived in the Republic of China, and spent the final decades of his life as a citizen of the People's Republic of China. From birth to death, Nee's life and social environment were dominated by the same cultural and political forces that led to the emergence of modern China, that is, the Chinese people's attempts to define themselves as a nation.

At the time of Nee's birth, the Qing Dynasty was on its last legs. It had proven itself unable to deal with foreign powers during the age of colonialism and had repeatedly lost armed conflicts, resulting in painful concessions and unequal treaties. Domestically, the Qing were also threatened by rising sentiments of ethnic nationalism. The Dynasty's rulers were of the ethnic minority known as the Manchus, ruling over a country that was over 90 percent ethnically Han. By 1911, the various threats to the state had culminated in what has come to be known as the Xinhai Revolution, in which key Chinese military units and provincial leaders quickly declared independence from the Qing, resulting in the abdication of the Emperor and the formation of a republic.

In the Republican Period that followed, the struggle for national salvation loomed over society and culture. Although it was now ostensibly a modern republic, China was internally fractured and the Chinese continued to negotiate from a position of weakness relative to the foreign colonial powers. Especially

[6] Chloë Starr, *Chinese Theology: Text and Context* (New Haven, CT: Yale University Press, 2016), 4–5.

for young Chinese people who were educated and informed, it seemed that their country was in a desperate situation. As a young native of Fuzhou, with a prestigious missionary education, Nee was in a prime position to take his place in the ensuing national drama. Many of his peers and coevals would play key roles on the public stage, shaping the future of the Chinese government and culture. Given these commitments, Nee's rejection of China as a "particular lens or narrative frame" and his general denial of Chinese "literary or philosophical traditions" were choices that were rich with significance, both in terms of his personal biography and as a signal that could be readily understood by his Chinese audiences and communities.

Nee's stand in this case paralleled that of Wei Enbo (1879–1919), the founder of the True Jesus Church, who also refused to participate in the patriotic currents of the age. Although Nee and Enbo formulated very different systems, both were attempts at "restoring Christ's original church and a timeless Christian authenticity transcending nationality."[7] By forgoing partisan leanings, both men tried to claim moral authority over Christians who allowed themselves to be co-opted by the affairs of state. It was exactly as a counter-cultural current to the dominance of political and nationalistic rhetoric that such claims maintained their most trenchant edge.

This context helps explain Nee's intense concern for preserving the Holy Spirit and the human spirit as guarantors of purity and holiness. Contrary to what other scholars have argued, it was not the case that Nee "barely paid attention" to the "national political drama" around him. Although he did not directly comment on political issues, his theology was specifically tailored to offer a spiritual alternative to the super-charged political atmosphere around him. From the moment of his conversion to the end of his life, Nee insisted on the possibility of a spiritual sphere separate from the compromises of earthly culture and politics. This basic preoccupation consistently explains Nee's own theological insights, his criteria for judging Western Christianity, and the complicated negotiations he made when the CCP finally forced him to confront the political ramifications of his "spirituality beyond politics."

Nee's selective use of Western sources also reflected his Chinese context. Chinese citizens often paired the quest for national salvation with a fierce resentment against Western incursions. Chinese Christians had to fight off bitter accusations that they were foreign lapdogs, collaborating with imperialists in a foreign religion. In such a context, it may seem odd that Nee chose to learn from Westerners at all, but, in fact, they gave him access to some of the most subtle and

---

[7] Melissa Inouye, *China and the True Jesus: Charisma and Organization in a Chinese Christian Church* (Oxford: Oxford University Press, 2018), 109.

scathing critiques of Western Christianity—those lodged from within the tradition itself.

Nee's theology was heavily indebted to two Western traditions, the Plymouth Brethren and the Keswick Convention,[8] two of the most self-critical strands of Western Christianity. Brethren ecclesiology indicted virtually all Western Christian churches, denominations, and associations (even, to some extent, their own) for their divisiveness, artificiality, political connections, and independence from God. The Keswick teachers spoke positively about the possibility of holiness and victory, but the basis of their theology was the assumption that almost no Western Christians were living up to the biblical standard of holiness.

Nee's use of these two traditions thus amounted to an attempt to de-Westernize Christianity using tools acquired and developed from the West itself. By applying the Brethren and Keswick critiques carefully, Nee believed he could strip away the illegitimate accretions of Western church practices and hold Christians to a higher standard of moral behavior. While this was not anti-imperialism in a political sense, it was still a bold claim. Nee purported to be following a more universal, pure, and holy version of Christianity than that practiced by the vast majority of Western Christians. Following the Brethren and Keswick writers, however, Nee claimed that his new vision of Christianity was not an attempt at one upmanship or establishing superiority, but for the uplift and benefit of the whole church of God.

Furthermore, in his desire to conduct a root and branch reform of the church, Nee mirrored another aspect of his modern Chinese context. China's twentieth century was an age of radical solutions, where the urgency of national humiliation spurred audacious attempts to overthrow or remake ancient institutions. The most successful of these attempts was pioneered by a group of Chinese inspired and guided by Soviet Communists in the aftermath of the successful Russian Revolution of 1917. At the outset, the CCP made common cause with the Chinese Nationalist Party, or Guomindang (GMD). With an authoritarian military leader in Chiang Kai-shek (Jiang Jieshi), the GMD emerged victorious as the leading power in China, and it soon consolidated its power by purging the Communists from its ranks.

The CCP that survived the purge was, by necessity, more focused on rural China, where the GMD's grip on power was weakest. The CCP's own emerging

---

[8] The Plymouth Brethren were restorationist movement that began in the United Kingdom in the early nineteenth century and that continues throughout the world today, most notably in Anglophone countries. The Keswick Convention is an annual conference that also continues to be held today and still has its devotees and followers, once again, primarily in Anglo-American evangelicalism. Nee was not especially indebted to Keswick theology nor to Keswick as a "school" of thought, but only to a specific, small group teachers and writers who were related to each other and to the Convention, even if those relationships could sometimes be distant and strained. For lack of a better unifying principle, calling them Keswick teachers or thinkers will suffice.

leader, Mao Zedong, had been an early proponent of mobilizing the peasant masses, and his adaptations of Communist thought proved to be more consistent, inspiring, and thoroughgoing than the GMD's vague alternatives—the fascist "New Life" movement and a cult of personality centered on Chiang. Throughout the vicissitudes of the Republican Era, the CCP continued to build its strength by offering the Chinese a relatively clear blueprint for national salvation, that is, a tightly organized party operating under a single ideological vision, leading the masses toward liberation.

While other educated Chinese worked toward socio-political rejuvenation, Nee channeled his energies toward a spiritual revolution. Nee did not become a champion of China, but he was a champion of the idea that the Chinese, too, could engage in demanding forms of the Christian tradition. They could live rigorous lives of self-denial, forsaking their natural inclinations, preferences, and human affections, representing God in unified, holy congregations that pointed toward the truth of the mystical body of Christ. If Nee believed that this testimony was lacking in the West, he was confident that it could be vibrantly represented in China.

By positioning himself in this way, Nee opened up a significant space for the Chinese to become serious, devoted Christians while escaping the ignominy of association with the West. Those Chinese who followed Nee maintained especially strong links to certain parts of the Western tradition. They prided themselves, however, on taking these elevated claims of the Christian tradition more seriously and following them more exactly than most of the Westerners themselves. In so doing, they understood themselves to be returning to the unadulterated practice of New Testament simplicity. They aspired to become more biblical than Western fundamentalists and more spiritual than Western mystics.

Of course, such a position contains an inherent check. It would "work" only so long as the claimants continued in genuine purity. Nee's followers may have been initially attracted to the example of a Chinese leader who could out-Christianize the missionaries, but they understood that in the long term, they were being asked to strip away their own chauvinism and to care only for a transcendent Christ, discarding their parochial preferences in favor of the universal church. Ironically, neither Nee nor his followers described his thought as particularly "Chinese" in any way. Nee's system only made sense and retained its vibrancy inasmuch as Nee was *not* seen to be particularly beholden either to Chinese society or to Chinese thought. Paradoxically, it seemed that Nee could only be a viable representative of a living tradition of Chinese thought to the extent that he shunned the specifically *Chinese* character of that thought. His followers believed that he offered an escape from being defined merely as Chinese—they could instead be the spiritual people of God.

This paradox also characterized Nee's relationship with other Chinese religions and philosophies. There are many ways in which Nee's patterns of ideas and behaviors seem obviously Chinese: He knew and read some of the Chinese classics; he kept abreast of political developments and adapted to them; and, later in life, he read Marx and studied Communism. Nevertheless, he rarely spoke of Chinese thought, whether classical or contemporary, except to contrast it disparagingly with the truth of the Christian Bible.

Even the ostensible rejection of Chinese religion, however, can be read as a feature of Republican China. Throughout the Republican Period, "superstitious" elements within Confucianism, Daoism, Buddhism, and other indigenous traditions were under strenuous attack by both religious reformers and atheists.[9] The most prominent legacy of this skepticism is the CCP's embrace of Marxist philosophical materialism. Thus, Nee's open hostility toward Chinese religion was one way in which his inclinations accorded with the mainstream attitudes of the educated class in his contemporary society.

Theologian Andrew Walls has argued that Christianity's relationship to culture can be understood in terms of two seemingly contradictory principles. The pilgrim principle denies that any human culture can fully manifest the divine, since all Christians are but "pilgrims" in time and space. Conversely, the indigenizing principle affirms that all human cultures can be a home for the gospel, in keeping with the traditional theology of incarnation in which God is taken to have fully become a human being in Palestine at the start of the Common Era.[10] While the pilgrim principle pushes Christians to reject human culture when it is unfaithful to the Christian standard, the indigenizing principle urges Christians to embrace human culture when it follows the truth.

Nee adhered to the pilgrim principle: He never credited any Chinese religious traditions for influencing his thought. His entire theological project was predicated upon the possibility that spiritual insight could flow directly from God, untainted by any contingent cultural element. Nevertheless, even though any hint of syncretism was deeply antithetical to Nee, his holiness- and purity-fixated theology also demonstrates the indigenizing principle: His work paralleled Chinese thought, and he likely would have conceded, at the very least, that some Chinese religio-philosophical traditions had created systems based on the universal truths that were best and most clearly revealed in the Bible.

At a high level of abstraction, there were crucial similarities between Nee's theology and some forms of Chinese thought. Just as some strands of Chinese

[9] See, for instance, Rebecca Nedostup, *Superstitious Regimes: Religion and the Politics of Modernity* (Cambridge, MA: Harvard University Asia Center, 2010) and Vincent Goossaert and David Palmer, *The Religious Question in Modern China* (Chicago: University of Chicago Press, 2011).
[10] Andrew F. Walls, *The Missionary Movement in Christian History: Studies in the Transmission of Faith* (Maryknoll, NY: Orbis Books, 2007), 7–9.

Buddhism are characterized by a holistic denial of difference,[11] Nee's theology denies that human perceptions of the distinctions between good and evil and true and false have ontological reality. Nee argued that the more meaningful distinction was between the eternal things of the spirit and the delusions of the independent human soul. Nee also seems to have been subtly influenced by Confucianism's emphasis on hierarchy, social reciprocity, and harmonious relationships, which elevated the group as opposed to the individual.[12] On a theoretical level, Nee valorized congregational life as a part of the mystical body of Christ, the goal of God's plan. On a practical level, Nee spent much time thinking about biblical models for authority and offices. Those who followed his ecclesiology invariably formed tight-knit groups of common life, not only meeting together for worship once a week, but offering mutual support and often even living in close proximity to share their Christian lives together. Historian Grace May has suggested that Nee might have been trying to replicate his ideal of the family life in the church.[13]

Furthermore, at least two very specific patterns recur in both Nee's teachings and Chinese religions. Firstly, Nee's Christian morality was often expressed in terms of a natural or spontaneous ability to follow God's will, a concept that has much in common with both the Daoist depiction of *wuwei* and the Confucian ideal of a sage. Secondly, Nee underlined the distinction between soul and spirit to discuss the illegitimacy of what he called the self. Nee defined this self as the sin-corrupted soul, holding on to its own identity, acting out of its own motives, independent from God. For Nee, this self was entirely problematic, something that would have to be overcome and denied on the path to spiritual maturity. This teaching had significant similarities to the Buddhist teaching of *anatta*, or "non-self," the belief that the self does not actually exist and that people's misconceptions about the self are an obstacle on the way to enlightenment.[14]

One other way in which Nee's life and work can be related to his Chinese context is subtle but inescapable. Nee's literary Chinese style is beautiful, clean, and simple—devoid of rococo stylings or flashy displays of learning. It is easy to overlook this fact because Nee's work so often appears in translation and its original simplicity lends itself easily to fluid translations. Nevertheless, Nee's oeuvre constitutes a significant contribution to Christian communication in what was

[11] An excellent exploration of some of these forms of holism can be found in Brook Ziporyn, *Evil and/or/as The Good*.

[12] This cultural distinction has been termed "collectivism" by psychologists, for instance, in H. C. Triandis, R. Bontempo, M. J. Villareal, M. Asai, and N. Lucca, "Individualism and Collectivism: Cross-cultural Perspectives on Self-ingroup Relationships," *Journal of Personality and Social Psychology* 54 (1988): 323–338.

[13] Grace Y. May, "Watchman Nee and the Breaking of Bread: The Missiological and Spiritual Forces That Contributed to an Indigenous Chinese Ecclesiology" (PhD Diss., Boston University, 2000).

[14] Peter Harvey, *An Introduction to Buddhism: Teachings, History and Practices* (Cambridge: Cambridge University Press, 2013), 57–62.

the emerging *baihua* or written vernacular style.[15] This book has sometimes opted for more literal, even wooden translations to convey fidelity to the original ideas and also to remind readers that these are, in the end, almost all translations.

Finally, Nee's debt to his Chinese context can be seen in his direct interactions with the CCP. As the CCP victory became increasingly apparent, Nee began to discuss economic themes, encouraging his followers to share their resources, hold property in common, and work in the rural countryside, all popular Communist ideas. After the liberation, the CCP moved to consolidate its monopoly of power over civil society. The party engaged in a series of social movements, designed to undercut alternative sources of authority ranging from private business to religion. As pressures mounted on Nee and other leaders, he responded by thinking deeply about the relationship between politics and Christian theology, formulating a synthesis that bridged the demands of the secular and spiritual as much as he thought possible. He was condemned and jailed anyway, but even Nee's behavior in prison exemplified his beliefs about authority and the limits of Christian obedience.

Watchman Nee and the History of Christian Thought

Watchman Nee's work must also be understood as part of the history of Christian thought, the long tradition of Christian writing and theologizing that extended from the earliest New Testament documents to the present day. In Nee's own self-understanding, his writing was directed both toward the congregations that followed him and to a conversation among the biblical scholars, devotional writers, and theologians he most respected. Even Nee's desire to contribute to this global discourse situates him in his particular time and place.

Historian Frank Dikötter has suggested that in Nee's China, "there were literally tens of thousands of creative individuals who were at the top of their fields, fully clued up with the rest of the world" and that these Chinese were all making respected, international-level contributions to pursuits ranging from astrophysics to jazz.[16] Like them, Watchman Nee was well "clued up" with contemporary Christian writers at the cutting edge of a variety of traditions. Like his fellow Republican citizens, Nee would make important interventions that advanced an international conversation, not as a passive recipient under colonial tutelage, but as an equal, with fresh insights and contributions of his own. Both the immediate impact and the continuing popularity of his work in these circles stand as

---

[15] Occasionally, Nee used the older, literary *wenyan* style in his early writings, but the vast majority of his work was in the more accessible *baihua*. Even Nee's ability to make this transition has rarely received comment.

[16] Frank Dikötter, *The Age of Openness* (Berkeley: University of California Press, 2008), 61.

important examples of China's growing engagement with the world and of Nee's unique voice in the Christian tradition.

This book is structured chronologically with special attention to the development of Nee's contributions to Christian theology. The first chapter of this book covers Nee's family background, his initial Christian conversion, his preoccupation with purity and holiness, and his tendency toward absoluteness, an unwillingness to compromise that was characteristic of his thought in general. Chapter 2 delves into Nee's first years as a Christian in Fuzhou, his interactions with Margaret Barber, an English missionary, and the development of his concept of "local churches." The third chapter, which covers the years following Nee's exodus from Fuzhou, examines the spread of his theology throughout China and Southeast Asia and the publication of his book *The Spiritual Person*, the most extensive and systematic of all his works and a significant, new contribution to the history of Christian thought. Chapter 4 begins after Nee's miraculous recovery from tuberculosis and covers the so-called Nanjing Decade, a period of relative social and political stability for most Chinese. Nee and his followers took advantage of this period to create a network of local churches that stretched across China and maintained a strong sense of group identity. Intellectually, Nee became the main proponent for an otherwise almost forgotten Protestant teaching concerning the possibility of Christian reward and punishment after death. He also created a more optimistic timeline for the Second Coming, identifying "the overcomers" as a group who would attain victory on behalf of the whole church, allowing Christ to return triumphantly, rather than in shame. Chapter 5 covers Nee's trip to the West, his return to war-torn China, his temporary excommunication by the elders of the church in Shanghai, and the development of his definition of spiritual maturity as "brokenness" or "pliability"—an intensely pro-social virtue that indicated an absolute humility, an inability to be offended, and the ability to work positively even with the most difficult of partners. Finally, Chapter 6 describes Nee's interactions with the CCP, his arrest, and his defense of a deeply compliant model of Christian behavior. Submissive to the end, Nee claimed to have "maintained his joy" until his death in prison.

Nee's rich theological legacy continues to inform contemporary global Christianities. The Conclusion of this book offers insights into the institutions that explicitly claim Nee as a founder, the wider publication history of his works, and the effect of his modified versions of Brethren ecclesiology and Keswick spirituality on world Christianity today. In the midst of some of the most dynamically fractious, rapidly self-propagating movements in Christian history, in which personal revelation and spiritual gifts are exuberantly practiced, his voice continues to be heard in a note of caution, a yearning for the ideal, spiritual unity of the church, and in a focus on the spirit, the cross, and victory marked by self-denial.

Nee's interventions in Christian thought have often caused controversy. Like members of the Brethren and the Keswick movement, Nee often made unfavorable judgments of other Christians, and at times, his language with regard to other Christians bordered on the incendiary. In his discussions on the Book of Revelation, he agreed with the Brethren that the Roman Catholic Church is the "great harlot" and that Protestant denominations are the "daughters of the harlot."[17] His rhetoric preserved the distinction between individual Christians, who deserved fervent love as genuine members of the household of the faith, and religious systems, but his explosive language, inspired by the Book of Revelation, demonstrated his disappointment at the persistence of Christian institutions that he felt stood in the way of true unity.

As the language of harlotry suggests, Nee's handling of gender has also been controversial. Nee's most influential co-workers were women (Ruth Li and Peace Wang), and it is possible to delineate almost the whole of Nee's biography as a series of successive interventions by women he held to be spiritual authorities. Nevertheless, in keeping with his attempt to maintain both literal adherence to biblical practices and his understanding of the importance of submission, Nee and his followers were known for their observance of head-covering for women as a sign of women's submission to men. While such head-covering was never enforced, it was widely practiced and was emblematic of a larger, fundamentalist cosmology of gender, in which male and female were seen as reflections of God and humanity. Nee found such connections fascinating, writing long commentaries on the Song of Songs, the Bible's premier poetic romance.[18]

This particular work has chosen to translate Nee's writings in gender-neutral language when appropriate. The most notable example of this is probably in regard to Nee's work, *The Spiritual Person*. The Chinese character Nee uses, *ren*, does not have an inherent gender, and so I have overturned decades of tradition to render the word more accurately as "person" or "human" in contemporary English.

Nee's writings on authority are yet another source of controversy. Especially given Nee's penchant for absoluteness, the book *Authority and Submission* can be read as a warrant for authoritarianism. Nee actually spends much of the book curtailing the boundaries of religious and secular authority, but taken out of context, his statements can sound categorical and could be used to justify abuse. Especially when coupled with Nee's criticisms of other Christian groups, it is no surprise that Nee's followers have often had a reputation for being sectarian and cloistered.

---

[17] See, for instance, Watchman Nee, NTSWJ volumes 4, 5, and 47.
[18] Although the book is quoted throughout his works, Nee, NTSWJ 23, offers an extended example of his exegesis on the topic.

The potentially negative consequences of this tendency may be intensified by a feature of contemporary Chinese religion. Historian David Ownby has described a broad swathe of Chinese traditions with the following: "At the most fundamental level, many of these groups appear to have been organized by and around charismatic masters, who generally claim independence from other recognized religions (or 'cultivation systems') and from one another."[19] The nearly universal importance of "charismatic masters" has meant that in some cases, Nee's own life story, personal ideas, and writings have taken on an outsized significance. For many of Nee's followers, the virtue of their "master" is an important component in their own religious identity and self-understanding, sometimes veering uncomfortably close to a cult of personality.

Still, if some of Nee's followers portrayed him as the archetype of the "charismatic master" who led them to salvation, Nee himself tried to guard against their excesses. He spoke forcefully against the danger of following human beings, writing that "the church should not be controlled by human wills, it should be led directly by the Holy Spirit."[20] Similarly, he inveighed against the clerical system because it meant that some "servants have been placed on a high pedestal and have been assigned the oversight of a congregation or a chapel."[21] Nee thus welcomed his own defamation and was upset when his followers treated him with special deference.[22] His writings reveal that he exercised far less control over his fellow co-workers and elders than did many other Christian leaders. For instance, on the eve of the Second Sino-Japanese War, he strongly urged his co-workers to evangelize the rural, inland regions of China, but the repetition of these exhortations and their vague nature suggest that his followers were free to ignore or interpret his advice as they pleased.

Additional Notes on Names, Sources, and Translations

One of the difficulties of writing about Nee and his followers is his refusal to attach a name to the congregations that followed his ministry. As was the case for so much of his thought, his wariness about names had both Western and Chinese antecedents. The Plymouth Brethren had also refused to adopt a name for themselves, seeing extra-biblical names as one root of sectarianism, and the significance of proper names is one of the enduring themes of Chinese philosophy.

---

[19] David Ownby, *Falun Gong and the Future of China* (Oxford: Oxford University Press, 2008), 26.
[20] NTSWJ 11, 157.
[21] CWWN 4, 396–397.
[22] CWWN 42, 447–448; CWWN 61, 51–52.

Although Chinese thinkers have disagreed on the desirability of ascertaining correct names and have also differed in their opinions concerning how accurately names reflect things, they have generally agreed that names are important means for maintaining social order and control.

Thus, one of Nee and his followers' contributions to the ongoing development of the Christian tradition is their persistent resistance to the adoption of any name beyond Christ and Christian. In English, they often refer to themselves in the lower case as the "church in Los Angeles," or the "church in London," insisting that they have no proper name. Nevertheless, as Nee's followers took on an increasingly distinctive and cohesive identity, outsiders began to refer to them with different names such as the "Christian Assembly" (*Jidutu Jiaohui*) and the "Little Flock" (*Xiao Qun*).

These were two of the earliest names by which Nee's followers were known. Both were based on his early publications. Nee first made a name for himself during the mid-1920s with a periodical called *The Christian*, which was disseminated throughout China. In Chinese, the term "Christian" in Christian Assembly is not an adjective but a noun, as in "the Christian." In the mid-1930s, as his Shanghai congregation grew, he printed a hymnal that took its name from a Brethren publication, *Hymns for the Little Flock*.

The fact that Nee and his followers used different terminology from most Christians to refer to their houses of worship (since they insisted that "the church" referred only to people) gave rise to another moniker, the "Assembly Hall" or "Meeting Place" (*Juhuisuo* or *Juhuichu*). This nondescript naming custom also followed Brethren traditions. Today, Nee's followers within China are primarily known as the Little Flock and the Assembly Hall.

While recognizing that Nee and his followers would prefer no name at all, for ease of reference, this work will use all three names with capital letters, as is customary for proper nouns in English. Thus, especially in the later chapters when Nee's followers began to crystallize around a distinct identity, this book will refer to the group interchangeably as the Christian Assembly, the Little Flock, and the Assembly Hall. Similarly, although the Christian Assembly saw itself as being no more than a faithful manifestation of the one, true church, this book will employ terms such as fellowship, network, or movement to describe the international phenomenon.

This book relies heavily on the Chinese and English compilations of Nee's works. These are, respectively, the *Ni Tuosheng Wenji*, henceforth referred to as NTSWJ, and the *Collected Works of Watchman Nee*, henceforth referred to as CWWN. When, as in the vast majority of cases, Chinese was the language of Nee's original speech or writing, the NTSWJ will be used. I have supplied my own translations into English. In a few cases, Nee spoke or wrote in English, and in those cases, the CWWN has been preferred. For a more detailed discussion of my evaluation of these sources, see the Appendix.

Finally, the biblical citations in this book are my own translations from the biblical Hebrew and Greek. I have attempted to re-create in English what I have understood Nee to be trying to do in Chinese, since Nee was also a capable student of the original biblical languages.

1

A Christian Conversion
in Republican China

The history of Christians in China reaches back at least to the seventh century, when Christians from the Syriac Church of the East arrived and eventually established flourishing congregations with a developed hierarchy. There were hints and legends, however, of even earlier missions, the most ancient of which was attributed to Thomas, one of Jesus's twelve original disciples. In any case, historical records suggest that both Syriac and Roman Catholic Christians were at work in China during the thirteenth and fourteenth centuries under the rule of the Mongol-led Yuan Dynasty. Despite all these efforts, none of these early attempts resulted in lasting Christian communities that could trace their lineages through the intervening centuries.

The permanent presence of Christians in China began with the Roman Catholics who arrived in the sixteenth century, during the European age of exploration. This time, Catholic missionaries succeeded in gaining a significant base of native converts, who were able to maintain the faith even after a period in which the Qing suppressed the religion and expelled foreign priests and missionaries. In the later Qing and Republican periods, foreigners were again allowed to return, and the number of Catholics grew steadily, while remaining a small minority of the Chinese population as a whole.

In the nineteenth century, foreign Protestant missionaries entered China in increasing numbers, starting from a scant few at the beginning of the century to several thousand by its end. Protestants were indirectly responsible for one of the most remarkable cases of Chinese Christianization when Hong Xiuquan, a frustrated, would-be official, began to see heavenly visions that he attributed to the Christian God, under the influence of some of the very first writings published by a Chinese Protestant. In 1851, Hong established the Taiping Heavenly Kingdom, which would eventually rule over tens of millions of Chinese, many of whom earnestly believed themselves to be participating in a Christian movement.[23]

---

[23] Recent monographs that have highlighted the Christian nature of Taiping claims include Thomas H. Reilly, *The Taiping Heavenly Kingdom: Rebellion and the Blasphemy of Empire* (Seattle: University of Washington Press, 2004) and Carl S. Kilcourse, *Taiping Theology: The Localization of Christianity in China, 1843–64* (New York: Palgrave Macmillan, 2016).

The Spiritual Person. Paul H B Chang, Oxford University Press. © Oxford University Press 2026.
DOI: 10.1093/9780197793664.003.0002

The Taiping Heavenly Kingdom would eventually be extinguished by the Qing Dynasty, and the Chinese Protestants who remained tended to be much more closely tied to the foreign missionary establishments, among whom the most influential were led by British and American institutions. Despite significant expenditures of money and personnel, the Protestant missions enjoyed only limited success. If the Roman Catholics represented only a small proportion of Chinese religion throughout the nineteenth and early twentieth centuries, the Protestant number was an even smaller fraction of the Catholic total. Nevertheless, in certain cities, especially where foreigners had a significant presence, Protestants were disproportionately over-represented. Furthermore, because of their long-term investments in education, Chinese Protestants were relatively influential in elite and literate circles.

Watchman Nee was born in Fuzhou, the provincial capital of Fujian and "one of the earliest and in numerical terms more successful centers of Protestant missionary work in China."[24] His family history seemed to be a signal proof of the missionaries' successes. Nee's paternal grandfather, Ni Yucheng (倪玉成, 1840–1890), had enrolled in a school opened by the American Board of Commissioners for Foreign Missions (ABCFM), a largely Congregationalist body. In 1857, Yucheng was among the first Chinese natives to be baptized by the foreign missionaries.[25] In 1876, he became the first Chinese person to be ordained by the ABCFM.[26]

Watchman Nee's father, Ni Wenxiu (倪文修, 1877–1941), was the fourth of Yucheng's nine sons. According to Angus Kinnear, Nee's biographer, Yucheng was among the last group of students to take and pass the province-wide examinations for government service, attaining the "second degree." Kinnear probably means to refer to the *juren* degree, which technically qualified its holder to advance to public office. By the turn of the century, however, many *juren* never received the coveted government posts. Thus, if Wenxiu attained the *juren*, his position as an officer in the Fuzhou customs office probably owed more to his English language abilities and connections with foreigners than to his familiarity

[24] Ryan Dunch, *Fuzhou Protestants and the Making of a Modern China 1857–1927* (New Haven: Yale University Press, 2001), xvii.

[25] Ellsworth Carlson, *The Foochow Missionaries 1847–1880* (Cambridge, MA: Harvard University Press, 1973), 66–67.

[26] Angus Kinnear, *Against the Tide: The Unforgettable Story of Watchman Nee* (Wheaton, IL: Tyndale House Publishers, 1978), 24, claims that Yucheng was the first ordained minister. The Hartwell papers that he cites do claim that he was the first ordained minister of the ABCFM. Charles Hartwell, *Jubilee Notes* (Fuzhou, China: Foochow College Press, ABCFM, 1904), 27 from the Hannah Louisa Plimpton Peet Hartwell Papers. MS 761. Mount Holyoke Archives and Special Collections, South Hadley, MA. Ryan Dunch, however, points out that the ABCFM was the last of the three missions to begin ordaining pastors because of its own theological preferences (Dunch, *Fuzhou Protestants*, 18).

with the Confucian classics, another sign of the rapidly changing times.[27] In 1905, just two years after Watchman was born, the government abolished the imperial examinations altogether, removing one of the pillars around which Chinese intellectual and political life had been structured for over one thousand years.

As another sign of Fuzhou's significant Christian history, Nee's mother, Lin Heping (林和平, 1880–1950), was also raised in a Protestant family. Her biological parents were poor peasants who maintained what she later called the *louxi*, or "ugly habit," of valuing males and belittling females (*zhong nan qing nü*). Her birth parents thus gave her up for adoption to the Lins, a wealthy merchant and his wife, who loved her "as life itself." When she was six, her adoptive father was stricken with a strange illness that doctors were unable to treat. His employer, the Methodist businessman Zhang Heling (張鶴齡, dates unknown), suggested having a pastor pray for the elder Lin's health. Upon his miraculous recovery, the family converted to Christianity, throwing out their idols and unwrapping Heping's feet, which had just begun to be bound.[28]

Nee was thus a third-generation Protestant Christian from both his father and mother's families. His deep internalization of Christian themes arose organically from the two families' significant religious heritage. This profound engagement with Christianity is one of the key markers of Nee's belonging to Republican Chinese society. As a Fujianese Christian, a son of Fujianese Christians, and grandson of Fujianese Christians, Nee naturally turned to Christian motifs and ideas to make sense of his own childhood and conversion.

Besides this cultural Christianization, the story of Nee's conversion reflects the Chinese Republican period in at least two other meaningful ways. Firstly, as a part of the heightened political consciousness of the era, Nee came to see true Christianity as necessitating the total rejection of secular politics. Secondly, in

---

[27] Dunch, *Fuzhou Protestants*, 41–42. Dunch focuses here on the accomplishments of the graduates of the Anglo-Chinese College. It is hard to ascertain the exact circumstances of Wenxiu's education. He is listed in the catalogue of graduates in neither Foochow College (ABCFM) nor Anglo-Chinese College (American Methodist). Wenxiu's father, Yucheng, was certainly associated with the ABCFM and Wenxiu's son, Watchman, was baptized as a Methodist, but it is not clear when Wenxiu changed his denominational affiliation. In any case, during Wenxiu's generation, even a few years of education in missionary schools could set young men and women on a path toward professional success and government service.

[28] Lin's parents are never named in her account, but her father's employer is the same Zhang Heling whose generous donation of ten thousand dollars was pivotal in founding the Anglo-Chinese College, which later bore his Chinese name (*Heling Yinghua shu yuan*). Lin Heping, *Enai Biaoben*, accessed on October 10, 2015, at http://found-treasure.org/cht/94/page94.htm. While the story of Heping's adoption and her biological parents' "ugly habit" may seem shocking, such tropes are cliché commonplaces in Chinese narratives. Since women generally became part of their husband's families upon marriage, daughters were often understood to be financial burdens while sons were financial assets.

keeping with the growing concern for women's roles in society, Nee evinced a lifelong willingness to learn from women.

This second theme began during Nee's youth. As a child, Nee was strongly influenced by Heping, who clearly dominated the household culture.[29] This may have established the recurring pattern in Nee's life. Both Kinnear and theologian Grace May have pointed out the importance of powerful women, including Heping, in shaping Nee's outlook and development.[30] In any case, the story of Nee's conversion to Christianity is inextricably tied to his relationship with his mother.

According to Heping, Nee's birth was itself an answer to prayer. Her first two children were daughters, and her mother-in-law mockingly suggested that Heping would never be able to bear sons. Desperate, Heping "poured out [her] fervent desire before the God who hears human prayers."[31] On November 4, 1903, her next child was born, eventually called "Watchman," but named Ni Shuzu (倪述祖) at birth. He was also given an English name, Henry, which may have been bestowed upon his christening in the Methodist church. Lin would go on to have four more sons and two more daughters for a total of nine children.[32]

Despite their illustrious Christian heritage, the Nee family was not known for its religiosity during the early years of Nee's life. In fact, the principal concern of the home was patriotism rather than piety. After the 1911 Xinhai Revolution, Heping made a "supreme effort to help the patriotic movement." She wrote that "At that time, the blazing fire raged, and I didn't care about my life, I made speeches everywhere." She sold her jewelry to donate money to the cause and involved herself in various political organizations. For her efforts, she received a medal of recognition and was chosen to be a part of the delegation that welcomed the first president of the Republic of China, Sun Yat-sen (Sun Zhongshan), on his visit to Fujian.[33] Her participation in these efforts offers further corroboration of historian Ryan Dunch's claim that Fuzhou Protestants were often at the vanguard of political activity in the formation of the new nation.[34]

For Heping, however, this political ascent was also a spiritual descent. According to her account, her new relationships with non-Christians caused her to degrade from being a nominal Christian (youmingwushi de jidutu) to total unbelief. Her new desires were "fame, position, power, clothing, etc."[35] Likewise,

---

[29] Kinnear, *Against the Tide*, 36–37. Kinnear describes Nee's father as a retiring man who "could not utter a word in public" (41).

[30] Kinnear, *Against the Tide*, 193. May, "Watchman Nee and the Breaking of Bread."

[31] Heping, *Enai Biaoben*. Also, NTSWJ, Vol. 26, 217–218. Hereafter, NTSWJ will be my abbreviation for *Ni Tuosheng Wenji*, or *The Collected Works of Watchman Nee*.

[32] Kinnear, *Against the Tide*, 14.

[33] Lin, *Enai Biaoben*.

[34] See Dunch, *Fuzhou Protestants*, 44–47.

[35] Lin, *Enai Biaoben*.

her oldest son was also consumed with secular pursuits and ambitions. One of Watchman's classmates later wrote that "During our junior and senior high school years, we [Watchman and I] were both nominal Christians." The young men had "knowledge of the Bible, and outwardly observed Christian customs," but in effect, they "loved the world and pursued the vanities of the world."[36]

Heping's Conversion

Things changed dramatically for both mother and son in February 1920 when Heping learned that the famous independent revivalist, Dora Yu (余慈度, 1873–1931), was coming to Fuzhou. One of Heping's great disappointments in life had been her thwarted ambition to become a modern medical doctor. Although she had excelled academically and had even made preliminary arrangements to study in the United States, her marriage had definitively ended those plans. Nonetheless, during her academic preparations, she had met Yu, who was on her way to Korea as a medical missionary. Even as an eighteen-year-old, Heping had been deeply impressed upon learning of Yu's success and subsequent decision. Although Yu had achieved Heping's dream of becoming a physician, the older woman had given up considerable wealth and status to drop her medical profession and openly devote her life to God.

By the time of Yu's arrival in Fujian in 1920, she had already led successful revivals throughout China and had even founded an institution to train other evangelists and Christian workers. Heping thus had a complicated reaction to the news of Yu's coming. On the one hand, Heping had dropped "even the outward mask of being a Christian" and feared Yu's condemnation. On the other hand, "among Christians, she was the one I respected the most."[37]

With a mixture of fear and eagerness, Heping began to attend Yu's meetings. She struggled with her decision, alternately attending a few meetings and escaping to play mahjong, a popular, tile-based gambling game. Eventually, on the fifth day of Yu's campaign, Heping was back in the congregation to listen to a sermon on "The Behavior of Nominal Christians." During her preaching, Yu frequently gestured at Heping, causing the latter no small amount of discomfort. And yet, inexplicably, Heping returned again and again until Yu spoke on "the love of God and how Jesus himself personally came to die on the cross for us." As Heping listened, her "stubborn, hard heart was unconsciously melted by this lovable Lord who had given up his life for me." She "wept bitterly" and offered herself to God, "even being willing to be a martyr to pay him back."[38]

---

[36] NTSWJ, Vol 26, 208.
[37] Lin, *Enai Biaoben.*
[38] Lin, *Enai Biaoben.*

When she returned home, she began confessing her sins to her bewildered husband, who at first protested that she had nothing for which to apologize. As she continued to enumerate all her faults and shortcomings in serving him and caring for him, Wenxiu was overcome with emotion. He, too, began to apologize, and soon both of them were weeping together. Although Heping also felt compelled to apologize to her oldest son, Watchman, then probably known as Shuzu, who was about sixteen years old, she resisted this impulse for a time.

One fateful day, Heping tried to hold her first worship service at home. With her new hymnal and Bible, she sat at the piano to play, but suddenly she felt "the Lord's Spirit speaking with authority in my heart." She was forbidden to play until she had apologized to Watchman. As before, she resisted, saying, "'Oh God, I am the mother, how can I confess my sins to my son? From today on, how would I be able to live in this house?'" Nevertheless, God's voice was "most clear." Mystified, Wenxiu and Shuzu watched as Heping sat frozen at the piano with tears welling up in her eyes. She turned, embraced her son, and begged him to forgive her for wrongly punishing him. Her narrative continues, "Everyone was astounded that I spoke this way, but my oldest son said, 'That time you beat me without cause, my heart really hated you.' I said 'Please forgive me.' He did not open his mouth."[39]

The next morning, Shuzu agreed to go to Dora Yu's revival meeting with his mother and probably continued to attend these meetings until the end of Yu's Fuzhou campaign. This series of events sparked an internal conflict that led to Nee's conversion to Christianity. Before the family revival, Nee had found Christianity to be despicable. To him, "it seemed that so many members in the church were merely nominal." Even the pastors were pathetic creatures, and "one did not ordinarily see them except when they came to ask for donations." Some pastors had apparently come to the Nee household and had thankfully accepted winnings that had been taken directly from the mahjong table, earning Shuzu's lasting contempt.[40] Now, though, he had seen the undeniable, visceral power of Christian conversion in an idiom exquisitely tailored to his time and place.

Republican China was open to change and revolutionary ideals in a way that people and nations rarely are. Youth, newness, and modernity were all crucial slogans of the era, shouted, debated, and printed on posters and publications. The dynamic appeal of the "new" can be explained by the common set of teachings, institutions, and customs that the "youth" opposed, often simplified and vilified as Confucian or feudal. No matter how this set of pre-Republican cultural elements is defined, they certainly included a reverence for the old and traditional—Confucius himself had described his project as one of retrieving

---

[39] Lin, *Enai Biaoben.*
[40] NTSWJ 18, 74.

ancient learning from a golden age. This respect for age had a practical and personal dimension. In every society influenced by Confucianism, parents and familial elders have been treated with great respect, and age-oriented hierarchies structure the life of the home and even, to a significant extent, society at large.

This cultural heritage helps to explain the intensity of Heping's struggle to apologize to her son. She found the experience difficult, almost inconceivably so, remarking that if she were to publicly admit her wrong, she wondered, "how would [she] be able to live in this house?" A public apology would invert the established hierarchy and cause her to lose an enormous amount of dignity or "face"—a central Chinese concept of social standing and respect. Although Shuzu's verbal response was brief and straightforward, his own actions suggest the power of her behavior. He began to accompany his mother to revival meetings and changed his view of Christianity so entirely that he went from despising Christian ministers to considering becoming one himself.

Clearly, the younger Nee was aware of the high cost of his mother's example, an example that only made sense within a deeply Chinese yet Christian matrix. It is quite possible that Nee's particular kind of conversion could only have occurred in a family like his, one that had been steeped in Christian theologies, practices, and communities for generations, without having ever left China. The Christian values of humility, dramatically exemplified by Jesus's counter-cultural sayings about the greater serving the lesser and the first becoming last, had been movingly transposed into a Chinese household to cross the taboos of generational authority.

Heping's intervention thus drastically changed the direction of young Shuzu's life, contributing to what Nee himself would have considered the most meaningful change in a life full of unexpected and extreme alterations. The family as a whole reoriented itself from politics and public influence to Christian work, while Nee's life took an unexpected turn in an age of openness, secularism, and revolutions. Nee would follow his mother into devout Christian service and return to the ancestral religion of his family with newfound fervor and modern insights.

Nee was spurred to consider Christianity because of the influence of his mother, and the preaching of Dora Yu was another, even more immediate catalyst. In the future, he would continue to be inspired by the examples of women. Nee's first and most important mentor would be the English missionary Margaret Barber (1866–1930), and the writer who most closely presaged his early teachings was the Welsh revivalist Jessie Penn-Lewis (1861–1927). Especially in his younger years, Nee was guided by a number of female figures of authority. During these years, Nee would repeatedly follow them, learn from their teachings, and even subject himself to their discipline and restrictions. As his own insights and reputation developed, he eventually struck out on new paths, largely leaving behind their direct oversight and indeed, the oversight of any person, regardless of gender. Nevertheless, until the end of his recorded ministry, he continued to publicly credit and openly admire the influence of his early female teachers.

This respect for female authority is difficult to name. In Chinese historiography, the term "feminism" has been embroiled in debates over the extent of its Western roots. It is often pejoratively described as "bourgeois feminism" and opposed to the putatively true feminism that can be found in Chinese Communism. Furthermore, although the term was being debated and used in Republican China, Nee himself never referred to it. For various reasons then, feminism is a difficult term to employ in this case. Regardless of the terminology, however, one of the major intellectual trends of the Republican era was a dramatic reassessment of the value and treatment of women, especially in contrast with Chinese "feudal" and "Confucian" traditions.

A significant group of Republican artists, writers, and political leaders from across the spectrum largely agreed that the historical Chinese appraisal of women as inferior to men was incorrect. Most espoused at least some kind of fundamental equality between the sexes. Still, much of the equality that women gained was, at this stage, ideological or symbolic. Although Republican Chinese women made significant strides in gaining access to education and institutions, on the whole, the nation's resources, power, and influence were overwhelmingly controlled by men. Even (male) writers and thinkers who passionately championed the cause of women often did so without much thought to the agency and voices of actual women, preferring to emphasize women's suffering and victimization in ways that created "a female construct to honor as a type of sacrificial lamb."[41]

Nee's willingness to listen to women and concede authority to them was both rare and consistent, with evidence beginning from the earliest records of his life. Although Nee never explained this particular tendency, its early appearance and the influence of his mother are suggestive. Perhaps even rarer is the fact that throughout the rest of his life, Watchman Nee continued to recognize and share authority with females as "co-workers," arguably the highest position in his understanding of church administration and something akin to the office of apostleship in other Christian traditions.[42]

---

[41] Hua R Lan and Vanessa L Fong, eds. *Women in Republican China: A* Sourcebook (Armonk, NY: An East Gate Book, 1999), xiv.

[42] Like apostles, Nee's co-workers exercised authority beyond a single local congregation and could travel from place to place. Among others, female Christians such as Ruth Li and Peace Wang functioned as Nee's co-workers for decades. As will be seen in later chapters, their authority among the congregations that followed Nee sometimes rivaled his own.

Nee's acceptance of female authority was not unqualified. Most of Nee's theological influences and co-workers were men. Nee also followed the Biblical injunctions from the Pastoral letters that portrayed elders, or leaders of local churches, as exclusively married men. Nevertheless, across the span of his Christian life and work, Nee maintained a respect for women that included submitting to their direction and sharing authority with them.

Watchman Nee's Conversion: Resistance

It is unclear if there was an immediate catalyst to Nee's final, climactic conversion experience. Over the course of a few months, his internal conflict developed and deepened. His first trip to Dora Yu's revival meeting occurred in February, but the final crisis came on the evening of April 29, 1920. Nee's initial struggle was marked by a significant unwillingness that bears explanation. Nee writes that "At first, I did not want to believe in the Lord Jesus and or become a Christian. However, not believing made me uneasy. Within, a struggle began."[43]

On the face of it, this reluctance is difficult to understand. Nee came from a Christian family, and his mother had already converted. If he despised some Christians and craven pastors, he admired both his mother and Dora Yu. Whence the internal struggle? Nee elaborated that the struggle was a "great conflict in the heart" that included two problems. Nee explained that "For many people, when they get saved, they address the issue of being saved from sin; but for me, the issues of being delivered from sin and the cause of my entire life were linked together." Thus, if he converted, "My previous plans all came to nothing, they were finished. My future was completely forfeit. For others this state of affairs might be easy, but for me, it was difficult because I had many ideals, dreams, and plans."[44]

Fundamentally then, there were two overlapping reasons for Nee's difficulty, both of which were centered not only on accepting Jesus but also, perhaps even more, on the corollary problem of the purpose to which Nee would devote himself, "the cause of my entire life." It was not that Nee despised Christians or Christ: In fact, he now esteemed both. The problem was that accepting Christ and becoming a dedicated Christian rather than a nominal one required a great sacrifice—the sacrifice of his entire future. The fact that Nee saw conversion as requiring total commitment touches on the absoluteness that was a core aspect of his personality. The fact that his future with its "many ideals, dreams,

---

[43] NTSWJ 26, 219.

[44] NTSWJ 26, 218, 220. The phrase I have translated as "the cause of my entire life" is "终生的事业" in Chinese. It is rather ambiguous and could mean something like "my life's career" or "the undertaking of my lifetime."

and plans" would "all come to nothing" also reflected Nee's understanding of the relationship between the Christian message and Chinese nationalism. Each of these claims demands further examination.

In terms of Nee's personality, belief in Jesus could not simply be a question of mental adherence. If Jesus were real and deserving of worship, then every aspect of Nee's life and plans needed to be adjusted. The decision of conversion touched upon an important facet of Nee's character, one that he himself might call "absoluteness" or *juedui* (絕對), an unconditionality that insisted on sparing nothing in service of a worthy cause. If Nee were to become a Christian, he did not think it would be enough to accept a set of beliefs or call himself a "Christian" as one marker of personal identity among many others. Instead, he was determined that all his abilities and energy would be redirected toward a new goal, dramatically remade by a new set of values.

Of course, many young people tend to see personal choices and values in stark, uncompromising terms. On top of this, the theme of heroic self-surrender had an especially powerful appeal in early twentieth-century China. Well outside Christian circles, the urgent need of national salvation seemed to demand the kind of resolute action and personal dedication that befit citizens of a country in the throes of existential crisis. Many other young people made calculations similar to Nee's, choosing higher goals that were all-encompassing and worthy of total devotion. Imprisoned in 1927, the Communist Zhou Wenyong wrote a poem on his cell wall:

> You can behead me;
> You can bend and break my limbs;
> But what you cannot eliminate is my revolutionary spirit.
> For the Party a brave man can give up his head;
> Committed to the collective a heroic man can let his body be torn apart.

Not to be outdone, Zhao Yiman, a female activist, made a similar declaration some years later:

> Casting aside my family I vow to struggle for other people;
> Crossing rivers and oceans I travel to world's end.
> Not all men are outstanding;
> for what reasons should women be regarded as inferior?
> For the rebirth of my nation I do not mind decapitation.
> May I shed my blood to fertilize the soil of China?[45]

---

[45] Both poems are quoted in Hung-yok Ip, *Intellectuals in Revolutionary China, 1921–1949: Leaders, Heroes and Sophisticates* (London: RoutledgeCurzon, 2005), 96–97.

Nee's absoluteness would outlive his youth and would continue to resound as a dominating characteristic of his Christian teaching. Over the course of decades, whenever he tried to exegete a Biblical passage, understand Christian principles, or promote certain practices, he would disregard the most obvious restrictions of inconvenience and personal cost. Instead, the content of Nee's Christianity consistently pointed to ideals that could not be changed or diluted. Even though Nee allowed for human weakness, he refused to stop teaching what he considered to be the Biblical standard, even when it set requirements that seemed impossibly high.

Politics and Religion

In regard to politics, Nee's uncompromising perspective makes most sense when it is considered, at least in part, in its Republican Chinese context. The Qing Empire had collapsed, and China was left without a strong, central government. It was not obvious how the Chinese people were to be politically organized and unified, while it was painfully obvious that China was far behind the developed nations of the world by almost every metric that mattered. Young Chinese flocked to science and politics to address these problems. While Nee never showed any particular interest in science, politics was another question. The second reason for Nee's reticence to convert to Christianity was his belief in the fundamental incompatibility between true Christianity and human politics.

On the face of it, there is no necessary opposition between politics and Christianity. Strictly speaking, it is hard to conceive of any religious claim that is truly free of any political implications. Conversely, there have always been Christians who have participated enthusiastically and directly in the affairs of state. In fact, two of the most notable figures of the Republican Era were Sun Yat-sen and Chiang Kai-shek, both of whom openly embraced Christianity while moving in the highest political circles. Nee's own family briefly contacted Sun to further the cause of national rejuvenation, all while maintaining their Christian affiliation. Others who saw themselves primarily as Christian ministers or teachers, such as T. C. Chao and Y. T. Wu, argued explicitly for Christianity as a means for China to gain political strength and cultural rejuvenation. Nee may have been personally absolute, but at least one option for his future could well have been absolute service toward both Christ *and* the Chinese people.

Though little is known about Nee's life before he became a Christian, there is evidence to suggest both an interest in politics and a foundational belief in the exclusivity of Christian fidelity and political involvement. Nee never explicitly explained the "many ideals, dreams, and plans" that "came to nothing" when he became a Christian, but one of his former classmates claimed that Nee "had deep attainments in Chinese literature" and that "he would frequently publish articles in the newspapers."[46] Nee himself wrote that because of his good judgment and intelligence, he "could likely have had great success" in the world.[47]

The need for "good judgment," the writing of articles for newspapers, and the "ideals, dreams, and plans" associated with Nee all suggest a future in some kind of politically engaged writing, which is consistent with the heavily political nature of much of Republican literature. Even writers who tried to avoid political perspectives often highlighted the failings of traditional Chinese culture, opening a space for reform, or calling attention to China's relative weakness on the world stage. Many other leading voices wrote forthrightly on political subjects, issuing passionate calls to action, some even arguing that all art should ultimately serve political ends.

Nee's mother's patriotic activities, his journalism, his familiarity with English, and his thorough command of both classical and vernacular (*baihua*) Chinese writing all show that Nee was deeply conversant with current events, and the current events of Nee's youth were especially incendiary. While Heping had written of making a "supreme effort to help the patriotic movement" with total disregard for her life, one of Nee's younger brothers, Shengzu, had actually joined a number of revolutionary societies and had died in a revolutionary demonstration.[48]

In 1919, less than a year before the night of Nee's conversion, news of the Treaty of Versailles had reached China, and students of Nee's age had led the national reaction of violent outrage. They were infuriated by the terms of the treaty, which granted Chinese territory in the Shandong province to Japan despite Woodrow Wilson's ideal of self-determination and Chinese participation in the war on behalf of the winning Allies. Throughout 1919, spontaneous student protests erupted in large cities throughout the country, including Fuzhou. In fact, Nee's own school closed its summer session that year "in order to prevent the schools from becoming merely centres for anti-Japanese propaganda."[49]

The politics of this period proved to be an important watershed for Christianity as well. Within the space of a few years, the mood and temper of Protestants in Fuzhou changed radically. In 1919, many Fuzhou Protestants still took the United States as a model of a Christian nation. They hoped for a cosmopolitan future in which Chinese Christians also led their country forward. As

[46] NTSWJ, 26, 208.

[47] NTSWJ, 26, 220.

[48] Kinnear, *Against the Tide*, 113–114.

[49] R. M. Gwynn, E. M. Norton, and B. W. Simpson, "*T. C. D.*" in China: A History of the Dublin University Fukien Mission 1885–1935. Compiled for the Mission's Jubilee (Dublin: Church of Ireland Printing and Publishing, n.d., 1935?), 56–57. Nee was not among the "'undesirable' boys" who were not "permitted to return" after that summer session, which suggests that he was not one of the more outspoken agitators.

China's relationships with many putatively Christian Western nations continued to sour, however, the disappointment of young Chinese quickly turned into bitter anger. As late as 1921, the Fuzhou YMCA was still "the leading public association in the city," but by 1923, its principal was stabbed on the street in broad daylight because of a perceived affront to Chinese nationalism.[50] The student-based Anti-Christian Movement would begin in April 1922, largely motivated by the belief that Christianity supported Western imperialism.

Nee's decision to convert to Christianity was forged in the same white-hot collision of ideals that gave birth to the modern Chinese national consciousness, often referred to as the May Fourth Movement, in reference to the date of the most notable student protests in Beijing. The unsparing hatred of imperialism, the fierce jealousy over autonomous sovereignty, and the burning desire for a lasting justice all had their analogues in the kind of Christianity Nee championed and espoused, even from the moment of his conversion. From the beginning, Nee envisioned a form of Christianity that would not be found complicit in imperialism and a church that would exercise sovereignty over its own affairs, all of which would serve the establishment of the kingdom of God, in which righteousness filled the entire earth. Although Nee's rejection of Christian political involvement has been almost universally noted by students of his thought, the fact that Nee understood and grappled with the political implications of this rejection has been overlooked.

Lamin Sanneh, a scholar of World Christianity, has suggested that a similar set of circumstances gave birth to particularly African theologies in their own contexts. Protestant missionaries were disproportionately influenced by counter-cultural trends in Pietism, which drew sharp distinctions "between faith and worldly institutions, between the cultivation of piety and the affairs of the workaday world." The missionaries therefore argued that the "government was the enemy of the gospel." For many Africans, it was easy to adopt and extend this critique by identifying the government with colonial rule and thus frame their resistance to imperialism in Christian, Pietistic terms.[51]

Of course, if Nee had simply accepted this calculus, it would have allowed him to support both Christianity and the prevailing political trends of his age. Like many of the Africans (and some of the other Chinese already mentioned), Nee could have taken up the banner of Christianity as an anti-colonial force in the service of indigenous independence. Nee's familiarity with politics and his belief that becoming a Christian meant a sacrifice of his literary future show that he had taken a further, more uncommon step. He believed, even before his

[50] Dunch, *Fuzhou Protestants*, 184–189.
[51] Lamin Sanneh, *Disciples of All Nations: Pillars of World Christianity* (New York: Oxford University Press, 2008), 163–164.

conversion, that the Pietist principle of spiritual-political division had to be applied to *Chinese* values and choices as well.

In other words, Nee understood conversion to Christianity to entail a fundamentally exclusive, complete devotion to Christ. If imperialist Christianity was an improper entanglement of politics and religion, so too was a preference for the Chinese people or Chinese national interests.[52] Christ possessed either supreme, unconditional authority or none at all. It is telling that Lin Heping's conversion also seemed to bring an end to her political aspirations and activities. As he would spell out in his later theology, Nee conceded that life on earth was unavoidably messy and that achieving true purity in this lifetime might be impossible. Nevertheless, for Nee, the *pursuit* of such purity was one of the purposes of the Christian life. Thus, even before his conversion, he had decided that the Christian faith should not be deployed in the service of national salvation.

As early as 1925, Nee was already talking thoughtfully about a total rejection of politics in his *Meditations on Revelation*. In a number of successive discourses on church history, Nee condemned the conversion of Constantine as opening the way for Satan's subtle plan of co-opting the church.[53] He also suggested that the church's embrace of politics caused it to forget the meaning of the cross, while exchanging its truth for wealth and power,[54] and criticized Christians for either forging alliances with state governments or usurping God's own authority by appointing their own church hierarchies.[55]

From the time before his conversion to the very first years of his written publications to the final years of his life, Nee wrestled profoundly with political questions and the proper role of secular and sacred authority in Christian life. Western missionaries may have introduced Nee to important partners in the long conversation about Christianity and power, but their disengagement from politics was generally unremarkable, part of their unquestioning acceptance of a long tradition of Christian political quietism in the service of holiness. The fact that these beliefs are "anti-political" has obscured the fact that for Nee, such an "anti-political" stance came at an enormous cost, something that would become excruciatingly clear at the end of his life. Nee's environment applauded his attempt to de-westernize Christianity, but at the same time, he resisted enormous pressures in refusing to take up the banner of Chinese national chauvinism.

---

[52] In some of his earliest published works, Nee expresses his opposition to imperialism and Westernization. On one occasion, he off-handedly concedes, almost as a matter of course, that "Certainly we must oppose imperialism and other lawless things." NTSWJ 7, 217. In another place, he suggests that both Chinese and Western cultural elements are included in the "world" from which Christians must separate themselves. NTSWJ 4, 234.

[53] NTSWJ 4, 276–278.

[54] NTSWJ 5, 10–11.

[55] NTSWJ 5, 70–71.

This fundamental guiding principle of an absolute separation of Christian faith and human politics would set a foundation for all of Nee's future Christian thought. Scholars who have remarked that Nee was thoroughly out of step with his times, or almost unrecognizable as "Chinese," have missed this critical connection between Nee and his times. For many young Chinese, the age seemed to demand total devotion to the cause of national salvation. Though countercultural, Nee's anguish in his conversion showed that he recognized the same stakes and the same ultimate incompatibility between Christianity and nationalism that many of his peers would soon press home during the Anti-Christian movement. In the end, one could support either the Chinese people's absolute sovereignty or Jesus's absolute sovereignty, but not both. The fact that the same question was so pointedly asked on both sides of the religious divide stems from a common source in the discourse of intellectual, socially engaged youths in early Republican China.

Watchman Nee's Conversion: Acceptance

Nee's personal conflict finally drew to a close, but it required both an extraordinary visual manifestation and a powerful spiritual recognition. Nee used the language of perception and sight to describe the vision he received on an April evening when he was struggling with the decision to convert. He writes:

> At first, I did not want to believe in the Lord Jesus or become a Christian, but that made me feel uneasy. Within me, a struggle began. Later, I knelt down to pray. At first, I had no words with which to pray, but after a little while, I saw many sins placed before me, and I knew that I was a sinner. In all my life, I have never had an experience such as this. On the one hand, I saw that I was a sinner, on the other hand, I saw the Savior. On the one hand, I saw the filthiness of sin, on the other hand, I saw that the Lord's precious blood could wash me clean, make me as white as snow. On the one hand, I saw the Lord's two hands bound to the cross, on the other hand, I saw the Lord stretching out his two hands to welcome me. He said to me, "I am here waiting to receive you." Such love subdued me, I could not resist it, and I decided to accept the Lord as my Savior. Before, I had laughed at others who believed in the Lord Jesus, but that evening, I could not laugh. I recognized my sin and wept, asking the Lord for forgiveness. After I confessed my sins, the burden of sin fell away from me. I felt free, and my heart was filled with joy and peace.[56]

---

[56] NTSWJ 26, 219.

This account weaves together a number of striking visual, theological, and emotional claims. Nee had a visceral recognition of his sinfulness while gazing on the figure of the crucified Christ. The colorful images he evoked of filth, blood, and snow were all classic biblical and theological hallmarks. In particular, both Roman Catholicism and Protestantism had long focused on Jesus's sacrifice on the cross as the central moment in God's treatment of sin. Although some Western Christians were suspicious of apparitions and miraculous visions, they were a common theme in non-Western conversion stories and in the burgeoning Pentecostal movement. If Nee was unaware of Pentecostal teachings in 1920 when he converted, by the time he related this testimony in 1936, he had already established deep relationships with a number of Christians influenced by some form of Pentecostalism, including Elizabeth Fischbacher, a British missionary, and Witness Lee (1905–1997), a Christian leader from North China.

In the Chinese context, Nee's vision could be considered relatively subdued. If anything, it is striking for its careful orthodoxy and strict adherence to biblical themes. In contrast, Hong Xiuquan (洪秀全, 1814–1864), the leader of the Taiping Rebellion, famously received a dramatic vision of celestial figures dressed in classic Chinese garb, whom he later interpreted as representing God the Heavenly Father and Christ the Son. Hong then claimed authority as God's own divine son, Jesus's younger brother, for a mission that included taking up arms and smashing idolatrous centers of worship.[57]

Nee's vision was also far less daring than the otherworldly experiences of Wei Enbo (魏恩波, 1877–1919), who founded the indigenous Chinese Christian movement, the True Jesus Church. In the opening decades of the twentieth century, Wei reported having "a series of miraculous experiences in which he was baptized personally by Jesus in a river outside the Beijing city gates, was girded with divine armor and weapons for the purpose of battling and subduing legions of demons, and was visited by Moses, Elijah, and the Twelve Apostles in order to receive inspiration in the task of 'correcting' Christianity and restoring Jesus' one true church."[58] One of Wei's associates received a vision in which he was instructed to call Wei "Little Jesus."[59]

Unlike Hong and Wei, who were first-generation adult converts, Nee described his conversion in terms that would have been readily understandable and acceptable to Christians in other countries. Evangelical testimonies from around the world frequently featured nominal Christians, or young people born

---

[57] Jonathan D. Spence, *God's Chinese Son: The Taiping Heavenly Kingdom of Hong Xiuquan* (Princeton, NJ: W. W. Norton, 1996), 46–50, 60–65.

[58] Melissa Wei-Tsing Inouye, "Miraculous Mundane: The True Jesus Church and Chinese Christianity in the Twentieth Century" (PhD diss., Harvard University, 2011), 2.

[59] Inouye, "Miraculous Mundane," 52.

into Christian families who come into personal experiences of faith from which they dated their salvation, the beginning of their "real" Christian experience.

It is instructive to compare Nee's family history with those of other non-Western Christians. Historian Niel Gunson has described conversion in the South Pacific as following a roughly generational pattern. The first generation of Christian converts might have respected missionaries as tribal chiefs, but they showed little remorse for their pre-Christian sins such as ritual infanticide. They also reported mystical visions that did not conform to standard Christian tropes and generally confounded the missionaries' hopes for ecstatic revival, although they still understood themselves to have adopted the Christian religion.

According to the missionaries' observations, the children of the first converts, the second generation, slid into a kind of formal religion. They had not committed infanticide and were relatively unconcerned with what they believed to be more mundane sins such as sexual immorality. With the passage of time, however, the Christian message could make an impact among these second-generation Christians and their children, the third generation. Eventually, among these later groups, archetypal Christian revivals began to emerge. Congregants were emotionally overcome, repented of their sinfulness and nominal Christianity, and began to relish religious services and meetings.[60]

Though there were obvious, significant differences between conversion in China and the South Pacific, the arc of the Nee family experience almost perfectly tracks that of the South Pacific Protestants. The first generation experienced what appears to be a genuine, if relatively unemotional, conversion. The second generation understood themselves to be religious as a formal duty or marker of identity. Eventually, the second and third generations experienced archetypal revivals, with emotional repentance for sin and a visceral embrace of Christian theology and practices.

Nor was the Nee family alone. Liang A-Fa, a first-generation Chinese Protestant, wrote a five-hundred-page "tract" that showed little evidence of the deep emotion or powerful experiences that many missionaries hoped for. Liang's theology was not shallow: He emphasized the divinity of Jesus and believed that Jesus's teachings could bring about the salvation of the world. Yet even though Liang's conversion was earnest, and he rejected other gods in favor of the "merits of Christ," his Christian conversion did not produce the obvious, expressive "heart piety" that would categorize later generations of Chinese Christians.[61]

Liang's experience can be contrasted with the effusive conversion narratives of Lin Heping, Watchman Nee, or their fellow Fuzhou revivalist John Sung

[60] Niel Gunson, *Messengers of Grace: Evangelical Missionaries in the South Seas 1797–1860* (Melbourne; New York: Oxford University Press, 1978), 217–236.

[61] Jonathan Seitz, ed., *Liang A-Fa: China's First Preacher, 1789–1855* (Eugene, OR: Pickwick Publications, 2013), xx.

(*Song Shangjie*, 1901–1944). During the Republican Era, Chinese religion was increasingly shaped by these second- and third-generation Christians who had internalized the Christian message at an almost instinctive, visceral level. Sung was a pastor's son who spoke about almost losing his faith to theological liber-alism during graduate studies at Union Theological Seminary. Contemplating suicide, he was saved by a vision of Jesus, who commissioned him to become a herald of the gospel. Sung returned to China to preach a fiery message, denouncing sin and exhorting thousands of Chinese to make emotional, public confessions.[62]

The intellectual legacy of the Enlightenment emphasized the importance of experience, and evangelicals built on that emphasis, especially with regard to the key experiences of conversion and revival. One of the most cherished evangelical themes was the emphasis on a personal, emotional encounter with Jesus. Evangelical missionaries often hoped that individual, non-Christian Chinese would repent for their sins in their conversions. The Chinese experi-ence, however, complicates this standard narrative. Mirroring and confirming the experiences of the South Pacific, the Chinese case suggests that the process of Christian conversion cannot be limited to an individual experience or even to the span of an individual human life.

While conversion can indeed occur on an individual level, if affective appeals and dramatic reactions are taken to be the standard of Christian success, some of the most stunning signs of progress are only seen after a longer process of Christianization. It seems that non-Christian communities often internalize and integrate Christian themes into their indigenous cultures over a period of gener-ations. It is only after the span of intervening decades that native children "spon-taneously" respond to and even craft effective emotional appeals, reworking evangelical themes of sin, repentance, and conversion in ways that resonate with native ears and native hearts. The Republican era was almost the earliest mo-ment that second- and third-generation Chinese Protestants could evoke their subjective embodiment of their parents' and grandparents' faith, and they did so repeatedly, and to lasting effect.

If Nee's conversion story reveals something of his deep roots in the Christian tradition, the emotional tenor of the story suggests Romanticism, another Western influence, had already spread widely throughout China, far beyond Christian circles—again, the dramatic testimonies of the young Communists, Zhou Wenyong and Zhao Yiman, are helpful parallels. In Nee's account, the pathos of the story reaches its highest pitch when "I saw the Lord's two hands bound to the cross," and "I saw the Lord stretching out his two hands to wel-come me." Coming immediately on the heels of his recognition of his own filthy

---

[62] Lian, *Redeemed by Fire*, 140–144.

sinfulness, he declared, "Such love subdued me, I could not resist it." The emotional invitation of a loving Savior beckoning toward sinners also echoed some of the most famous contemporary evangelical themes. The American evangelist Dwight Lyman Moody (1837–1899) gained world renown for appealing to audiences with his use of sentimental anecdotes and examples, matched with stirring music. One of his most famous lines was to call out sinners, welcoming them to "come home."[63]

In Nee's case, his emotional response to these classic Christian themes is evidence of his own position at the terminus of a long process by which Christianity had become so ingrained in Chinese minds as to provoke heartfelt responses to sin. Jesus was able to appear and speak to a patriotic, young Chinese man who was alone in his room and convince him to give up his dreams of literary glory and national salvation.

Nee spoke of his conversion as a spiritual event, almost outside the bounds of time and space, but he also left more tangible clues as to his historical moment and context. Nee's willingness to learn from women, his total rejection of secular politics, and his deep internalization of Christian themes are all markers of his belonging to the Republican period of China. His conversion, however, was also uniquely his own, irreducible to either his Chinese contexts or the Christian traditions in which he took part. In the coming years, he would continue to blaze his own trail, contributing both to Chinese society and the Christian tradition, with fresh and surprising insights as bold and unique as his initial conversion.

[63] George Marsden, *Fundamentalism and American Culture* (New York: Oxford University Press, 2006), 36.

2

Fuzhou

Church and Conflict

After his conversion in April 1920, Nee would spend about four more years in his hometown of Fuzhou before departing in the first half of 1924. During these first years of his Christian life, Nee fixed the foundations for a number of important positions from which he would never really deviate, although he would continuously refine the details and specifics. He set an ecclesial course that was dependent neither on Western Christians nor on other Chinese Christians. He made deep, personal sacrifices to remain faithful to his vision of Christian ministry. And finally, he learned the crucial principle of self-denial that would hold all these themes together and would serve as a crucial compass for his own future conduct and ministry. All of these matters can be explained by examining the first years of Nee's Christian life in Fuzhou.

Nee's dramatic and sudden Christian conversion made for some hard transitions in his life. He had loved fine clothing, buying lottery tickets, and going to see movies.[64] But now he understood all of these as distractions from his Christian calling. He was still enrolled as a student at Trinity College in Fuzhou, only because he believed that his studies—now motivated by a higher sense of purpose—could serve God. The most pressing initial question that confronted Nee could be called one of Christian socialization. Significantly, his conversion had been an intensely private, personal matter, and the catalyst for his conversion had been a traveling evangelist. These facts did not naturally lead to any established congregation in Fuzhou.

As with many Chinese (and other non-Western) Christians, the Nee family was not particularly bound to denominational structures. Nee's paternal grandfather had been ordained by the American Congregationalists and his school was run by British Anglicans, while the family had associated itself primarily with American Methodists—it was probably a local Methodist preacher who had accepted the Nee family donations from the mahjongg table. Still, as a young man, Nee would have felt the need for social connections intensely,

---

[64] NTSWJ 26, 208, 221.

The Spiritual Person. Paul H B Chang, Oxford University Press. © Oxford University Press 2026.
DOI: 10.1093/9780197793664.003.0003

and as a Christian, he believed that God's commands regarding the church were clear.

In many ways, the story of Nee's years in Fuzhou shows how he was "socialized" into Christian relationships and behaviors by his various relationships with his mentors, peers, and followers. The specific patterns of cooperation, independence, mutual concern, and friction that would characterize the rest of Nee's Christian life can all be seen in their earliest iterations during his years in Fuzhou. In addition, these relationships also goaded Nee into what would become a lifelong habit of trying to understand his experiences by looking to the Bible and to Biblical interpreters. Through these Biblical exegetes and commentators, Nee absorbed important ideas from the wider Christian tradition and crafted his own novel contributions.

The first of these connections, and certainly the most important, was Nee's early association with the independent, self-supporting English missionary, Margaret Emma Barber. It was probably through Barber that Nee was introduced to the writings of the Plymouth Brethren, whose conception of the church as a spiritual, sovereign entity, removed from political and cultural currents, fit in well with Nee's own tendencies. Nee's theological reliance on Dissenting British Protestants would continue throughout his intellectual career. Their Bible-based objections to state-sponsored religion were deeply congenial to Nee's own attempts to resist what he understood to be the inappropriate co-option of religion by nationalism in his own country.

Nee's most creative contributions to the Christian theology of the church, or ecclesiology, can also be seen in light of a resistance to the overwhelming Republican emphasis on the "national" as the basis for patriotism and good citizenship. Beginning in Fuzhou and for the rest of his life, Nee tinkered with both the intellectual justification and the actual practice of church organization and propagation. In the end, he formulated a flexible model that split the difference between congregational autonomy and central control. For many, it represented the ideal church and offered a sense of stable community in the midst of the general political chaos of the Republican years.

Basic Questions on the Church—Baptism, Denominations, Bread Breaking

For Nee, the obvious first step for a Christian life began in his own home, with his newly converted mother, Lin Heping. Unsurprisingly, she ardently supported her son's newfound Christian commitment, and every Thursday, she also hosted a Bible study at their home. Watchman quickly joined the group. Nee, however, was only sixteen years old, and "the ones who came to the Bible studies were almost all old and elderly people, so that I was like a little child, and I couldn't seem to find anyone around my age to talk to."[65]

Nee was thus grateful when, after two or three weeks, another younger person joined the Bible study. Leland Wang (*Wang Zai,* 王載, 1898–1975) was five years Nee's senior, and in many ways, the two men were ideal companions. Both were intelligent, energetic, and devoted. Both had recently given up promising careers for Christian ministry, possibly making a similar calculus with regard to the incompatibility of Christianity and politics. Wang had been a naval officer but had just resigned his commission to become a full-time revivalist. A Fuzhou native, Wang had returned to his hometown and found himself unoccupied and hungry for Biblical teachings at almost the same moment that Nee began to seek fellowship for his own Christian journey.

The friendship was strengthened soon afterward in 1921 when Wang's and Nee's paths converged on the issue of baptism. Both Nee's recent conversion and his intense study of the Bible caused him to reflect on his childhood baptism. Although he had received a baptismal certificate with his name and the signature of the Methodist bishop who baptized him, he would still have "dared to do anything [evil or immoral]" prior to his actual conversion. It thus appeared to Nee that the baptism had no effect and that the certificate was worthless. Nee was also convinced that the form of his baptism was wrong. Whereas the bishop had scattered cold water upon Nee's head, the Bible recorded that after Jesus's baptism, he had "come up out of the water," strongly implying baptism by immersion, not sprinkling.[66]

Nee's growing convictions seemed to be confirmed by all the Christians who were most important in his life. In May 1921, Lin Heping approached her son and asked him for his opinion on whether she should be baptized by immersion. Nee responded enthusiastically, "I have also just been considering being baptized by immersion." In fact, he had already looked into the matter and found that an English missionary named Margaret Barber (1866–1930) lived a short two-hour journey from their home. Significantly, the Nees may have been aware that when Dora Yu had come to Fuzhou to conduct her revival meetings, she had also been baptized by Barber. Perhaps buoyed by their common sentiment, mother and son decided not to delay at all and went that very day to be baptized by Barber. Upon his return, Nee's very first order of business was to tell his new friend, Leland Wang, who responded with hearty approbation, "very good, very good!" It turned out that Wang too had once been baptized by sprinkling before

---

[65] NTSWJ 18, 76.
[66] NTSWJ 18, 75. As Nee would later come to realize, the Greek term *baptizo* itself means to "immerse" or "dunk."

becoming convinced that he should be immersed. As Nee recalls, "We two were so delighted because we had received the same light."[67]

The fact that his mother, Wang, and Dora Yu had all reached the same conclusions may have fortified Nee when his decision was first challenged. The Bible study at the Nee's home had been led by an "old pastor" whom Nee respected deeply, having the opinion that "in Fuzhou, he was number one in knowing the Bible." After sharing news of his baptism with Wang, Nee went to this pastor as well, expecting a warm reception since "he used to tell us that everything must be done according to the Bible." The pastor admitted that immersion was scriptural but chided Nee for being "such a stickler." Instead of questioning his own decision, Nee began to question the pastor and all his other teachings on the church, resolving to "put aside all human authority, and henceforth to carefully study the Bible instead."[68]

This further Bible study fostered even more questions with regard to the church. Nee began to doubt the fundamental legitimacy of the entire Western denominational system. He later recalled that the discrepancies between the Bible and Western Christianity seemed obvious at the time. "Today there are so many denominations, but in the Bible there are no Methodists nor Presbyterians nor any other denominations. Why am I a member of the Methodist church? God's word does not speak this way, why then do I practice this way?" He came to believe that both "the system of pastors" itself and the way Christian meetings were generally conducted were against "the principles of the Bible."[69]

Like many non-Western Christians, Nee was forced to grapple with the dissonance between Western church traditions, his own Bible study, and the Christian practices he witnessed in his own non-Western context. Although the Nee family had a long history of working with Western missionaries, the lasting divisions between different Protestant denominations were still rooted in the alien history of Europe and North America. Especially in Asia, where Protestants were a tiny, relatively new religious minority that had to survive among much larger and better-established traditions, the reasons for these denominational divisions could seem frivolous and even offensive.

Furthermore, the form of Protestantism that captivated many Asian Christians in the nineteenth and twentieth centuries was a deeply biblical evangelicalism. Its ethic of respect for the Bible as the ultimate authority could easily be turned against church denominations. Sometimes, as with Nee, this led Asian Christians to dramatic conclusions. Japanese Christians in the *mukyokai*, or "No-Church" movement, went so far as to argue for a Christianity without the church. One

[67] NTSWJ 18, 75–76.
[68] NTSWJ 18, 76.
[69] NTSWJ 18, 77.

leader in that movement criticized Western Christians for being "churchmen" who held to a "Church faith" that egoistically pushed people to "opt for one de-nomination [and] cut themselves off from those in other denominations."[70]

Closer to home, the Chinese Protestant leader Cheng Jingyi (1881–1939) had captivated international audiences at the 1910 World Missionary Conference in Edinburgh with his frank denunciations of the denominational system. Cheng famously explained that "your denominationalism does not interest the Chinese," who "had never understood it, could not delight in it, though they often suffered from it."[71] In response, leading lights in the international and Chinese missionary communities had supported Cheng in his mission to create a unified, non-denominational Chinese church. As Nee and Wang began to form their own conclusions based on the study of the Bible, Cheng moved on a grander scale, acting as chairman of the National Christian Conference in 1922 and founding the Church of Christ in China in 1927. Both organizations were meant to work toward the end of divisions between denominations in China. Unfortunately, these attempts at union suffered the fate of similar attempts in the West—consensus broke down over the difficult details of finance and control, as well as the deepening theological divide between liberal and fundamentalist Christianity.

Nee's own solution relied on an even more fundamental critique of Christianity as a whole. As Nee's mention of not only the denominations but also of the "system of pastors" suggests, he was prepared to make sweeping changes. He admitted that at this early stage, his critiques were generally embry-onic and hazy.[72] Still, his ideas were definite enough that he convinced his family to agree with his decision to have their names removed from the Methodists' membership records, much to the Methodists' understandable consternation.[73] Whatever he believed about the church, it was clearly going to be independent of Western systems and traditions.

In the first half of 1922, Nee began to think about another focal point of church practice, that is, the Eucharist. Characteristically, he preferred to refer to the rite by its more strictly biblical moniker, "the breaking of bread" (擘餅). Since the time of his salvation, he had "never been to receive the so-called Holy Communion," because he was bothered by the many unscriptural practices of the churches in which communion was offered. Nee objected to the fact that the Methodists offered communion only four times a year, that they allowed

---

[70] Tsukamoto Toraji, as quoted in John Howes, *Japan's Modern Prophet: Uchimura Kanzo, 1861–1930* (Toronto: UBC Press, 2005), 369–370.

[71] W. Nelson Bitton, "Report of the Proceedings of the World Missionary Conference in Edinburgh from June 13th to 23rd," *Chinese Recorder* 41 (August 1910), as quoted in Lian, *Redeemed by Fire*, 35.

[72] NTSWJ 18, 77.

[73] NTSWJ 18, 82.

congregants who were sinful or not even Christian to receive the elements, and that they insisted that only an ordained pastor could preside over the meeting and break the bread. And yet Nee also recognized that the biblical record clearly showed that the early Christians came together frequently to break bread. Thus, he was caught in a conundrum. "At this time, I was very, very troubled. The Bible said that I must frequently break bread to remember the Lord, and I wanted to go, but I had no place to go."[74]

Once again, he sought out his friend Leland Wang. After their Thursday Bible study, the two had a private conversation, and Nee shared many of his burgeoning insights, listing the many unscriptural practices that seemed to surround the Christian practice of communion. As in the case of baptism, Nee found Wang to be a kindred spirit. Wang took Nee's hands and responded enthusiastically, "What God has been leading you in has been just the same for me. Last night, I couldn't sleep at all, I just kept praying and studying—should believers break bread? Is breaking bread something that a pastor must preside over? The conclusion of my prayer and study was that the Bible did not say in any place that only an ordained pastor can break the bread." The two quickly decided that they should not hesitate and agreed to break bread together on the coming Sunday, which, again, Nee referred to using the strictly Biblical term—"the Lord's day."[75]

Although the outward circumstances seemed to strongly confirm his beliefs, Nee was still hesitant. He and Wang decided to hold the initial ceremony in Wang's home because Nee feared that "If my mother knew of these things, she might say that we young people were being rebellious." Nee spent all of Friday and Saturday in eager anticipation, and finally, on Sunday evening, he told his mother that he had to go to Wang's home to "take care of a very important matter." If any doubts remained, they were washed away by the ecstasy of the event. Nee writes:

> That night, the three of us (Brother Wang, his wife [Ada], and I), were in a little home, breaking bread together and drinking the cup together. I must tell you, to my dying day I will never forget, even in eternity I will never forget—I have never been so close to heaven as I was that night! That day, heaven was truly near the earth! The three of us could not stop weeping! Only that day did we realize the true significance of breaking bread to remember the Lord. When I was young, after I had been baptized by sprinkling, I had taken Holy Communion. At the time, I said 'The bread is a bit sour and the grape juice is a bit sweet.' I only remember that one was sour and the other sweet, I didn't understand anything else. Only on this occasion did I come to know that [Communion]

---

[74] NTSWJ 18, 78.
[75] NTSWJ 18, 78–79.

is in the presence of God, and is most precious to God. We learned for the first time what it meant to worship, what it meant to remember the Lord. We were speechless, we could only praise and thank God![76]

The three communicants then decided, upon the basis of further Bible study in Acts, that they should meet together weekly, an obligation that Nee took very seriously, writing that "From that day on, I have broken bread every Lord's day unless I was sick, on the road, or detained by some unexpected circumstance." When his mother discovered shortly thereafter what Nee was up to, she did not oppose him, only commented that they had been "quite bold." After a few months though, she also began to join them to break bread together.

Nee experienced these humble but happy gatherings as a powerful promise, a taste of the church as a concrete manifestation of the ideal Christian society, a bridge between heaven and earth. These experiences also encouraged him in his lifelong experiments with church practices, testing out the best ways to follow Biblical teachings faithfully. Although Nee had initially pressed for answers to the question of baptism and bread breaking primarily for his own conscience's sake, his answers soon became pressing, public issues. In the years following his conversion, Nee and his friends led a number of evangelical campaigns that eventually converted hundreds of their fellow Fujianese, new Christians who naturally looked to their young leaders for direction.

Consecration and Revival

Immediately after his conversion, Nee began to try ardently, if ineffectively, to convert his classmates. He went to Barber for help, and one of her associates suggested that he could never be an effective evangelist without being "filled by the Holy Spirit to receive power from above." For Barber, this process required that a person give herself to God unreservedly and forsake any intervening sins. Thus, Nee "went to at least two or three hundred people to confess offenses... But despite passing through various kinds of dealings, I still could not gain [spiritual] power."[77] Finally, Nee realized that the problem was his love for a young woman, Charity Chang (張品蕙, 1902–1971), whom he would marry many years later.

Nee and Chang had been childhood friends.[78] Their long acquaintance and the gradual nature of its change may account for the somewhat vague timeline Nee supplies regarding the development of his feelings for her. In any case,

[76] NTSWJ 18, 79–80.
[77] NTSWJ 26, 225.
[78] On the Nee and Chang families' long friendship, see Kinnear, *Against the Tide*, 37, 80–81.

Nee explains the problems that these feelings created, leading to another crisis early in 1922.[79] In Nee's words, the confrontation opened with a passage of the Scripture:

> One day, before I was to preach, I opened the Bible to search for a topic and happened upon Psalm 73:25: "Whom do I have in heaven but You? Whom do I desire upon the earth besides You?" After I read it, I said to myself, "The writer of this psalm can say these words, but I cannot." At that time, I realized there was a distance between me and God.[80]

Nee casually admits that he was preaching as an eighteen-year-old who had been converted for fewer than two years. It is possible he started some form of public preaching from the first months of his conversion, at least in the Bible studies held in his home. Nee was obviously a gifted speaker and teacher. The Protestant world of Fuzhou was both small and intimate. Since Western denominations were struggling to maintain their legitimacy amidst mounting societal pressure and disrepute, they were desperate for native talent wherever it could be found. Unsurprisingly, informal arrangements proliferated in unpredictable ways, apart from the hierarchies of ordained pastors, denominational boards, and established elders.

In any case, Nee's sermon preparation ran into a significant obstacle. He began to question "whether she [Charity] or the Lord would have first place in my heart." His feelings were all the more problematic because Charity was then decidedly uninterested in religious matters. She greeted his attempts to convert her with mockery, much as he himself had treated Christians before his own conversion. Although their lives seemed to be heading in opposite directions, Nee remarked, "once young people have fallen in love, they find it very difficult to give up the one they love."[81]

Nee recalled an intense back-and-forth between God and himself. He asked God to "be patient and give me strength until I could give her up." He tried to bargain and even "considered going to evangelize in the desolate boundaries of Tibet and proposed many other ideas," hoping that God might accept an alternative. Nevertheless, "No matter how I prayed, I could not get through." Finally, Nee submitted, choosing to "deny myself, to lay aside natural love, and love Him with a single heart." Looking back, Nee recognized that he had learned a precious

---

[79] This confirms Witness Lee's account that these things took place "When Watchman Nee was a teenager" in *Watchman Nee: A Seer of the Divine Revelation in the Present Age* (Anaheim, CA: Living Stream Ministry, 1991), 97. Although Nee gives the 1922 date in his own account (NTSWJ 26, 227), he also claims that it was "About ten years before our marriage [in 1934]" that he was in love with Charity (NTSWJ 26, 226).

[80] NTSWJ 26, 225–226.

[81] CWWN 26, 458; NTSWJ 26, 226.

lesson—that personal emotions had to bow before God's will. Retroactively, he thanked God for "chopping off my natural life with a sharp knife so that I might learn a lesson which I had never learned before in this lifetime."[82]

Nee seemed to remember the date of his breakthrough as clearly as that of his initial conversion, writing that on the evening of February 13, 1922, "I was filled with His love and I was willing to let her go. I loudly declared, 'Let her go! She will never be mine!'" Nee records that he experienced the joy of heaven: "I saw the world shrink, as if I were alone, mounting the clouds and riding the mists through heaven." The very next week, "people began to be saved." With the sacrifice of his heart's desire, Nee's ministry was born.[83] He was now fully given over, or "consecrated" to be filled with the Holy Spirit.

The revival began with Nee's successful conversion of his classmates at Trinity College. Many of the students who had once rejected his message now converted, and some even went to become fellow leaders in the revival. Eventually Nee and Wang were joined by others who had been Nee's schoolmates since childhood, such as John Wang (no relation to Leland), Wilson (Leland's younger brother), Faithful Luke, and Simon Meek. The experience of the Fuzhou revival proved formative for these young men as well, as they all went on to devote their lives to Christian ministry.[84] Luke's and Meek's English names were idiosyncratic and seem to have been chosen for Christian effect, and it is possible that Nee adopted the moniker "Watchman" around this time.[85] Adopting new personal names throughout one's life was a relatively common Chinese custom, especially among educated men. Although Nee never explained his choice of a name, his established interest in Jesus's second coming suggests that he saw his personal mission as agreeing with the Bible's frequent warnings toward vigilance and watchfulness in that regard.

Having turned their campus into a hotbed for Christian activity, the young men then turned their attentions to the city at large. They set up twenty-four-hour prayer watches and paraded around the city, accompanied by music and wearing white vests and banners upon which were written slogans like "Jesus is Coming" and "Believe in the Lord Jesus Christ." At the end of the march, they

[82] NTSWJ 26, 226–227.

[83] NTSWJ 26, 227.

[84] Kinnear, *Against the Tide*, 65–79. James Chen, *Meet Brother Nee* (Hong Kong: The Christian Publishers, 1976), 18–19. Leland Wang's Testimony accessed on November 1, 2016, at http://www.joyfulheart.com/maturity/no-bible-no-breakfast.htm. Although Nee says that there were five other schoolmates, Leland Wang mentions only the four and I have been unable to find the name of the last revivalist.

[85] In Chinese, Nee was already using the stylized Christian name (倪柝聲) by which he became known in his written articles. In traditional Chinese culture, the taking of courtesy names and art (or pen) names, was common and the young men appear to have applied the practice to their English names as well. Nee's first English name upon his christening had been Henry.

would gather all the curious onlookers and preach to them.[86] Soon, the young men were at the head of a Christian congregation of hundreds.

Margaret Emma Barber—A Unique Mentor

As the revival developed and matured, the young leaders looked increasingly to Margaret Barber for spiritual direction. Barber had a strong, idiosyncratic personality, and she may well have influenced Nee more than any other single, living person, even though he spent fewer than four years in Fuzhou directly under her influence. Unfortunately, much of her life story is shrouded in mystery.

An unlikely set of circumstances and events led Barber to be stationed in Fuzhou, not far from Nee's home, at exactly the time when he most needed religious guidance. By 1922, Barber had already spent about fifteen years in China on her third and final visit as a missionary. She had completed two previous tours as an Anglican under the auspices of the Church Missionary Society. Upon her return to the United Kingdom after her second missionary trip to China, she left the Church of England to be baptized by immersion and joined an independent, evangelical congregation called Surrey Chapel.

Surrey Chapel was founded by Robert Govett (1813–1901) and was led for decades by his successor, David Morrieson Panton (1870–1955). Both men published extensively, outlining their complementary visions in a unique set of literalistic, Biblical interpretations. While many of their teachings were common to other evangelicals of their era, they were virtually alone in propounding something like a Biblical, Protestant version of purgatory. Based on the "millennium" mentioned in the Book of Revelation, Govett and Panton argued that Jesus's return would initiate both the resurrection from the dead and a period of one thousand years in which some Christians would enjoy a millennium of bliss while others would be subject to a millennium of discipline. Eventually, Govett, Panton, Barber, and Nee would comprise something of an intellectual lineage, embodying and propagating Surrey's unique perspective. At the time of Nee and Barber's meeting, Surrey Chapel supported only two missionaries to China, Barber and her companion, Margaret Ballord.[87]

---

[86] Kinnear, *Against the Tide*, 68–9. NTSWJ 26, 235.

[87] Ballord's name appears as "L. S." in Wing Hung Lam's [林榮洪], *Shuling Shenxue: Ni Tuosheng Sixiang de Yanjiu* (Hong Kong: China Alliance Press, 1985), 22 and "M. L. S." in James Reetzke's *M. E. Barber: A Seed Sown in China* (Chicago: Chicago Bibles and Books, 2007), 109, and Kinnear's *Against the Tide*, 57–58. In a letter taken from the Norwich Records Office (NRO) 76/85, however, she signs her name "Margaret Ballord." Margaret Ballord to David Panton, April 6, 1931. Reetzke claims that she was Barber's niece (109), but this was almost certainly not the case. In the "Report of the Foreign Band 1930" from NRO 76/82, Ballord is simply called Barber's "friend and helper."

As it happened, then, Barber was one of the few Western missionaries who could have wholeheartedly sympathized with Nee's objections to common Christian practices on the grounds of their being unscriptural. His absolute character and careful attention to Biblical mandates, regardless of convenience and cost, could hardly have suited her own tastes more perfectly. Her years in China had not seen much outward success, but she was busy cultivating an inward spirituality that hewed closely to biblical mandates and prized quality over quantity. If the aspiring minister needed a pattern, the experienced teacher was also happy to find a worthy student.

Until her death in 1930, Barber mostly stayed in the Fuzhou area, where she spoke the local dialect and was familiar with the climate and surroundings. The first decade of Nee's ministry thus coincided almost perfectly with the last decade of Barber's life, in which she served as an independent missionary, connected with Surrey Chapel. She seems to have been living with Ballord in a small, rented bungalow when she first met and baptized Nee. She also maintained some correspondence with another figure who would inspire Nee, the Welsh laywoman revivalist and Bible teacher, Jessie Penn-Lewis (1861–1927).

Unfortunately, while Barber's first two missionary trips to China were carefully recorded in numerous letters to the Church Missionary Society, almost no written biographical or autobiographical record of her life during this last, longest mission to China survives. If Barber also wrote regular reports to Surrey Chapel, no record of that correspondence survives. Historian Jay Riley Case has argued that scholars should pay more attention to the "antiformalist" evangelical missions that eschewed scrupulous recordkeeping and institution building in favor of simply contacting people and winning souls. Because they had little need to connect with hierarchies and funding sources in their sending countries, they often enjoyed far closer relationships with the individuals and cultures where they were stationed. This social and cultural intimacy made them far more successful at converting native peoples while also rendering them invisible to official documentation.[88]

Barber's missionary career strongly supports Case's claims. Her first missionary trips offer a rich paper trail but appear to have had little lasting impact. Her last missionary trip might easily have completely disappeared from the record had one of her native converts not been so impressed that he wrote about her repeatedly. And yet, if for nothing but her guiding influence on Watchman Nee alone, Margaret Barber's last mission to China should be considered one of the most important in Chinese Christian history. Still, the absence of her own

---

[88] Jay Riley Case, *An Unpredictable Gospel: American Evangelicals and World Christianity, 1812–1920* (Oxford: Oxford University Press, 2012), 7–15.

writings means that the story of her relationship with Nee must be told almost entirely from Nee's perspective alone.

At every turn, Barber had encouraged Nee to follow a strict, self-sacrificial Biblical piety. She baptized him by immersion, she encouraged him to seek a filling of the Spirit that caused him to give up his romantic interest, and she disparaged official church membership, cementing his break with the Methodists. Nee's entire career would take place decidedly outside of what historian Daniel Bays has called the Sino-Foreign Protestant Establishment, or the complex set of institutions and persons that controlled the vast majority of the resources available to Protestants in China at the time.[89] As an interesting Chinese parallel to Case's thesis, although the Sino-Foreign Protestant Establishment garnered more headlines and represented Chinese Protestantism to the world, it is likely that Nee and other anti-formalist Chinese Christians ended up affecting the religious beliefs and practices of their fellow Chinese far more significantly. In any case, as Nee and his co-revivalists forged an unknown path, they found a mentor who had maintained a similar streak of conscientious independence for many years.

Problems in the Revival

Nee and Leland Wang had shared many joyful and meaningful experiences, but leading a revival was quite different from participating in a Bible study or agreeing to follow the Bible on questions of baptism and bread breaking. There were many practical points to consider, and in most cases there was no clear biblical solution. Leland and Nee evidently came to dominate the small group of revivalists. Nee later admitted ruefully that "We had a co-workers' meeting every Friday and the other five would all listen to the two of us argue."[90]

Leland's growing reputation was based on both his own eloquence and on his "famous surrender of worldly success to the service of God," having resigned a naval commission to preach as an itinerant evangelist.[91] Wang was certainly one of the more vibrant and influential Chinese Christians to emerge during the 1920s. He would go on to have a successful international preaching career, traveling widely throughout China and the Sinosphere. Like Nee, he would find special success in Southeast Asia, where the common Fujianese connection helped both men make inroads into large, well-established, diasporic Chinese communities.

[89] NTSWJ 18, 82. Bays, *A New History of Christianity in China*, 92ff.
[90] NTSWJ 26, 228.
[91] Lian, *Redeemed by Fire*, 159. Lian also points out that a naval commission in China was less glamorous than it might have seemed, which may have helped with Wang's decision.

Often, when two strong personalities are forced to work in close proximity, social friction is the result. Nee and Wang's different temperaments may also have had an effect. Whereas Wang was exuberant and extroverted, Nee was reserved and analytical. The two men's youth may also have been a factor. In 1923, Nee would have been only twenty, and Wang, twenty-five. In any case, Wang and Nee disagreed strenuously and often. Nee admitted that "I frequently lost my temper."[92]

In a sense, the young Christian group was a victim of its own success. In 1936, even after Nee had already rebuilt and expanded his following to include many congregations throughout China, he still looked back fondly to his work in the early 1920s, claiming that he "had never seen a revival greater than this one." He continued:

Back then, people were being saved every day. It seemed that no matter who they were, as soon as we contacted them a bit, they would get saved. Every morning, I would get up early at five o'clock and as soon as I arrived at school, no matter where I looked, I saw people holding and reading their Bibles. In all, more than a hundred people were reading their Bibles there. Previously, reading novels had been very fashionable, now people had to read novels secretly. Now, reading the Bible became something very honorable. . . .

Every day, about sixty people marched around carrying [gospel] banners. The entire city of Fuzhou only had a population of about one hundred thousand. As we went out every day in this way, marching and carrying banners, with dozens passing out gospel flyers daily, the entire city of Fuzhou was shaken.[93]

For a small group of students to overturn the culture of their own college must have seemed an impressive achievement. Furthermore, the nucleus of six or seven young men was also able to inspire dozens of others to join them in their vocal processions throughout the town. It must indeed have seemed to the revival leaders that the whole city was shaken, even though most of the city's hundred thousand inhabitants were probably unaware of their activities.[94] Nor were they the only young Chinese who had grand ambitions to change the world with only a small group of committed followers. In 1921, the Chinese Communist Party planned to make China into a modern socialist nation with a party membership of only sixty nationwide.[95]

[92] NTSWJ 26, 228.

[93] NTSWJ 26, 237.

[94] Unfortunately, no church records exist to fix a definite number for those who were saved, baptized, or regularly meeting with the congregation. At least one early follower corroborates Nee's story. See Chen, *Meet Brother Nee*.

[95] Jonathan Spence, *The Search for Modern China* (New York: W. W. Norton, 1990), 322–323.

Of course, the rising number of conversions begged an important question: What was the next step for this group of burgeoning Christian ministers? None of them had much taste for foreign Christianity. Nee notes that the headmaster of Trinity "admired everything we did," only "our attitude towards the Anglican church grieved him" because the group resolutely "refused to belong to any denomination."[96] Here, Barber may have played a role in encouraging the young evangelists to maintain a strict denominational independence from her own natal tradition.

When Nee had gone to Barber to ask about his own family's being removed from the Methodist membership rolls, or "book of life," she had replied rather acerbically that "I am afraid that among the names in that book of life many are dead and not a few are perishing." Adding, for clarification, that "If your name is in the heavenly book of life, what can an earthly book of life do for you? And if your name is not recorded in the heavenly book of life, what benefit is the earthly book of life to you?"[97]

While all the leaders of the revival generally agreed with Barber's idea of independence from Western denominations, they had very different ideas of what that meant when it came to practical specifics. Wang and most of the revival leaders wanted to continue in what might seem the most logical course of action. Since the people of Fuzhou were welcoming, the revivalists should continue to "be zealous in revival and gospel preaching work" because "the fruit of such work could easily be seen."

Nee, however, had been studying the book of Acts and had come to the conclusion that "God's wish is to establish local churches in every city." For Nee, this understanding was not only an exegetical doctrine. He spoke of his realization as a mystical vision with enormous practical effects, writing that "What the Lord showed me was extremely clear. Soon, he would raise up local churches in many places throughout China. Whenever I closed my eyes, I saw the emergence of the local churches."[98]

This disagreement went to the heart of the conflict between Nee and Wang. In the end, although both felt called to Christian ministry, they had very different understandings of its purpose. Wang was primarily interested in saving souls and following an established pattern for native preachers such as Dora Yu and other revivalists, including Cheng Jingyi. He hoped to found a flourishing independent church, while also maintaining warm and mutually beneficial contacts with the established Protestant bodies. Wang would be given the honor

---

[96] NTSWJ 26, 237.
[97] NTSWJ 18, 82.
[98] NTSWJ 26, 238–239.

of baptizing Ruth Bell, Billy Graham's future wife, and he eventually received an honorary Doctor of Divinity degree from Wheaton College.[99]

Nee, on the other hand, was already starting to show his penchant for mysticism and the more radical reform of Christian ideas. Not satisfied just with amassing converts, formally independent from but amenable to the Western denominations, Nee returned to his "vision of the birth of local churches." This vision had historic and universal dimensions that can only be understood by studying Nee's sources in Western Christianity. In the end, what may be called Nee's ecclesiology represents one of his most original contributions to the history of Christian thought. Nee began with some of the West's most self-critical voices and ended up with what he considered to be a more Biblical, less culturally captive version of the gospel.

The Vision of the Local Churches: Watchman Nee's Ecclesiology

At first glance, Nee's teachings on the church may strike some observers as both so extraordinary and so critical that it may be supposed that these ideas must have emerged from some kind of revolutionary or subaltern resistance to Western norms. However, the subtle and trenchant nature of these critiques actually grew out of a long debate within the West itself, as embodied by the teachings of a small group of British Christians often referred to as the Plymouth Brethren.[100] Nee carefully translated these Brethren ideas into Chinese and convinced many Chinese Protestants that this ecclesiology was a faithful interpretation of the Bible's own message.

The Plymouth Brethren were founded when a number of theologically similar groups coalesced in the late 1820s and early 1830s. Initially, these groups were primarily clustered in Ireland and Western England. A number of common themes united the first Christians who became the Brethren, including their study of unfulfilled prophecy, their radical Protestant adherence to the principle of *sola scriptura*, their pacifism, and their pessimism regarding the direction of secular and ecclesial history.[101]

---

[99] Lian, *Redeemed by Fire*, 162.

[100] Both the original "Plymouth Brethren" and the contemporary groups designated by that name would refuse to name themselves as such. As we will see, they considered all denominational monikers to be divisive. Nevertheless, for the purposes of analysis, it is impractical not to name them at all. There are many other Christian groups that use the generic English name "Brethren," which they would prefer (for instance, see brethrenonline.org and brethrenhistory.org). Thus, "Plymouth" has the benefits of granting further differentiation, recognizing one of the movement's early bases of strength, and pointing to the movement's source in the United Kingdom. The group is now international and quite a bit larger, with probably a few million total members.

[101] James Callahan, *Primitivist Piety: The Ecclesiology of the Early Plymouth Brethren* (Lanham, MD: Scarecrow Press, 1996), xii–xiii. Despite this internal diversity, many scholars have primarily focused on Brethren teachings related to eschatology. See David Bebbington, *Evangelicalism in*

Although Nee adapted a number of these disparate themes, for him, as for many of the Brethren, the church lay at the heart of all these concerns. The concept of the church captivated Nee. Besides Christ himself, it is possible that no other subject occupied as much of Nee's attention throughout the course of his life. From his earliest recorded work to his latest, Nee spent an immense amount of time and energy thinking about the nature of the church and trying out different methods of church organization, propagation, and worship, all topics generally considered under the heading of "ecclesiology."

For Nee, the church was at the very center of God's purpose and work. If Christians properly understood the church, they would understand how they could best live and behave with respect to everything else in the universe. This included both the invisible order (God, Satan, angels, and evil spirits) and the visible order (themselves, other Christians, secular society, and government authorities).

Trying to uncover Nee's own understanding of the "local churches" at this earliest stage in Fuzhou is difficult.[102] Nevertheless, his rationale for leaving the Methodist denomination, the aversion to Anglicanism he shared with his fellow revivalists, and the nature of his most serious conflict with Leland Wang all make most sense in the light of Brethren ideas, which were sharply and uncompromisingly critical of Western church structures and clergy.

It is clear that soon after the Fuzhou conflict was resolved, Nee began to publish openly and extensively on his understanding of the church, and that these writings were clearly and heavily indebted to Brethren teachings. According to Witness Lee, in the beginning stages of Nee's work in China, the influence of the Brethren on Nee's followers was so thorough that some even referred to them as "the Chinese version of the British Brethren."[103] In 1925, Lee also wrote to Nee, asking him for help to "understand the Bible verse by verse." Nee referred Lee to the *Synopsis of the Books of the Bible*, written by one of the Brethren's founders, John Nelson Darby (1800–1882).[104] By the end of that year, Nee

---

Modern Britain: A History from the 1730s to the 1980s (New York: Routledge, 2004), 86–91; Marsden, *Fundamentalism and American Culture*, 48–62; Paul Boyer, *When Time Shall Be No More: Prophecy Belief in Modern American Culture* (Cambridge, MA: The Belknap Press of Harvard University Press, 1994), 80–112; and Matthew Avery Sutton, *American Apocalypse: A History of Modern Evangelicalism* (Cambridge, MA: Harvard University Press, 2014), 16ff.

[102] Before 1925, Nee wrote very little—only scattered articles for denominational magazines and a few issues of his own publication, *The Revival*, which was meant to provide spiritual food for the young Fuzhou congregation. Neither venue was particularly conducive to spelling out a controversial, intricate, Brethren-inspired theory on the nature of the church.

[103] Witness Lee, *The History of the Church and the Local Churches* (Anaheim, CA: Living Stream Ministry, 1999), 62.

[104] Lee, *Watchman Nee: A Seer*, 285. Comparing this reference with another of Lee's in *Elder's Training, Book 10, The Eldership and the God-ordained Way* (Anaheim, CA: Living Stream Ministry, 1992), 117, gives the date of 1925.

began an in-depth study of the book of Revelation that was profoundly indebted to Brethren ecclesiology. One year later, Nee publicly acknowledged Darby's *Synopsis* as "the best commentary" available.[105]

Taken together, all of these facts indicate that Nee had deep roots in Brethren thinking. In fact, he had probably begun to read their work during the early 1920s. This may have come about as a result of Nee's contact with Barber. In 1910, Barber herself had written a letter decrying the "superficial unity" to be found in Christianity, and her dismissive attitude toward the Methodist book of life is also highly suggestive.[106] Whether Nee was introduced to the Brethren through Barber or independently, by the mid-1920s, he was thoroughly steeped in their ecclesiology.[107]

Thus, while Nee's use of the phrase "local churches" might seem to be a generic reference to local congregations, for Nee, the "local churches" included a significant body of specific ecclesiological beliefs and practices, largely derived from axioms laid down by the Brethren. Furthermore, the stakes involved in getting the local churches right were so high that Nee was willing to confront his Fuzhou companions and endanger his part in a promising new revival.

To begin with, Nee believed that his understanding of the church was the clear teaching of the Bible. Nee wrote that "The greatest goal of the Reformation was to show that, besides the Bible, nothing is trustworthy."[108] In the spirit of that Reformation, Nee, like the Brethren, was willing to use biblical principles to oppose even other Protestant ideas and organizations that they felt to be unbiblical.

Crucially, Nee and the Brethren agreed that the church was at the heart of the biblical message and furthermore, that the vast majority of Christians, whether Catholic, Protestant, or independent, were not following the biblical commands on the church. Nee believed that if Christians "allow the Bible to solve all problems," they would see that "neither Lutheran doctrines, Calvinist teachings, the Anglican Church, nor the Genevan Church have led us back to the original standing of the church. They had not yet come to know the truths of the body of Christ and the spiritual house built with living stones." Such groups transgressed

---

[105] NTSWJ 7, 156–157.

[106] Reetzke, *M. E. Barber*, 138–139 and Jessie Penn-Lewis, *The Overcomer*, Vol. 2, December 1910.

[107] In December 1925, *The Christian*, another magazine he had founded, began to publish "Meditations on Revelation," which was Nee's extensive exegesis on the first three chapters of the book of Revelation. In particular, "Meditations on Revelation" focused on his prophetic interpretations of the seven churches described in the second and third chapters of Revelation. Like his Brethren teachers, Nee understood these seven local churches to be both historical and prophetical. By thinking about the church in this way, church history and practice were put into a cosmic timeline. It was the state of the church that would move God's hand, leading to Jesus's second coming, and eventually, to the end of time. Nee's exegesis is especially indebted to the Brethren historian, Andrew Miller, *Miller's Church History* (London: Pickering and Inglis, 1974).

[108] NTSWJ 5, 84.

the basic unity of the spiritual church and "divided the church along national boundaries."[109]

This rationale helps to explain Nee's idea that being involved in the Methodist Church in any way made him complicit in its sins. As a denomination, Methodism divided the spiritual body of Christ, participating in the sin of division. For him to remain attached to Methodism, even nominally, was to share in its sin. This stance was virtually identical to the Brethren position. Early Brethren had defended their choice to leave their original congregations and denominations on the grounds that "Separation from Apostasy [is] Not Schism."[110] Since the original congregations and denominations were unbiblical and divisive, they were apostate. In such a case, faithful, obedient Christians had no choice but, paradoxically, to separate themselves from the denominations to pursue true unity.

Just as Nee was convinced to leave the Methodist denomination because of Paul's exhortation to unity in 1 Corinthians, so too, the Brethren left their original congregations in the name of church union. The Brethren writers frequently gave unity pride of place in discussing the hallmarks of the true church. One argued that the first "departure from the simplicity of the faith of Christ" was "internal disunion."[111] Another stated his objection to "division, and sectarianism . . . whether it assume the character of the Establishment or of Dissent."[112] In the Parliamentary Returns, their peculiar emphasis on ecumenism coupled with their refusal to denominate themselves caused them to be entered in the rolls as "Catholic, not Roman."[113] The Brethren touted their catholicity and unity even as they denounced Anglicans, Dissenters, and the rest of post-Apostolic Christendom for "disunion," "division, and sectarianism."

This apparently self-contradictory position can be explained by a widespread Protestant belief in the invisible church. Historian Grayson Carter elaborates:

> Central to Evangelical ecclesiology was the idea of the "Church of Christ," the invisible body of all regenerate souls to which alone could be given the adjectives, "one, holy, and catholic." Here, at the theoretical level, all Evangelicals were agreed. While they prized the visible Church into which they were ordained,

---

[109]   NTSWJ 5, 84–85. See also NTSWJ 5, 152–154.

[110]   Henry Borlase, "Separation from Apostasy Not Schism," *Christian Witness* 1 (1834).

[111]   Benjamin Newton and Henry Borlase, *Answers to Questions Lately Considered at a Meeting, Held in Plymouth* (Plymouth: J. B. Rowe, 1834), 301 as quoted in Callahan, *Primitivist Piety*, 93.

[112]   William Kelly, ed. *The Collected Writings of John Nelson Darby, Ecclesiastical*, Vol. 1 (London: George Morrish, n. d.), 31.

[113]   James Bennett, *History of Dissenters, During the Last Thirty Years (from 1808–1838)* (London: Hamilton, Adams, 1839), 30.

Evangelicals maintained that its interests should be subordinated to those of the real church, the "Church of Christ," or the invisible body of all believers.[114]

From an evangelical perspective, the true or "real church" was composed of those who had passed through the watershed experience of conversion and were to be counted among God's elect. Anglicans, Roman Catholics, and Magisterial Reformers all agreed that the earthly church was inevitably a mixed body, filled with both saints and the unrepentant. For various reasons, both utilitarian and dogmatic, loyalty to the visible churches was promulgated by apologists within these traditions. Nevertheless, most British evangelicals, who treasured the value of adult conversion or regeneration, had to admit that the members of the "one, holy, and catholic Church of Christ" were to be found across the denominational lines of many visible congregations. The discrepancy between these mixed, visible congregations and the pure, spiritual church weighed heavily on some consciences.

Like the Brethren, Nee placed a higher emphasis on this doctrine of the true, invisible church than other Protestants. In particular, like many who followed in the traditions of radical reformers, such as the Mennonites and Anabaptists, the discrepancy between the invisible and visible churches weighed heavily on his conscience. Even if it were only possible in small groups, these radical reformers sought more tangible manifestations of the true church's unity and catholicity. In Nee's case, following the Brethren, he was especially anxious to eschew any denominational names and markers. If all the groups in organized Christianity enforced divisions in the body of Christ, the only ecumenical option was to leave them all.

Visible unity and catholicity comprised one part of Nee's vision of the local churches. Visible holiness was another. Here again, Nee drew on the biblical record to discredit the mainstream practices of Western Christianity. Just as contemporary Christian practice seemed to Nee to be woefully lacking as far as unity was concerned, so too, Christian congregations appeared to have compromised the purity of apostolic practice. Even though Acts described tight-knit groups of true believers, Christian congregations seemed to care more for success, power, and organization than for purity. As a result, other compromising practices proliferated.

For instance, Nee believed that it was the responsibility of every Christian to "contact God *directly*," and that in the New Testament, the "intermediary priesthood has been forever abolished." In this light, both "the 'system of priests'" in the historical Roman Catholic Church and the 'system of pastors'" in

---

[114] Grayson Carter, *Anglican Evangelicals: Protestant Secessions from the* Via Media, *c. 1800–1850* (Oxford: Oxford University Press), 9.

the contemporary Protestant churches" were only "different expressions" of the same erroneous teaching.[115] Obviously, the vast majority of Christians were not prepared to give up ordination, whether of priests or pastors.

Likewise, Nee saw the early churches as being untainted with secular politics, and indeed, when politics is mentioned in the book of Acts, its influence is generally cast in a negative and craven light. On such grounds, Nee condemned both the Roman Catholic Church for getting involved in politics and the Protestant Reformers for not trusting enough in the "immeasurable capacity and unlimited intelligence" of God, and instead relying on "the patronage and support of worldly powers."[116] It is not surprising, perhaps, that the congregations that have followed Nee, like those of the Brethren, have often been condemned for their sectarianism.

This sharp, unbridgeable gulf that Nee and the Brethren maintained between the secular and ecclesiastical spheres was to have immense consequences for Nee and his followers. Nee lived through some of the most politically turbulent decades in modern Chinese history, but his works scrupulously avoided any mention of political affairs. Even when lives and congregations were at stake, Nee did his best to maintain an apolitical stance, a position that became extremely costly at the end of his active career. It is possible that the political chaos of Republican China made the Brethren ecclesiology more attractive to Nee. A church that stood apart from political powers offered the hope of a lasting haven in the midst of a rapidly shifting political landscape, which often had brutal consequences for losers.

In any case, Nee concluded that the Biblical standard of holiness had been thoroughly corrupted, allowing sin to have its place in what were supposed to be holy congregations, interposing mediatorial clergy between God and fellow Christians, and becoming corrupted by relations with secular authorities rather than maintaining a sanctified distance. Nee's local churches would hew to the New Testament Christian teachings on unity and purity to the greatest extent possible, at the cost of isolating themselves from other Christians and minimizing their influence on mainstream society.

Conflict and the Cross

While Nee cherished his personal vision of church doctrine and practice, Leland Wang had different ideas. Although we do not have Wang's record of the controversy, it is possible to reconstruct something of his point of view. He was an

[115] NTSWJ 4, 239–240. Emphasis in the original.
[116] NTSWJ 5, 67–68.

older, married man who had given up a reputable profession to join his younger brother and his brother's schoolmates to evangelize China. Perhaps because he was the only one with a house of his own, the initial revival meetings had been held in a pavilion on his property. Since their preaching had been successful and had gained hundreds of converts, Wang naturally wanted to continue a successful work that God had seemed to bless. In Nee's later recollection, the other five young men agreed with this obvious course of action, and they "always stood on [Leland Wang's] side and opposed me. No matter what I did, they always said I was wrong."[117]

Nee had his own reasons to be proud. Simon Meek, one of the five schoolmates, later told Nee's biographer that Nee was the "planner and ringleader" for many of their ventures.[118] Nee explained that he was used to positions of leadership, writing "In my school and in my class, I was always ranked first, in the matter of serving the Lord, I wanted to be ranked first as well. Thus, when God made me second, I did not submit. Every day I told God that I couldn't take it. I received too little glory and authority, everyone sided with the older co-worker."[119] Like Wang, Nee had also given up a promising future upon his conversion, and he was deeply earnest in his desire to follow his intricate vision for the local churches. Nee suggests that the gravity of the situation pressed upon him heavily. He "rarely laughed at that time" and "frequently lost [his] temper."[120]

Every Friday, as the seven "co-workers" met, Nee and Wang monopolized the proceedings with their arguments. On Saturday, Nee would appeal to Barber, hoping that she would justify him. Instead, Barber took the opportunity to humble Nee further. Again and again, she told Nee that since Wang was five years older and "The Scriptures say that the younger should obey the elder," Nee had no choice but to obey Wang.[121]

Thus, Nee recounts that "On Friday afternoon, I would argue, and that evening I would weep. The next day, I would go to Missionary Barber to vent my grievances, thinking that she would vindicate me. But on Saturday evening, after returning home, I would be weeping again."[122] Even when Nee wanted to baptize fellow students from Trinity who had believed as a result of his own preaching and prayer, Barber forbade him. Instead, she ordered him to submit to Wang and allow Wang to perform the baptisms, arguing again that Wang's age made him more qualified. Nee, sensing a loophole, suggested that a third brother who was

---

[117] NTSWJ 26, 232.
[118] Kinnear, *Against the Tide*, 69.
[119] NTSWJ 26, 232.
[120] NTSWJ 26, 228.
[121] NTSWJ 26, 228.
[122] NTSWJ 26, 229. Nee frequently referred to Barber with the honorific title 教士, which could be translated "clergy," "churchwoman," or "missionary."

older than both himself and Wang might be allowed to baptize. Barber was un-moved and "still insisted that Leland perform the baptisms."[123]

Barber consistently opposed Nee over the course of "a year and a half" throughout his arguments with Wang.[124] Her behavior might seem capricious and even cruel to an outside observer, and it is easy to imagine that persons more level-headed than the young Watchman Nee would have been infuriated by this treatment. In fact, it seems befuddling that Nee continued to come to Barber and to seek her approval. Evidently, Barber possessed a mysterious quality that both subdued and attracted Nee. All the existing accounts of this early revival suggest that she seemed to have this same effect on the whole group of the young men, all of whom deferred to her spiritual seniority.

In later years, Nee recalled Barber's authority with a number of fascinating descriptions. One of his most vivid memories employed a theological concept he called "life." He wrote, "God does not only want us to gain His life, He also wants His life to flow out of us. Sister Barber was such a person. As soon as people touched her, they touched life. If you sat down and fellowshipped with her, in a minute or two you would sense the flowing out of life. If a person with life just sits there, others can sense the supply from them."[125]

At other times, Nee spoke of Barber possessing a kind of prescience that could be powerfully convicting. Nee wrote that "A few times Missionary Barber seemed to be like a fortune-teller. She would talk about how a particular brother was in a certain kind of situation. Afterward, the evidence showed that every-thing she had said was true."[126] Similarly, he wrote that "Many people who knew Missionary Barber can testify that she was very special. If you went to her, sat in her presence for a while, and then left, you would realize that you had erred. You would realize that you did not have what she had and would aspire to gain what she had." Thus, Nee recounted that early in his Christian life, he had been proud of his Bible knowledge, and "I went to go talk to her about [what I had read]. After I prayed a few sentences with her, before she even corrected me, I saw my own pride. I knew that I did not have what she had."[127]

Thus, in his disagreements with Leland Wang, Nee was trapped. He admired Barber and wanted to learn from her and gain her approval, but she resolutely opposed him. Later, he suggested that over the course of these years, he went to her "forty or fifty times" and she "did not agree with me once." If Nee was frus-trated, Barber too, may have felt that the lesson she was trying to impart was not taking. Nee described the moment of their breakthrough on a number of

---

[123] NTSWJ 57, 10.
[124] NTSWJ 26, 229.
[125] NTSWJ 44, 141.
[126] NTSWJ 41, 224.
[127] NTSWJ 42, 12–13.

occasions, but in his most thorough description of the affair, Nee had clashed with Leland yet again. In describing the aftermath, he wrote:

> I felt that there was no righteousness in this world. I went again before Missionary Barber to discuss Leland's mistakes. I spoke for half an hour to an hour, full of righteous indignation. I could not suppress the righteous indignation of my youthful temper and kept speaking and speaking. Then, Missionary Barber said to me, "For months now, you have been coming here, mostly to talk about how Leland was wrong. Even if I say that Leland is wrong, what good will it do you? Do you want to talk about right and wrong or do you want to bear the cross?" After a while, she spoke again, "Look at yourself. Is this the attitude of a lamb?" She called my name loudly and said, "Watchman Nee! Is this how you bear the cross?" I immediately began to cry. I crumbled. From that time on, I no longer accused people. I feel that I owe her a lot. Today, I no longer have the opportunities I had then to learn such precious lessons. Although the dealings I received from her hand were bitter, these dealings were my blessing.[128]

On another occasion, Nee reiterated that this was "the most precious lesson of my life."[129] Nee had begun to share Barber's vision of "bearing the cross"—one that idealized Jesus's meek, silent response to misunderstanding and human opposition. His open arguments with Leland Wang stopped, and he would return to this experience again and again for the rest of his life as an important touchstone.

If Nee's conception of the local church was to be practiced, the demand placed on the individual members was significant. Although the local churches were to be reflections of the universal church, they had no ultimate, eternal significance of their own. In eternity, after all, all the "local" restrictions of space and time would be transcended. Nevertheless, in practice, the local churches were to be pure and harmonious, unified within each city, and unified also with all the other local congregations throughout the earth. Furthermore, they were to maintain this standing without the interference of a hierarchical clergy. This meant that the individual members and churches had to discipline one another. For members to be restricted in their disciplining of one another, humble in their receiving the discipline of others, and magnanimous to avoid offenses and church schisms was a tall order. Without such self-restraint, Nee's vision of the local churches could not be practiced. In learning his "most precious lesson" from Barber, Nee realized that the way of the cross—absolute self-negation—was the only path forward.

---

[128] NTSWJ 59, 20–21.
[129] NTSWJ 26, 229.

Nee immediately had crucial opportunities to test the depth of his new convictions and understanding of the cross. Although he had been convinced by Barber's rebuke not to argue with his co-workers, he still felt that God had expressly commissioned him to establish local churches. The root of the disagreement between Nee and Wang remained, and they continued to work in contradictory directions without open confrontation. As a figure of growing renown, Wang frequently left town to preach in other meetings and congregations. Nee writes, "When he was away, I worked according to my vision. When he returned, he undid what I had done, working according to his vision." Nee did not give details but explained only that "one way was that of focusing on revival and preaching, while the other way was that of establishing local churches." Some of the other co-workers "were not satisfied" with Nee and eventually, "God allowed the church in Fuzhou to fall into a trial. In order to avert a schism, I left Fuzhou."[130]

One of Nee's co-workers told a much more dramatic and specific account of the schism. James Chen was a long-time leader of a congregation that followed Nee in Hong Kong. He first met Nee in 1926, when he was converted by Nee's itinerant preaching in the aftermath of the conflict in Fuzhou.[131] He later recounted that the final question that divided Nee and his friends was their desire to "invite an ordained minister for the purpose of having themselves ordained as ministers." Nee opposed this practice, claiming that "a minister is a gift given to the church by God (Ephesians 4:11) and not a position created by man," and arguing that the "system of ordination" was an unscriptural, erroneous tradition. Nee then preached a message warning that "once the ark had left Shiloh, there was no return, thus alluding to the fact that we should not backslide to old ways."[132]

As might be expected, Nee's sermon "incited resentment in his fellow-workers," who excommunicated Nee and "announced it publicly." Chen records that there was a significant backlash to this drastic decision and that Nee was "well loved because of his eloquence and his ability to shed light on the Scriptures in his preaching." Nee's supporters went to discuss the matter with "the leading brothers," and their anger soon began to focus on Leland Wang, whom they recognized as "the key figure in the expulsion decision." In the heat of the argument, some of them rushed at Wang, seeking to attack him, when Nee jumped in front of him and "spoke loudly, 'Don't touch him! If you want to beat him, beat me first! He is loved by God, and loved by me too. He is our brother! I have forgiven him. You should also do the same. At any rate, you must not lay your

---

[130] NTSWJ 26, 238–239.
[131] Chen, *Meet Brother Nee*, 29–30.
[132] Chen, *Meet Brother Nee*, 18–19.

hands on him.'" Chen recounts that Wang was "deeply moved, and shed tears on the spot" and that "The demand for ordination was no longer raised." Still, it was at this point that Nee recognized that his presence had become a divisive factor and left Fuzhou of his own accord.[133]

It is understandable that ordination could become an explosive issue among young Christian workers with no official status. Most, if not all of the young men involved in the revival, would eventually devote their lives to full-time ministry. Like Nee, his classmates had also given up promising futures for an uncertain career. They all agreed on formal independence from denominations and the Sino-Foreign Protestant Establishment. There is no indication, however, that any of the other revivalists had either made Nee's radical decision to live by the "faith principle," that is, to depend on God for their income, or come to Nee's conclusions about the unscriptural nature of the hierarchy. Since they had not traveled down those paths, Leland Wang's method and future seemed much brighter than Nee's.

Wang had agreed that clergy were not required to preside over the Holy Communion, but this did not necessarily imply that the clerical system was inimically wrong. Wang maintained both his independence *and* close ties with denominational Christians and the Protestant establishment. Although establishment Christians were slow to cede actual power to native Christians, they did make smaller concessions to indigenization, such as sponsoring the preaching tours of independent Chinese revivalists, or paying for them to preach in their denominational congregations. Ordination could have given the young men firmer footing and recognition from other Christian congregations. Wang would go on to have great successes overseas, widely feted by Chinese and Western Christians alike. Nee would be opposed repeatedly for his ideas on the church and would eventually pay an enormous price for his convictions. It is hard not to sympathize with the concerns of the other Fuzhou revivalists.

The first period of Nee's ministry had come to an end and appeared to result in total personal failure. Nee had been converted and had given up the prospect of secular employment in order to devote himself to Christian ministry. With a small group of his childhood schoolmates, he had spearheaded a heady revival in which hundreds were saved, many of them by his own preaching among his classmates and the people of Fuzhou. His friends wanted to continue with "revival and evangelism," possibly seeing ordination as a way to solidify their careers and status. Nee, however, insisted on "establishing local churches" according to his vision of an exacting, scriptural way to practice church unity and purity. Nee then chose exile over schism, allowing himself to be cut off from the congregation that he himself had helped to establish.

---

[133]   Chen, *Meet Brother Nee*, 19–20.

In the coming decades, Nee would be banished at least two more times from groups in which he clearly held a founding, leading role. In each conflict, Nee allowed himself to be marginalized without mounting a defense or rallying his supporters. Especially as his stature grew, it is hard to believe that he could not have won significant support, or even banished his opponents, if he had been inclined to try. Nee's apparent passivity during these crucial moments has become part of an enduring puzzle, making it even more difficult for later historians and biographers to sort out the facts.

Self-abnegation is not a common quality in leaders, but for Nee, it was a crucial, non-negotiable part of the Christian message. Barber had introduced him to a theology of the cross, which demanded a radical form of self-denial, and Nee had begun to see that this was the only means by which church unity could actually be achieved and practiced. The combining of a Brethren-based ecclesiology with this mystical, demanding conception of the cross was one of Nee's most novel contributions to Christian thought.

Nee later trained his own co-workers to absorb and embody this same principle. He warned them that their usefulness depended upon the depth of their experience of the cross and their willingness to submit even in the face of great wrong and injustice.

> If you cannot pass through the trials of the cross, you cannot become a useful vessel. God only delights in the spirit of the lamb, gentle, humble, peaceable. Your great ambitions, high aspirations, and abilities are all useless before God. I have walked this path, I must constantly confess my own mistakes. Everything I have is in God's hands. The problem is not whether one is right or wrong, but whether one is like the cross-bearer or not. In the church, right and wrong have no place, what counts is bearing the cross and accepting the breaking of the cross. Thus only can the life of God flow and accomplish God's will.[134]

Nee's idea that the cross invalidates questions of "right and wrong" is a curious one. Biographically, the notion can be derived from Nee's assessment of his own behavior. Even when he was on the "right" side of the argument against Leland Wang, Barber exposed his proud, uncharitable attitude. Intellectually, however, the claim that the Christian life did not depend on notions of right and wrong was another of Nee's contributions to an ongoing conversation. As with his ecclesiology, Nee inherited a particular set of Western Christian ideas on ethics and behavior and then developed these ideas on the basis of his own Bible study, creating a theology that had special resonance in his own context and adaptability for many other audiences.

---

[134] NTSWJ 26, 229–230.

On the one hand, Nee left Fuzhou with little to show for his time there. On the other hand, he had received a detailed vision of the local churches derived from his own Bible study, his understanding of Brethren theology, and his training under Barber. To this, he had added the innovation of the "local church" that allowed for the Brethren's pessimistic idealism to be put into enthusiastic practice and potentially resolve the age-old contradictions between congregational and universal unity. Possessed of the vision and blueprint of the local churches, Nee was ready to implement what he had seen. To these he also added a particular understanding of the Christian life, one that eschewed outward success in favor of inward attainments.

The combination of local churches and self-denial allowed for a deeply communal form of Christianity. During his time in Fuzhou, Nee was constantly involved in Christian meetings, from his mother's Bible study to his first communion at the house of Leland and Ada Wang to Barber's mentorship and the meetings with his co-workers. Except for the larger gatherings in their rented building, all of these meetings took place in the participants' homes, suggesting a high degree of intimacy and sociability.

Wherever Nee established churches in the future, the congregations would follow suit, meeting throughout the week, often in one another's houses. One scholar of Nee's life has suggested that his placement of the home and hearth at the center of congregational life capitalized on the traditional Chinese emphasis on family.[135] This form of daily church practice, where members might regularly spend many hours each week together heightened both the potential for conflict and the demand for unity and harmony.

Even though he was eventually rejected by his companions, Nee first glimpsed the possibilities of such a life in Fuzhou. As a result of his Fuzhou experiences, Nee also believed that he now had the secret to fostering a congregational life that could overcome all differences in personality and vision. Every member of the church simply had to take the way of the cross. Even if he had to begin anew, he was now equipped with Barber's lessons and also the secret of her attractive wisdom and equanimity. He was prepared to embark on a Christian path that would allow "the life of God [to] flow and accomplish God's will."

---

[135] May, "Watchman Nee and the Breaking of Bread."

3

Constructing a "Spiritual Person"

After Watchman Nee left Fuzhou in 1924, he was suddenly very alone. His excommunication from the congregation and subsequent departure from the city largely cut him off from the Christian society he had previously enjoyed. Lin Heping (Nee's mother), Leland Wang, Margaret Barber, and his fellow schoolmate revivalists all remained in Fuzhou while he began to move from place to place, never staying in any location for more than a few months. With a few significant exceptions, he would never again be quite as solitary or unsettled as he was during the years between 1925 and 1927, which would turn out to be a period of both intense suffering and impressive productivity.

Nee took advantage of his solitude to distinguish himself and refine his distinctive message. If his childhood friends had been a source of support, they may also have been something of a limitation. Nee's biographer, Angus Kinnear, suggests that the schism "shook [Nee] from his rest in Christ and plunged him deep in discouragement."[136] In his own writings, though, Nee leaves no record of being depressed at his expulsion from the Fuzhou group. The parting of ways may have freed Nee from having to compromise his developing set of convictions. He set about advancing his work with remarkable drive and confidence. Instead of falling into obscurity, Nee wrote and published more than ever, and his burgeoning ministry began to garner a significant reputation and a sizable following. He had lost Fuzhou, but he was gaining a much wider audience.

Nee's surprising persistence in the face of adversity may have owed something to the lessons of self-denial he had so freshly learned under Margaret Barber's tutelage. One of the first things Nee wrote after his expulsion from the Fuzhou congregation touched on the importance of genuine humility. In this article, Nee argued that "Humility is not thinking less of oneself; it is not thinking of oneself at all. Humility is not to look down on oneself, but not to look at oneself at all. All truly humble people are truly dead to themselves." Nee believed that he could be so deeply identified with the cross that he would be able to ignore all personal insults, slights, and setbacks because he was "truly dead" with

---

[136] Kinnear, *Against the Tide*, 91.

The Spiritual Person. Paul H B Chang, Oxford University Press. © Oxford University Press 2026.
DOI: 10.1093/9780197793664.003.0004

Christ. Nee had also concluded that for the "truly humble person," there was no place for wavering or indecision, writing that "True humility before the Lord does not withdraw at a crisis or pull back from advancement in the name of false meekness." Shorn of the burdens of self-pity, regret, and doubt, Nee was paradoxically freed to "strive forward while acknowledging his uselessness and powerlessness."[137]

The paradoxical figure who embodies both dynamism and a total lack of self-consciousness is a familiar trope in Chinese religion and philosophy. Daoist and some strands of Confucian thought famously uphold the ideal of *wuwei*, which connotes a kind of effortless excellence, action that transcends intention and artificial exertion.[138] As Nee represented himself and his experiences in terms of total freedom from self-regard, he was using language that would have been culturally familiar to Chinese audiences and widely identifiable as a sage, a generic figure of ethical superiority and wisdom who was able to uplift the conduct of others, presumably his readers and followers.[139]

Nee would never have referred to himself as a sage since the terminology was so deeply associated with Confucianism and Daoism, whereas Nee's brand of evangelical Christianity clearly depicted Christ as superior to all other religions and religious figures. Nevertheless, the years between 1925 and 1927 were the last stage in the process of Nee's formation and emergence as a sage-like figure. In 1924, he was known mainly to a small circle of Fuzhou Christians. After 1928, he was increasingly acknowledged by Christians throughout China to be a master of Christian doctrines and practices, and his teachings were widely believed to lead to true moral excellence.

In other words, if one ignores the specific designation of Christianity, by the time he was twenty-five, Nee was clearly recognizable as a sage. Even though he and his followers preferred to use exclusively Christian terms to refer to their relationship, other Chinese, at least, would have considered them to be following well-trodden cultural paths. This chapter will explore Nee's emergence as an influential Bible teacher and Christian leader despite his youth and relative isolation.

---

[137] NTSWJ 7, 220.

[138] There is a passage in the *Analects* in which Confucius uses the term approvingly, at Book 15.5. It has been argued that this is a late assertion, but Benjamin Schwartz points out that other parts of the *Analects* share a similar perspective. *The World of Thought in Ancient China* (Cambridge, MA: The Belknap Press of Harvard University Press, 1985), 188–191.

[139] The term "generic" is used in two senses. Nee's behavior corresponded to the "genre" of the sage, a universally recognizable pattern of behavior in Sinophone culture. Nee's behavior also corresponds to that of a sage in a "generic" or general sense. The cultural production around sages is vast and varied among different thinkers and traditions. Here, the term is only meant as a broad reference to a person of exemplary moral excellence whose life and teachings uplift others.

The "Faith Principle"

To begin with, on a wholly practical level, Nee was able to survive expulsion from Fuzhou because he had learned from Barber how to "live by faith," that is, to live without a regular means of support. At the time, Nee seemed to be aware of only two Christians in China who were living by the same principle, Barber and Dora Yu.[140] In the context of evangelical piety, the "faith principle" was an established rule that had important implications.

When Barber had first considered returning to China for her last missionary journey, she had consulted with a respected, older missionary who had counseled her that as long as God was sending her, God would also see to all her needs, financial or otherwise.[141] Barber was a member of Surrey Chapel, and the Chapel organized a group of supporters whose subscriptions helped finance foreign missionaries. Nevertheless, it appears that Barber never received a definite salary, and it is unclear how regularly she was paid.[142] Not surprisingly, she was forced to rely on God, sometimes coming to desperate circumstances. Nee recounts that on one occasion, after Barber had "spent her last yuan," she had written the poetic lines, "God's cup overruns / In the end, a surplus comes."[143] For Nee, such a response showed a certain greatness of soul, which hinted at the real purpose of living by faith.

Barber's example and his own desire to remain independent forced Nee into a difficult position immediately after his initial conversion. Later, Nee dated the start of these concerns to 1921 and 1922, around the same time he was struggling with his love for Charity. Nee recognized that he could have chosen to be a "preacher in a denomination," which would have yielded him a "fixed monthly salary." Instead, he felt that he had to "walk in the Lord's way" and "only depend upon Him for my livelihood."[144]

For Nee, the first step along this path was to speak to his parents about their expectations. This precaution provides a small insight into Nee's adaptation of the Christian message to what he saw as ethical behavior in a Chinese family. In that culture, parents' significant investments in their children often came with the expectation of reciprocal support for them in their own old age. Nee recounts:

One evening I spoke with my father about his financial support for me. I said, "I have been praying for a few days and I feel that I must tell you that I can no

---

[140] NTSWJ 30, 236 and NTSWJ 26, 254.

[141] NTSWJ 30, 236.

[142] Surrey Chapel, "Report of the Foreign Band 1930," Norwich Records Office (NRO) 76/82 and 76/85.

[143] NTSWJ 30, 246. This was Nee's translation of Barber's English poem, which began "There is always something over / When we taste our gracious Lord."

[144] NTSWJ 26, 253.

longer spend your money. I know that you have spent a lot on me. On the one hand, I know that you have done so out of fatherly responsibility. On the other hand, I am sure that you expect that I will one day make money to support you as well. I must tell you now that I am becoming a preacher. I will not be able to repay you in the future nor can I plan to have a certain amount to give to you. Although I have not completed my education, I want to learn how to depend on God." After I had spoken this, my father thought it was a joke. But from that time on, when my mother would give me five or ten yuan, she would write on the envelope, "For brother Watchman Nee." She was not giving me money as a mother.[145]

Nee followed up this story with a few autobiographical vignettes taken from his early years of ministry. Each of these vignettes pointed to a similar lesson. In every case, Nee came to dire financial straits. Once, he was pickpocketed. In another instance, God specifically commanded him to give money to one of his co-workers even though he did not have enough for himself. Nee recalled that on other occasions, God called him to a mission or a project that he did not have the resources to carry out. Every time, Nee refused to ask for human help. In fact, God forbade Nee from borrowing, begging, or otherwise making his needs known. At one point, Nee even rejected an offering from a would-be supporter who claimed that someone else had already taken responsibility for his needs, but who did not specify that this "someone" was God. Nee reported that frequently, the devil tempted him, mocking his unreasonable behavior and trying to cause him to waver. Through every difficulty, he persevered and, in the end, God providentially, almost miraculously provided. Nee suggested that he had "ten to twenty more cases" that would serve to prove the same point.[146]

Nee later concluded that "In spiritual work it is necessary that one's livelihood not be fixed." This was because "In spiritual work, it is necessary to have fellowship with God, to have the revelation of God's will, and to have God's heavenly provision." From Nee's perspective, the lack of a settled income would force the Christian worker to fellowship with God, seek God's will, and depend on God's provision.[147] Barber's conduct showed Nee a vibrant pattern for this kind of life. Barber was certainly one of Nee's examples when he argued that depending on God for support went hand in hand with a life of constant, absolute intimacy, in which outward circumstances repeatedly forced a Christian to turn inward, examining her own conscience for anything that might hinder God's unstinted approval. For Nee, living by faith was the earliest iteration of a lifelong

[145] NTSWJ 26, 253–254.
[146] NTSWJ 26, 254–260.
[147] NTSWJ 30, 230.

theme: Dependence on God was a non-negotiable requirement, trumping all rational expectations and calculations.

Living by faith could foster misunderstanding and suffering, but misunderstanding and suffering could also be helpful. Ideally, all these hardships caused a Christian earnestly to seek God's presence, rather than find temporary relief in the material comforts of life on earth. Nee's insistence on this principle of faith empowered a financial independence and independence of direction that matched his physical isolation. Nee became used to turning down other sources of support, whether they be individuals or institutions, allowing him to distinguish himself, both as a leader and as a target of criticism.

Reading and Publication

On another practical level, the success of Nee's work in these early years of independence can be explained by his careful investment of time and his prodigious mental energy. In general, he moved in three basic directions that would continue for the rest of his life. He read and learned, he published his own work, and he preached widely. To begin with, Nee gathered material for his publication and preaching by reading the Bible and Christian literature at a furious rate.

Early in his Christian ministry, Nee dedicated himself to reading through the New Testament once each week over the course of an entire year.[148] It is possible that he engaged in this course of intense reading during the mid-1920s when he was suddenly deprived of congregational duties. Nee also amassed a library of over three thousand Christian books and periodicals over his lifetime.[149] His book-buying activity was so notable that in 1926, his Western suppliers began to ask him why he wanted these books. This exchange initiated a sequence of events that would eventually connect Nee directly to the Plymouth Brethren and lead to his first visit to Europe and the United States.[150]

Based on his studies and experiences, Nee also continued his writing and publication. His first periodical, *The Revival*, had been published and financed on an irregular basis between 1923 and 1925.[151] In 1925, he replaced *The Revival* with a new magazine called *The Christian*. Nee would go on to publish twenty-four issues of *The Christian* between 1925 and 1927, and it was clear that he

---

[148] Witness Lee, *CWWL 1978*, vol. 2, 570.

[149] On Nee's library, see Witness Lee, *Watchman Nee*, 25 and *Life-Study of Proverbs, Ecclesiastes, Song of Songs* (Anaheim, CA: Living Stream Ministry, 1995), 55 and Jennifer Lin, "The Secret Flock of Watchman Nee: Curiosity About a Famous Relative Becomes an Unexpected Voyage of Discovery," *The Philadelphia Inquirer Magazine* (March 12, 2000).

[150] NTSWJ 18, 97–99.

[151] NTSWJ 18, 84–85. In 1928, he would stop printing *The Christian* and resume his publication of *The Revival*, giving it a second run of thirty-six issues going up to 1934.

had developed his skills in planning and production considerably. Although no known copies of this first run of *The Revival* exist, Nee had correspondents and subscriptions for *The Christian* as soon as it started. Thus, it is possible that a warm response to *The Revival* convinced Nee that a more organized publication could also succeed.

Perhaps in keeping with the ethos of the "faith principle," Nee had not even asked for subscription fees for *The Revival*. As a result, he was only able to print issues as he had the funds. In contrast, the first issue of *The Christian* suggests a system of fees, asking for seventy cents for a yearly subscription of twelve issues, at a time when many urbanites would have made about a dollar a week.[152] Nee also suggested at the outset that for every ten copies ordered, one would be free, so that the "financially poor" could solicit other subscribers to "receive a copy free" for themselves.[153]

The content of *The Christian* also showed that Nee wanted to offer readers a more systematic approach than his earlier publications. *The Revival* had touched on various topics under the rather vague, overarching theme of "the deep things of God."[154] In contrast, *The Christian* began with a definite plan. Odd-numbered issues would be typical "magazines"[155] with an eclectic collection of articles, "signs of the times," and a "question and answer box." Even-numbered issues would be specifically devoted to biblical exposition. Nee more or less kept to this plan and, during the first sixteen issues, he even maintained a nice parallel structure with odd issues containing substantial articles on Genesis while even issues were entirely devoted to Revelation. *The Christian*'s subscribers thus received extended exegeses sequentially explaining the difficult and controversial bookends of the Bible.[156] Around this time, Nee also founded the Gospel Book Room to handle his publications.

These changes between *The Revival* and the first issue of *The Christian* were the fruit of lessons learned through Nee's work in publications during the interim. In 1922, Nee and his cohort in Fuzhou had invited an older Christian named Ruth Li (Li Yuanru, 李淵如, 1894–1969) to help in their revival. In 1924, Nee went to visit and work with her in Nanjing, where she was editing a Christian magazine called *Spiritual Light*. Although Li was initially resistant to Nee's ideas

---

[152] NTSWJ 7, 338. On urban salaries and the costs of printed materials, see Perry Link, *Mandarin Ducks and Butterflies* (Oakland, CA: University of California Press), 1981, 12.

[153] NTSWJ 7, 338.

[154] NTSWJ 8, i, 1.

[155] The Chinese term *zazhi* indicates a "mixed" publication composed of different features and topics, as opposed to an essay or monograph.

[156] Nee's writings on Genesis dealt with a number of knotty questions raised by the book. For instance, following some other conservative Christians of the time, he reconciled literal readings of Genesis with contemporary science and archaeology by positing that there was an indeterminate gap of time between Genesis 1:1 and 1:2. His use of the book of Revelation to discuss his ideas on the church is largely covered in Chapter 2.

with regard to the church, she was eventually convinced, and by 1927, she had quit her position to devote herself to Nee's work. For the rest of his publishing career, she would be one of his primary editorial assistants.[157]

Nee's additional expertise notwithstanding, early issues of *The Christian* still show evidence of a number of difficulties. Some were common obstacles faced by many new publications. Early issues thus apologize for problems in proofreading and typesetting. Another asks readers to "increase the usefulness of *The Christian*" by recommending it to "believers within and outside your province."[158] Nee admits that "It is not an easy thing to publish a magazine" and repeats his initial plea for his readers to "have a share in this work" by "doing your best to introduce this paper to others."[159] By the second issue, he found it necessary to raise the cost of a subscription to one dollar a year, and he also asked those readers who had not yet paid to send their subscription fees to the Gospel Book Room.[160]

Nee also faced problems due to the general chaos in Chinese society and the general lack of infrastructure. In the third issue, he tells readers that all subscribers should have received their copies, but if not, "it may be due to the current political situation."[161] Even sending and receiving money could present significant complications. Some subscribers were apparently unable to send in their fees because "the post office is not issuing money orders." Nee suggested a workaround in which subscribers would "use a check from a foreign bank, or spend five cents on a special postal stamp [for sending money by mail]."[162]

Despite these difficulties, Nee was certain that there were many "seekers of the Lord's truth." The only problem was that "they have not subscribed to the magazine because they do not know about it."[163] Nee had evidently judged the temper of the times correctly. By the seventh issue, sent out in the spring of 1926, he was able to announce that "the magazine has greatly increased its circulation" and that a number of back issues were already sold out. By the tenth issue, *The Christian* had thirteen hundred subscribers and was possibly covering its costs.[164]

---

[157] Lee, *Watchman Nee*, 104–106.

[158] NTSWJ 7, 339. On typographical errors, 341.

[159] NTSWJ 7, 342. There are other similar pleas at 348–349 and 351.

[160] NTSWJ 7, 338.

[161] NTSWJ 7, 342.

[162] NTSWJ 7, 348.

[163] NTSWJ 7, 342.

[164] NTSWJ 7, 348, 351. In the 1910s, a magazine of about 55,000–85,000 characters might break even at three thousand copies for sixty cents a copy. By the 1920s, there had been significant technological advances in print. Furthermore, *The Christian* usually ran at around 30,000 characters and, of course, Nee did not have to pay the author or copyeditor any royalties. Link, *Mandarin Ducks*, 11–12, 86–91.

The Success of The Christian

Nee's success in publishing and preaching went hand in hand. As readership of *The Christian* increased, Nee's growing fame and connections led to numerous invitations to travel and speak. Throughout the 1920s, he preached and held revival meetings not only across his home province of Fujian but also in the populous Southern Chinese provinces of Zhejiang and Jiangsu. Those provinces included important cities such as Shanghai, the burgeoning giant of commerce and industry, and Nanjing, which would soon become China's political capitol.[165]

In the latter half of 1924, Nee had also accompanied his mother on a preaching tour through Malaysia and Singapore, establishing his first international contacts among the significant Chinese diasporic communities in Southeast Asia, among whom Fujianese were well represented. Some of these Chinese communities were quite prosperous, and although Nee did not discuss the financing of his trip, it is possible that he and his mother were sponsored by their hosts. Whatever their financial relationship, Nee and these diasporic Chinese communities enjoyed a strong relationship. Chinese from Malaysia and Singapore would continue to write to Nee and invite him to visit until the end of his life.

On this first trip, Nee probably distributed his writings, because the Southeast Asian congregations began to order his publications. The very first issue of *The Christian* included fees not only for Chinese readers but also for overseas subscribers: one US dollar or two shillings six pence for a twelve-issue subscription.[166] Likewise, the first query in *The Christian's* inaugural "Question and Answer Box" was from "Huang" in Singapore, who asked about the apocalyptic schedule of the book of Daniel.[167]

Huang's question centered on the interpretation of Daniel 8:14, which suggests that "on the two thousand three hundredth day, the sanctuary must be cleansed." Huang argued that "According to *Modern Mysteries Explained*, published by the Seventh-day Adventists, this is a long period of time and is related to the last things." Huang, however, had his doubts, asking "How should this actually be explained?"[168]

Huang's question presupposed not only that the Adventists were incorrect, but also that Nee would be able to solve a knotty prophetical problem. In response, Nee suggested that Adventist biblical interpretations were generally "forced."[169]

---

[165] Kinnear, *Against the Tide*, 99. NTSWJ 18, 89–93.
[166] NTSWJ 7, 338.
[167] NTSWJ 7, 69.
[168] NTSWJ 7, 69. The Adventist publication Huang references is a Chinese translation of *Our Day in the Light of Prophecy*, a work by William Ambrose Spicer, who was the president of the Adventist General Conference at the time.
[169] NTSWJ 7, 70.

As evidence, Nee cited an Adventist publication that defended the year 1844 as the beginning of the end times—a reference to their distinctive "heavenly sanctuary" theology, which grew out of the "Great Disappointment."[170] Nee also appeared to have his own copy of *Our Day in the Light of Prophecy.* He cited other examples from the book that highlighted the very point Huang had raised, in which a day could be understood as a year based on passages such as Ezekiel 4:6 and Numbers 14:34. Nee argued that in both of those cases, contextual biblical references had been improperly expanded to apply as a general principle of prophetic interpretation.

As an alternative, Nee suggested a more rigorously literal interpretation that maintained Daniel's understanding of days as actual days. His solution avoided Adventist interpretations while maintaining its own implications for both history and the future. Nee suggested that Daniel's prediction referred to the fact that Antiochus Epiphanes had desecrated the second temple for two thousand three hundred days and that the coming Anti-Christ would do the same. The exactness of the biblical interpretation with regard to the ancient Greek ruler preserved the Bible's status as an infallible source of truth, while the future promise safeguarded the "blessed hope" yet to come.[171]

This brief interaction gives some sense of the way the three modes of Nee's ministry could support one another. His extensive study allowed him to answer difficult questions, his preaching in Singapore piqued interest in his work, and his ongoing publications nurtured communities of followers. For many Chinese, Nee became an authoritative voice. His facility with English allowed him to channel a vast corpus of Western works that were inaccessible to most Chinese Christians. Nee was particularly masterful in his exegesis, where his knowledge of Western theology was supplemented by his familiarity with the Bible. Even when Nee's arguments undercut rival interpretations, they still maintained a deep confidence in the biblical texts and could shore up the faith of wavering Chinese Christians, assuring them that literal readings of the Bible could fully conform to the facts of history.

There was also a powerful symbiosis between Nee's writing and his preaching. When Nee first began publishing *The Revival*, his ostensible purpose was to create material to teach and sustain the new Christians who had been converted as a result of his and his friends' evangelizing. Now, with the growing circulation of *The Christian*, the synergy began to flow in the other direction as well. Individuals and congregations purchased and spread Nee's writings and began to practice his ideas. They began corresponding with Nee and invited him to

---

[170] The Seventh-Day Adventists were founded by followers of William Miller. The failure of Miller's predictions has been called the "Great Disappointment."

[171] NTSWJ 7, 71.

come and speak to them. Nee's vision of local churches throughout China was beginning to take shape.

The Beginning of the Local Churches

Much of Nee's outreach was embodied by his literary production and, as the interaction with Huang suggests, his writings could touch on abstruse matters of doctrine and exegesis. Unsurprisingly, his followers tended to be more literate than the average Chinese citizen. During the Republican Period, an unprecedented class of literate citizens was emerging. Historian Peter Zarrow has described "the study societies, state and private schools, arsenals, officials' secretariats, the new media" that gave institutional structure and support to an emerging social base of persons who were not part of the official hierarchy but still operated in the "newly opened public sphere."[172] Nee himself was part of this class, and naturally, they had an affinity for his work.

If Nee's support was disproportionately educated, however, it was not exclusively so. Some of Nee's ideas could also be readily understood even by poor, barely literate, or very new Christians, giving his work a broad base of appeal to match its depth. A few examples can be seen in the participants of Nee's "trainings." Throughout his life, Nee conducted a number of these trainings, which consisted of his selecting and inviting local leaders from around the country to join him for several weeks of intense topical Bible study and spiritual formation.

Pan Qingdao was an indirect participant in one of Nee's later trainings. Pan was brought along by a contingent of Wenzhou Christians to translate and negotiate the language barrier, since they were only able to understand their own local dialect. Another trainee was Zhang Lijiao, who had never received any formal education. She learned to read by using the phonetic symbols in her Bible and, even in her old age, continued to read with their help. Nevertheless, she had a local reputation as a successful evangelist who had itinerated, preached, and taught the Bible in villages throughout the area for many years.[173]

The experiences of such followers hint at the breadth and nature of Nee's appeal. Evidence suggests that many Chinese Christians were able to quickly accept and propagate Nee's teachings from relatively marginal social and economic bases. In fact, by 1927, Nee decided to stop printing *The Christian*, in part because he felt that his message was already, if anything, too well understood. In the last

---

[172] Peter Zarrow, *After Empire: The Conceptual Transformation of the Chinese State, 1885–1924* (Stanford, CA: Stanford University Press, 2012), 22–23.

[173] Interviews with Pan Qindao and Zhang Lijiao on March 13, 2013.

issue of *The Christian,* Nee noted that he had already made certain points abundantly clear. "If we continue to belabor the point, we will make *The Christian* into a publication that specializes in talking about leaving denominations and baptism by immersion."[174]

Both baptism by immersion and leaving the denominations were obvious, practical teachings that could be readily understood and carried out—they were accessible theology for even the illiterate. Nee had a special knack for using plain language to explain complex theological issues. For instance, when one subscriber named Guo asked Nee about the legitimacy of the Christian and Missionary Alliance, Nee was able to distill the Brethren ecclesiology into three simple points. A Christian group could be considered a divisive sect if it had a special name, if it held to a "charter other than the Bible," and if it did not include all regenerated believers. Since the Christian and Missionary Alliance had a name, held to its "special fourfold gospel" and "its system did not include all born-again believers," it could only be considered a sect, even if it was "one of the best denominations."[175]

Given the fevered climate of Republican patriotism and resistance to Western domination, the time was obviously ripe for resistance and independence. As one of Nee's correspondents noted, "During this time of radical changes in the international situation, it is time to reform the church."[176] When he introduced the first issue of *The Christian,* Nee also admitted that "Lately, the indigenous church has been a popular topic." He repeated this basic observation about the temper of Chinese Christianity a number of times in the following issues.[177]

From beginning to end then, the tenure and mission of *The Christian* were influenced by Nee's convincing resistance to many forms of Western Christianity. The magazine showcased Nee's ability to engage with Western claims on multiple levels, whether disputing Seventh-day Adventist claims by deploying careful exegesis or broadly pointing out that all denominations were fundamentally illegitimate. Nee's audience understood and responded enthusiastically. Even as he critiqued other Christian claims, Nee was simultaneously able to use the pages of *The Christian* to outline his own positive project: a detailed vision of the local churches as representatives of a pure, unified church.

Between these critical and constructive ideas, Nee's writings laid the groundwork for his basic solution to the problem of Christianity's Western roots. He would de-Westernize Christianity, rejecting many Christian ideas, practices, and institutions with Western roots, while also avoiding Chinese chauvinism. In their place, Nee wanted a spiritual, heavenly church. In the context of Republican

[174] NTSWJ 7, 372.
[175] NTSWJ 7, 195–196.
[176] NTSWJ 7, 366.
[177] NTSWJ 7, 357. See also 109–110, 341–342.

China, Nee's views can be understood as, at very least, a claim that ordinary Chinese people could follow the Bible according to the strictest interpretations of its mandates, whether they touched on prophecy, church organization, or baptism, and that in so doing, they could surpass most of the Western Christians from whom they had inherited their religion. At the same time, Nee refused to countenance any claims of Chinese ethnic or national superiority, or even to propose a gospel influenced by Chinese culture. In Nee's eyes, the purity and unity that a select few Westerners, such as Barber and the Brethren, taught could only be maintained and even surpassed if he was as strict with his own biases and culture of origin as they had been.

The Shadows of Death

Nee's accomplishments in these years give little indication that he was working under a cloud. As a matter of fact, the intensity of his pace was, in part, spurred by his fear that he had little time left. As early as 1924, probably upon his return from his Southeast Asian trip, Nee became aware of a problem. He reports having a "slight pain in my chest" and "a slight fever." After a medical examination, Nee learned that "I had contracted a serious case of tuberculosis and that I would need an extended period of rest."[178]

Tuberculosis often led to death, and Nee immediately recognized the severity of the situation. The night he received the diagnosis, he was unable to sleep and his "mood was depressed." On the one hand, Nee was not afraid to die. He also accepted the situation and "believed that the Lord could not be wrong." On the other hand, Nee was an ambitious twenty-one-year-old with much unfinished business. Above all, he wanted to complete God's commission to him in the time he had left. Of course, the nearness of the end put the question of God's intentions in sharp relief. Nee spent the next six months earnestly considering his path before coming to a definite understanding regarding "the Lord's will." As he sought divine leading, his growing popularity only exacerbated the problem. News of his affliction spread through the network of churches and Christians that admired him. Nee writes that "At the time, letters came from everywhere, not to speak words of consolation, but to rebuke me for working too hard and for not taking care of my life."[179]

Nee eventually concluded that God intended for him to move in two important, closely related directions for the little time he had left on earth. At the end of his period of soul-searching, Nee was visited by an unexpected contingent of

[178] NTSWJ 26, 242–243.
[179] NTSWJ 26, 243.

"more than thirty brothers and sisters." As he spoke to them "about the question of the church," Nee realized that God had caused him to suffer specifically to force him to return to his "first vision" rather than to take "the way of a revival preacher."[180] Nee's first vision, of course, was that of the church, in particular, his unique understanding of the local churches.

Nee's service to the church could include some fairly traditional outlets, like preaching and sermons. Although doctors had warned him to rest, Nee could not remain entirely inactive, still taking time "to study the Bible" and preach. Some of his supporters' admonishments concerning his overwork may well have been warranted. Nee recalls that on one occasion, he was "invited to lead a gospel meeting." His health had deteriorated precipitously, but he persisted, even though he had to lean against lamp posts to rest and gather strength as he walked.[181]

Beyond his preaching and general publications, however, Nee began to sense that he had a special commission to write a specific work. Nee later recalled his greatest concern at the time: "I thought about all the things I had learned in the Lord's presence over the years and the lessons I had experienced. All remained unwritten. Should they accompany me to the grave?"[182] He began to conceive of a large work that would contain the most important of these lessons and would set them down in a comprehensive manner. This work would become *The Spiritual Person*.

Thus, in the four years between 1924 and 1927, as Nee read and preached and wrote, he was also ruminating over his experiences to find material for his spiritual bequest to the church.[183] The lessons he learned during this period took on a special significance and anchored an otherwise unfixed, uncertain life. Even if one discounts his short preaching tours, Nee rarely stayed long in any single place, making his productivity all the more impressive. He spent at least half of 1924 with his mother traveling across Southeast Asia. In May 1925, he rented a small hut at Maxian (馬限) in the Mawei district, where Barber's home was also located, a short distance away from what was then Fuzhou proper.[184] He may have chosen the location to benefit from more frequent counsel with Barber, but he did not end up staying there long.

Then, in 1926, he left for Nanjing to stay at the home of a friend but, once again, he departed shortly thereafter to rest in the countryside in Wuxi. Fighting related to Chiang Kai-shek's Northern Expedition in March 1927 forced him to

---

[180] NTSWJ 26, 243.

[181] NTSWJ 26, 244.

[182] NTSWJ 26, 240. 不過我想到我多年在主的面前所學習的、所經歷的功課，都沒有寫出來，難道把這些都帶進墳墓裏去麼？

[183] NTSWJ 12, 5–7.

[184] Kinnear, *Against the Tide*, 97–98. Nee refers to his "rented home" at "Luoxing Pagoda" in NTSWJ 18, 89.

move again. This time, he came to Shanghai, where the foreign presence had long guaranteed some level of stability. Shanghai was just then coming under Chiang's firm control, and the city would become Nee's home and his headquarters for most of the rest of his life.[185]

The Context of The Spiritual Person

In Shanghai, galvanized by the fear of dying before he could contribute his work to the church, Nee finally finished and published *The Spiritual Person*, the culmination of the project he had been planning for four years. Often referred to as Nee's *magnum opus*, *The Spiritual Person* is an impressive accomplishment, especially given the pressing circumstances of Nee's health, the constant threat of war, and the constraints of his itinerant life. Its mystical bent may represent a reaction to his straitened circumstances. In a world that seemed to promise only suffering, Nee believed that the secret to human existence could be found deep within. Although understanding *The Spiritual Person* requires some effort, it is well worth examining in detail. Studying the premises and arguments of Nee's longest single work simultaneously explains much of Nee's place in the history of Christian thought, the reverence with which his followers have held him, and the criticisms he has received.

While many of Nee's other works were "homiletic or expositional,"[186] *The Spiritual Person* is not structured around congregational needs or biblical texts. Rather, it is systematically arranged according to Nee's understanding of "biblical psychology."[187] In contrast, most of the other works published under Nee's name today were derived from his oral preaching and exposition. To create *The Spiritual Person*, Nee personally put pen to paper and organized hundreds of pages of material. The book is the closest thing to a constructive theology that Nee ever created.

Despite these characteristics, Nee did not intend for it to be a theological treatise at all. In fact, he found such theological knowledge to be potentially perilous. In an extensive postscript to his preface, he suggests that "The more profound a truth is, the more likely it is to remain a theory. This is because the more profound the truth, the more difficult it is to reach without the work of the Holy Spirit." The danger was that a person who "could not reach it" would "think of it

---

[185] NTSWJ 26, 240–242. See Spence, *The Search for Modern China*, 352–354 for the larger historical context.

[186] NTSWJ 12, 8.

[187] NTSWJ 12, 9. Nee may have derived this term from Jessie Penn-Lewis, *Soul and Spirit: A Glimpse into Bible Psychology* (Fort Washington, PA: The Christian Literature Crusade, n.d.). Nee's use of the term "心理學" clarifies that he specifically means to designate "psychology" as a field of study.

as a kind of theory." An intelligent reader might receive the teachings of this book "only in the brain" and think that she had "gained it all." Nee cautioned, "This is most dangerous. Because of this, we may fall deeper every day into the deceit of the flesh and the evil spirits."[188]

Instead, for Nee, the "system" of The Spiritual Person was to be understood more along the lines of carefully and intentionally placed signposts that simultaneously mapped the contours of the human being and the journey of spiritual experience. The entire book was a practical handbook for spiritual travelers. Although Nee sometimes talks about the experiences of unregenerate unbelievers, they are only brought up as examples to underscore his understanding of certain biblical teachings. The book is not addressed to the unconverted, but rather, to earnest Christians who are seeking, even desperately hungry to actually participate in holy, spiritual experiences. Thus, in the preface, Nee also emphasized the fact that the Lord had delayed him from writing it for three years because many of things he felt that God was commanding him to write "had not yet been fully verified in my experience at that time." Only after he could personally "learn, verify, and experience the Lord's truths" and convert the "spiritual theories" into "spiritual facts" had God finally allowed him to begin writing. Nevertheless, Nee admitted that during these three years, "not one day passed without my putting the writing of this book on my heart."[189]

It was an intensely personal journey and, as the phrase "biblical psychology" might suggest, it contained an intensely personal message. The Spiritual Person is rigorously focused on the experience of the individual believer and has almost nothing to say about the church in any way. Nevertheless, the work should not be read in a vacuum. It is important to recall that during the writing of The Spiritual Person, Nee was simultaneously writing and publishing issues of The Christian that meticulously outlined his Brethren-inspired ecclesiology. Nee's ideas and writings on the church always constituted a central pillar of his thought and work. In fact, Nee claimed that God prompted him to write The Spiritual Person by reminding him of his "first vision" of the local churches. Thus, in Nee's own thinking, The Spiritual Person was a guide to individual Christians with a view toward fostering healthy churches.

It is important to emphasize the underlying link between Nee's writings on the church and his writings on spiritual life because of later developments in the reception of his work. Nee would become well known throughout the world, and his writings would be widely disseminated. In North America and Europe, however, his reception developed a particular bias. Most Westerners knew Nee only as a devotional writer. Many Western evangelicals appreciated Nee's book,

---

[188] NTSWJ 12, 18.
[189] NTSWJ 12, 6.

The Normal Christian Life, which sold hundreds of thousands, if not over one million copies, in the United States alone. Like *The Spiritual Person*, *The Normal Christian Life* makes relatively little mention of the church, focusing instead on developing a Christian's personal experiences of victory and the cross. Even more scholarly Western evangelicals who wrote graduate theses and dissertations on Nee's work tended to ignore or occlude the ecclesiological dimensions of Nee's legacy.[190]

The Structure and Thesis of The Spiritual Person

The Spiritual Person is written in ten sections, which are organized around repeated discussions of what Nee delineates as the biblical perspective on the three parts of each human being: the human spirit, human soul, and human body. Nee covers each of these three parts three different times. The order of Nee's three separate analyses roughly corresponds to his understanding of actual Christian experience, which means that Nee's readers are taken on a journey through the human being even as they progress through the stages of a Christian life.

Although the structure of the book might seem repetitive, with Nee covering the same general territory at least three times, each section introduces significant new material to develop his major themes. *The Spiritual Person* contains a wide range of anecdotes, scriptural exegesis, detailed descriptions of spiritual experience, and careful doctrinal qualifications and analyses. In the end, however, its central thesis can be given quite succinctly. Nee's central argument is that although the human soul (Chinese: *hun*, 魂) and the human spirit (Chinese: *ling*, 靈) may be difficult to differentiate in both doctrine and experience, the Bible clearly and consistently teaches that they are, in fact, different faculties.

It is unclear how Nee settled upon the use of the two Chinese characters, *ling* and *hun*. *Ling* was probably chosen for its association with the Holy Spirit (Chinese: *Sheng Ling*, 聖靈) in the Chinese Union Version (CUV), the most popular Chinese translation of the Bible. Nee certainly wanted to preserve the semantic consistency involved in both the Holy Spirit and the human spirit as translations for the Greek *pneuma*. The choice of *hun* is more obscure. The CUV's inconsistency in its translations was one of the reasons for Nee's writing of *The Spiritual Person*. In at least two places, however, where the CUV was

---

[190]   There are many such works. Some examples include Bassett, "The Formulation of a Basis for Counseling from a Christian Theory of Personality"; Barthélémy, "De l'anthropologie à l'éthique"; Baudraz, "De la Sanctification selon Watchman Nee"; Yuan-wei Liao, "Watchman Nee's Theology of Victory: An Examination and Critique from a Lutheran Perspective" (PhD diss., Luther Seminary, 1997); Phillip W. Sell, "A Theological Critique of the Spiritual Life Teaching of Watchman Nee" (Master's Thesis, Dallas Theological Seminary, 1979).

forced to make a distinction between spirit and soul, it translated spirit as *ling* and soul as *hun*.[191]

In any case, Nee's point was that the distinction between these two invisible parts of the human being was important to maintain. Nee conceded that this distinction might not be apparent to human perception and that even advanced, spiritual Christians might be deceived. Nevertheless, Nee argued that in God's eyes, there was an unbridgeable, ontological chasm between Christian life and work that originated with the spirit, and all other work, which could only be fleshly or soulish by default and was therefore disapproved.

In a characteristic passage, Nee wrote that Paul "classified all Christians as either spiritual or fleshly." According to this stark dichotomy, the "spiritual Christian is a Christian who has the Holy Spirit dwelling in his human spirit and ruling over everything" while the fleshly Christian "includes the whole of the unregenerated person, that is, all the things included among their sinful spirits, souls, and bodies." In sum, a fleshly Christian was "a Christian who follows his soul and body to sin, behave, and conduct himself."[192] The vague language Nee used to define the evocative term "fleshly" was deliberate. Although Nee admitted that the flesh could include the usual litany of ugly and obvious sins, his understanding of the flesh was far-reaching and potentially more insidious.[193] Nee based his teaching on John 3:6 in which Jesus teaches "That which is born of the flesh is flesh." Following this broad definition, Nee concluded,

> What every human being is originally, all that they have by nature when they are born from their parents—all of this is fleshly. No matter how good a person is, no matter how virtuous, no matter how competent, no matter how benevolent, no matter how intelligent, he is still fleshly. No matter how evil a person is, no matter how impious, no matter how stupid, no matter how useless, no matter how vicious, he is also fleshly. Humans *are* flesh. This means that *everything* a person is from birth, no matter what (with no distinction between good and evil), it is all fleshly.[194]

Thus, the flesh referred to the entirety of the natural human state, which, even in its most exquisite, refined, and moral manifestations, is utterly condemned by God. Exactly because the flesh included such a comprehensive range of activities and ideas, Christians frequently tried to "fix, improve, train, or tame the flesh" by all manner of ethical, ascetic, educational, and religious practices and

---

[191] 1 Thessalonians 5:23 and Hebrews 4:12.

[192] NTSWJ 12, 63–4. Nee cites 1 Corinthians 3.

[193] See NTSWJ 12, 92–95 for an example of one of Nee's discussions on the more obvious manifestations of the flesh.

[194] NTSWJ 12, 67.

regulations. God, however, had no hope in the flesh. He refused to ameliorate the flesh and instead condemned it to death. In opposition to humankind's "indescribably numerous methods to overcome the flesh," God's salvation was simple and stark: the cross of Christ.[195]

Nee's understanding of the human being's tripartite nature gave him rich and varied materials with which to depict a broad and subtle range of human behaviors, interior states, and proclivities, but the most important axis of *The Spiritual Person* is the absolute distinction between everything that proceeds from the regenerated human spirit and everything that proceeds from the rest of the human person. In Nee's understanding, the true work of God begins in the deepest part of the human being, the spirit, where God is one with the human being. Only activity that proceeds from this internal union is approved by God.

For Nee, spiritual union is also the true meaning of conversion. Nee writes that "Our being united with Christ's death and our gaining his resurrection life as a starting point happen in our spirit. Regeneration takes place completely in the spirit, it has nothing to do with the soul or the body."[196] Similarly, in another place he writes that "The resurrected Lord is the life-giving Spirit (1 Cor. 15:45), so his union with the believer is his union with the believer's spirit." Once "we accept his death as our death" and "his resurrection as our resurrection," we are freed from "all that is natural and temporary," which "pass away in death, allowing the spirit to be joined to the Lord as one Spirit, in the freshness of resurrection, with absolute purity, and without any mixture at all."[197]

Nee clearly has an actual unity of spiritual substances or persons in mind. Such a unity is irrevocable and can form the basis for the Christian's assurance of eternal salvation. Nee writes that in the process of regeneration, his preferred term for initial conversion, "the life of God is put into the human spirit by the Holy Spirit. Because this life is the life of God, it can never die. So, all who have been regenerated, having this life, are said to have eternal life."[198] Nee believed that the divine life of God himself could provide the basis for an endless supply of grace and strength for true Christian service, not to mention transcendent peace and joy.

Nee also claimed that God's purposes depended on Christians understanding their human spirits. Although Nee recognized that God could work in many other ways, he argued that God was related to the human being most directly through the channel of the human spirit. Nee wrote, "Thus we see in the scriptures that only the spirit can serve the Spirit (Rom 1:9, 7:6, 12:11), only the spirit can know the Spirit (2 Cor 2:9–12), only the spirit can worship the God

---

[195] NTSWJ 12, 96–97. In particular, Nee cites Romans 6:6–7 and Galatians 5:24.
[196] NTSWJ 12, 55.
[197] NTSWJ 13, 22–24.
[198] NTSWJ 12, 62.

who is Spirit (John 4:23–24), only the spirit can gain revelation from the God who is Spirit (Rev 1:10, 1 Cor 2:10). Therefore, we must remember: God has ordained the means of the human spirit to deal with humanity and wants to use the human spirit to accomplish his plan."[199]

In Nee's view, Christians who did not know the difference between their spirit and their soul and who did not know how to live and work from the spirit could never truly satisfy God's desire, or even their own Christian calling. According to Nee, it was unfortunate that most Christians believed the spirit and the soul to be identical even on the level of doctrine. This meant that in practice, they had little impetus or ability to distinguish between real promptings of God in the spirit and distracting external stimuli in the soul or body. Like non-Christians, most Christians spent their lives mostly reacting to their physical environments. At best, they might be ruled by their own apparently good human characteristics.

Nee explained that "Even before they believed in the Lord and were regenerated, many people were already loving, patient, and gentle. Their love, patience, and gentleness were natural, of the flesh, and of the self. They were not spiritual." Even when they were "merciful, patient, and gentle," their work had nothing to do with the "Spirit of God" but rather comes only from "their own capacity."[200] All non-spiritual modes of life and work are at best glittering counterfeits with dire consequences, even if those consequences might not be known or understood in this lifetime.

At times, Nee seemed to offer the spirit as a simple, easily accessible solution. He wrote, "To speak honestly, in experience, the spirit and the soul are easy to distinguish." Those who wanted to follow the spirit "only had to follow the direction of the intuition in the spirit" by "waiting quietly for the voice of the Holy Spirit in the [human] spirit." In contrast, "The soulish way of life is completely the opposite of this. It takes the self completely as the center. When a believer is soulish, he acts according to the self. This means that his actions all come out of his *self*."[201] Upon closer inspection, however, Nee spoke of such things at the level of theory, pointing to spiritual or ultimate realities that were difficult to discern in practice.

Nee explained that in practice, since the soul can have all kinds of apparently good impulses and characteristics, the critically important distinction between spiritual life and soulish life can easily be obscured. Nee used the term "self" to describe the fallen, egotistical soul, and he pointed out that the self may not be sinful according to common understandings of sin. While "Sin is foul, opposes God, and is totally despicable," the self may be "dignified, wanting to help God,

[199] NTSWJ 12, 55.
[200] NTSWJ 12, 161.
[201] NTSWJ 12, 166–167.

and lovable." Thus, although "Studying the Bible is a good thing," it is possible to study the Bible in a way that is "full of the self's activity," conducted by one's "own intelligence" so that it is wholly an "action of the self." Similarly, "pursuing spiritual progress is certainly not a sin," but Nee lamented, "Oftentimes, this kind of pursuit is out of the fleshly self. It may be because we do not like falling behind others, or because there is some advantage for us in spiritual progress."[202]

Thus, even though Nee pointed out that the spirit and the soul are diametrically opposed and are "easy to distinguish," he almost immediately qualified this statement by describing the soul as the "shell of the spirit" in the way the "body is the shell of the soul." In their natural state, the soul and the spirit are "tightly woven together" so that "the soul frequently influences the spirit." Because of this, the benefits of a Christian's spiritual union with God might be difficult to recognize or appreciate. "A regenerated person may originally have a kind of unspeakable peace in their spirit, but because the spirit and the soul have not yet been divided, even a small stimulus . . . will disturb the peace and tranquility in the spirit."[203]

Nee's work contained a basic, inherent tension. On the one hand, his "biblical psychology" clearly distinguished between the three parts of the human being. The division of these three parts even lent its structure to the overall organization of *The Spiritual Person*. And, in fact, his whole work highlighted the basic, crucial, and non-negotiable distinction between the flesh and the spirit. For believers, the flesh mainly encompassed the fallen soul and body, which were constantly perturbed, while the regenerated spirit was the place of unity with God and a source of "unspeakable peace." The two could not be more different in theory. On the other hand, much of the motivation for and focus of the book derived from the difficulty of untangling these deeply intertwined parts in practice. In the life and experience of those to whom he preached, the spirit and soul were basically indistinguishable. Many of Nee's followers would have assumed that the environment affected the body, which acted on the soul, and even the slightest stimulations of the soul would "disturb the peace and tranquility" of the spirit.

The Western History of the Soul/Spirit Distinction

On the face of it, the distinction between soul and spirit can seem like an arcane theological debate. Since Nee conceded that the soul and the spirit were often very difficult to distinguish, what was the point of insisting on a fundamental

---

[202] NTSWJ 12, 160–161.
[203] NTSWJ 12, 168.

difference between the two in the eyes of God? When Nee was on his deathbed, beset with requests and letters from churches around the Sinosphere, why did he devote such an enormous amount of time and energy to spelling out the intricate details of this theological anthropology in trying to serve the actual needs of local churches? Understanding Nee's Western interlocutors only heightens the idiosyncrasy of his position.

In *The Spiritual Person*, Nee claimed a distinguished pedigree for his idea. In the preface to his book, he wrote the following:

> As far as the teaching of the distinction between the soul and the spirit is concerned, I am not one of the originators. Andrew Murray said, "The one thing that both the church and the individual should fear the most is the overuse of the will and the mind of the soul." [Frederick Brotherton] Meyer also said that, "If I didn't know how to distinguish between the spirit and the soul, I don't know what my spiritual life today would be like." Others such as [Otto] Stockmayer, [Jessie] Penn-Lewis, [Evan] Roberts, Madame [Jeanne] Guyon, etc, have given the same testimony. Because we have received the same mission from the Lord, we have freely used their works. Because their work has been used so much, I will not explicitly list the source in each citation.[204]

Nee cited the works of a select, international group of Christian authors and teachers, active in the late nineteenth and early twentieth centuries, who were associated with a British gathering known as the Keswick Convention. This coterie of like-minded primarily Anglophone evangelicals—figures like Murray, Meyer, Stockmayer, Penn-Lewis, and Roberts—probably introduced Nee in turn to older, similar traditions of Christian spirituality, including earlier, Roman Catholic mystics such as Jeanne Guyon. In this passage, the relevant point for Nee was that all of these thinkers argued for a "trichotomous" understanding of the human being as composed of three parts (spirit, soul, and body), as opposed to the "dichotomous" position, which holds that the human being is composed of two parts (soul and body).[205]

Nee's listing of multiple trichotomous authors obscures just how much he was an outlier, even within this group. *The Spiritual Person* spends far more time and space discussing the distinction between soul and spirit than all the works by all the authors on Nee's list combined. While Nee did not misrepresent their arguments regarding the soul and spirit, none of these Western writers shared Nee's preoccupation with "proving" the doctrine's importance.

---

[204] NTSWJ 12, 10–11.
[205] In keeping with his aversion for technical theological language, Nee never adopts this terminology, but for the sake of convenience, they are helpful here.

The closest analogue to Nee's ideas in his list of progenitors was Jessie Penn-Lewis (1861–1927), the Welsh writer whom historian Grant Wacker has described as being "one of the most influential voices in higher life circles in Britain, if not in the English-speaking world."[206] Unfortunately, today Penn-Lewis is mostly forgotten among scholars, if not entirely among higher life evangelicals themselves. More than any writer before Nee, Penn-Lewis seized upon the distinction between soul and spirit and elaborated upon it as an important biblical teaching with far-reaching consequences. Of all Nee's predecessors, Penn-Lewis was the most careful to consistently distinguish between the terms "soul" and "spirit" in her written works, and only she devoted an entire written work to explain the difference between the two, the aptly named, *Soul and Spirit: A Glimpse into Bible Psychology.*[207] Although Nee seems to have adopted the phrase "Bible Psychology" from Penn-Lewis, the difference in their subtitles is telling. If Penn-Lewis's work was a "glimpse," a short booklet of eighty-four pages, Nee's *The Spiritual Person* was an exhaustive treatise—comprising over seven hundred pages in English and over three hundred in Chinese.

As for the distinction between soul and spirit itself and its theological justification, the Keswick authors belonged to the general tradition of biblical evangelicalism. This meant that they were relatively unconcerned with Christian tradition or extra-biblical systems of theology. For evangelicals, the Bible was the final arbiter for all Christian teaching. Therefore, if the Bible supported their arguments, it was more than enough reason to propound them. Here again, Nee both followed and outdid his Keswick teachers. Andrew Murray and Frederick Meyer were trained in classic languages at British universities, while Penn-Lewis frequently referenced various biblical scholars and the importance of reading the Bible in its original languages.[208]

All of these writers believed that one of the difficulties in convincing "the generality of Christians" that the Bible taught a systematic distinction between soul and spirit was the fact that most Christians knew no Greek and were thus at the mercy of inconsistent translations. Penn-Lewis declaimed the fact that "'the Greek word which signifies "pertaining to the soul"' is sometimes rendered 'natural' and sometimes 'sensual.'"[209] Such seemingly minor choices in translation could greatly influence how a biblical passage was interpreted or understood.

---

[206] Grant Wacker, "Travail of a Broken Family: Radical Evangelical Responses to the Emergence of Pentecostalism in America, 1906–1916," in *Pentecostal Currents in American Protestantism* (Urbana, IL: University of Illinois Press, 1999), 29.

[207] Penn-Lewis, *Soul and Spirit.*

[208] Penn-Lewis, *Soul and Spirit,* 1–3.

[209] Penn-Lewis, *Soul and Spirit,* 1. Here Penn-Lewis is drawing from George Hawkins Pember, yet another nineteenth-century evangelical (and a Plymouth Brethren affiliate), who propounded the trichotomous position in his book *Earth's Earliest Ages.*

For instance, both Penn-Lewis and Nee focused on the second chapter of 1 Corinthians, in which Paul lauded "the human spirit" as the only thing that "knows the things pertaining to human beings" just as "the Spirit of God" alone "comprehends the things pertaining to God." From a trichotomist perspective, Paul thus not only suggested a link between the two spirits but also suggested that a special kind of spiritual knowledge exists, one that transcended "human wisdom" and spoke of "spiritual things" with "spiritual words . . . to spiritual people."[210]

Trichotomists such as Penn-Lewis and Nee interpreted Paul as drawing a contrast between the spiritual human and the "*psychikos*" human. English translations almost universally render the Greek word as "natural," "sensual," "selfish," or even, tautologically, some form of "unspiritual."[211] Nee argued, however, that *psychikos* was, in fact, derived from *psyche*, the etymological root of psychology and that the word should be translated as "soul." Tellingly, one of Nee's most important followers, Witness Lee, eventually oversaw a project to retranslate the New Testament. In Lee's Recovery Version, the Corinthian passage explicitly contrasted the "spiritual" person with the "soulish" one.

Penn-Lewis and other Western Christians who had ready access to a wealth of biblical scholarship were galvanized by these biblical "discoveries." Penn-Lewis claimed that "The ignorance of Christians concerning the distinction between 'soul' and 'spirit' is very general, and is a primary cause of the lack of full growth in the spiritual life in many devoted and earnest believers."[212] She argued that the distinction between soul and spirit, as grounded by the original languages, seemed to offer a hidden code by which to interpret the biblical message. From her perspective, such knowledge might be manifestly obvious for those who can read Greek, but for those who were not "able to go direct to the Greek Testament," learning of the soul-spirit distinction would "enable them to grasp the truth, and receive spiritual understanding of spiritual facts set forth in the Scripture as necessary for their growth in life and godliness."[213]

Nee worried that if even the average Western Christian was in the dark, then the lack of Greek knowledge among Chinese Christians was greater by far. To remedy this problem, he began *The Spiritual Person* with a meticulous taxonomy that dealt with every Biblical occurrence of key terms referring to different parts of the human being. Each reference was traced back to the original language and indexed with the Chinese Union Version's translation of these words. Nee ended up supplying over 2500 Biblical citations, including every appearance of the Hebrew and Greek root words for "spirit" (*ruach/pneuma*), "soul"

[210] 1 Corinthians 2:11–13.
[211] 1 Corinthians 2:14.
[212] Penn-Lewis, *Soul and Spirit*, 1.
[213] Penn-Lewis, *Soul and Spirit*, 2.

(*nephesh/psyche*), "flesh" (*basar/sarx*), "heart" (*leb/kardia*), and "mind" (Greek only: *nous*).

Nee's goal was to give readers with no knowledge of Hebrew or Greek a way to check the evidence and draw conclusions for themselves. He was confident that the Bible supported his findings and that audiences would recognize the same pattern that he had seen. Nee's scrupulous efforts managed to invert what he saw as the initial situation. Today, it is much more likely that a Chinese Christian has heard about the biblical justification for distinguishing between soul and spirit than a Western Christian.

This particular triumph carried its own cultural resonances. Although Nee was clearly working out of an international tradition of English-language evangelicalism, China had its own tradition of speculation with regard to the metaphysical self. Some early Chinese writings, dating from the Warring States Period (ca. 475 BCE–221 BCE), included subtle philosophical speculations about the nature of the human being and the cosmos. Most of these schools of thought imagined human bodies, minds, spirits, and souls to lie on a continuum of existence along with the matter and energy of the universe, without drawing sharp distinctions between any of these elements.

The long Chinese intellectual tradition that followed reinforced and revised these relationships in ways far too numerous and diverse to offer a meaningful historiography here. Still, as in the West, influential thinkers often offered new configurations or perspectives on the basic relationship of the human being to itself or to the world at large. For instance, one of the last universally acknowledged masters of the Confucian tradition, Wang Yangming (1472–1529), founded the philosophical "School of the Heart" (Chinese: *Xinxue*, 心學), which challenged existing understandings of the relationships between knowledge and action and the mind and the world.

In choosing *ling* and *hun* to represent the spirit and soul, Nee was rather brilliantly making an intervention in basic Chinese etymology that would have been instantly recognizable to nearly all Chinese-speaking people. Chinese "words" are generally composed of two characters, each of which provides part of the meaning for the word as a whole. Sometimes these characters have complementary meanings, so that when combined, *dian* (電, electric or electronic) and *nao* (腦, brain) create *diannao*, signifying a computer. At other times, they are duplicative so that *bang* (膀, arm) and *bi* (臂, also meaning arm) intensify or clarify one another, so that *bangbi* simply means arm. The common Chinese phrase *linghun* is often taken to be duplicative in the latter sense, so that two supposedly synonymous characters are meant to stand for the seat of human selfhood, an ethereal entity that is potentially separate from, or higher than the physical, material body, and thus also, potentially immortal or linked to supernatural forces. By drawing a distinction between *ling* and *hun*, Nee's challenged a common-sense assumption, and positioned himself as a teacher, offering insight into the composition of the human person and people's interior states of being.

The Chinese Reception of the Spirit/Soul Distinction

The Spiritual Person surpassed all previous attempts to explain the trichotomous position, and Nee's concordance of biblical terms was the most systematic attempt to study the matter from a biblical perspective. His novel innovations in this regard all seemed to follow the same trend. Each of them intensified his predecessors' claims. He was the first to try to prove that the entire Bible held a consistent trichotomous anthropology, and he was also the first to suggest further subdivisions, maintaining that both the human spirit and the human soul were themselves composed of three constituent parts. Nee argued that the spirit was made up of intuition, fellowship, and conscience while the soul was comprised of emotion, mind, and will.

All of these departures from previous teachings beg the question: What were the stakes for Nee? When he announced the publication of *The Spiritual Person*, Nee claimed "The most difficult thing for believers today is that in seeking progress on their spiritual journey, they cannot find the way forward, so they grope in the darkness." Nee felt that *The Spiritual Person*, with its broad scope, adequately addressed "every question related to spiritual things that believers want to know but cannot answer." These answers included "hearing God's voice, knowing God's will," and dozens of other topics including "regeneration, salvation, sanctification, denying the self," and "fellowship, prayer, reading the Bible," and even, "warfare with Satan, evil spirits, demon possession."[214]

Nee was convinced that when Christians properly understood their own beings, their spirits, souls, and bodies, they would have the basic interpretive key to make sense of almost all their other questions and shed new light on many important Christian doctrines. For instance, he argued that hearing God's voice and knowing God's will depended on discerning between the spirit and the soul. God was one with the human spirit, while the human soul was frequently influenced by the selfish ego, the flesh, and evil spirits.

Nee's further division of the human spirit and the human soul into their respective component parts was designed to help seeking Christians to understand their own experiences and advance their spiritual growth. If they understood that the spirit included the intuition, for instance, then it was possible that direct knowledge from God would breach rational thought and conflict with their emotions.

---

[214] NTSWJ 12, 1–2.

Thus, in the eyes of Nee and his followers, *The Spiritual Person*'s careful delineations of the parts of the human being were anything but abstract theological positions. Instead, they were a set of practical, concrete tools by which any Christian could come to grasp God's eternal plan as spelled out in the Bible and to follow God's ongoing revelation and guidance as known by the Holy Spirit. Nee believed that the Christian, thus enlightened and guided, could participate in a life of true spiritual work, supporting the church and defeating Satan while maintaining a joyous love for Christ that was balanced, unshakeable, and long-lasting. All of this potential could be realized simply by understanding oneself and one's true nature and position before God: that is, maintaining the distinction between the human soul and the human spirit.

Other Christians may have perceived these issues as abstruse and irrelevant at best. Nee wrote and published at a time when Chinese theologians such as Y. T. Wu and T. C. Chao were arguing for Christianity as a means of Chinese national salvation. In general, such perspectives pushed back against fundamentalist Christianity's focus on individual holiness. In contrast, Nee's central argument seemed to be moving in the exactly opposite direction by suggesting that serious Christians did not distinguish between their internal faculties *enough* in the quest for true holiness. At the same time, Nee's critiques could be seen by other conservative Christians as divisive and controversial. He was potentially invalidating their good Christian practices as merely soulish or selfish, devoid of true spirituality.

Nee's was clearly a mystical argument, directed toward the individual human spirit. Ironically, however, Nee disliked the concept of introspection. He argued in *The Spiritual Person* that "This 'spiritual depression' happens mainly because believers turn inward toward themselves." He argued that to consider oneself too much risked "taking the self as the center in praying to and worshipping God" and could be caused by "the intrusion of the power of darkness." Instead of becoming obsessed with one's own spiritual condition, Nee argued that Christians should look outward and upward, to Christ's heavenly, victorious position and thus be "unfettered above the clouds."[215]

But Nee's objections in this case were contradictory. For Nee, the significance of looking to the outward, heavenly Christ lay partly in the fact that this same Christ was also simultaneously joined to the human spirit within. Even though the gaze needed to be fixed on the transcendent Christ, the comfort of Christ's transcendence lay in the fact that the Christian also shared in Christ's glorious, celestial position. Nee wrote that ideally, Christians would "often preserve their spirits in a kind of condition of being constantly leaving the world and ascending to the heavens" such that they could "become citizens in the heavens in

[215] NTSWJ 13, 192–193.

experience."[216] When Christians looked "outward" and were conscious only of Christ, at that same moment they were paradoxically also seeing something of themselves—their position and nature in Christ.

The extraordinary claim that a deep part of the human being can exist in harmony with an ineffable, ultimate reality has a long and illustrious history in Chinese thought.[217] All of the major Chinese religious traditions contain some form of mystical thought, often coupled with meditation, self-reflection, or other modes of inward-focused discipline to perfect the union between the human being and the higher or truer states of reality. Such patterns of thought and behavior can be traced from ancient records to contemporary China.

Historians such as Prasenjit Duara and David Ownby have traced the history of various "redemptive societies" during the Republican period. These societies were complex organizations which combined religious, philosophical, and sometimes political themes with civic service or mutual benefit. Redemptive societies were active throughout Nee's lifetime and counted millions of members throughout China during the 1920s. Although their teachings were esoteric and varied, interior discipline and unity with a transcendent order were two common themes.[218]

The redemptive societies are also a useful analogy because they often reveled in the intricate details of their religious beliefs and practices. Their sacred writings and teachers could illuminate complex paths to unity with the divine or ultimate. These byzantine components sometimes included internal maps of the human being, celestial pantheons, higher planes of existence, ritual practices, and mantras. Specific comparisons are difficult to make since Nee neither cited nor used sources other than the Bible and Western Christian writings. In fact, Nee suggested that even the more common Buddhist and Daoist practices such as meditation and breathing exercises could be infiltrated by evil spirits.[219] Nevertheless, when Nee offered *The Spiritual Person* as a detailed guide to the human being that would help people find oneness with God and live proper human lives, the breadth and detail of his engagement would have attracted rather than deterred many potential adherents.

If the form of *The Spiritual Person* was congenial to Chinese religious expectations, the content was even more so. By emphasizing the distinction between

---

[216] NTSWJ 13, 237–238.

[217] Alexander Chow has recently written a monograph on Chinese Christianity that takes this concept as its central conceit, tying various forms of Chinese Christianities to China's other religions. He includes Watchman Nee as the representative of one of his major types of Chinese Christianity. See Chow, *Theosis, Sino-Christian Theology and the Second Chinese Enlightenment.*

[218] For instance, see Duara's description of *Yiguandao*, and *Daoyuan* in *Sovereignty and Authenticity: Manchukuo and the East Asian Modern* (Lanham, MD: Rowman and Littlefield Publishers, 2003), 108–109.

[219] NTSWJ 10, 55–56.

soul and spirit, Nee promoted a kind of Christianity that strongly resonated with at least two major themes of Chinese religion: holism and effortlessness.

The philosophical idea of holism can be defined in many ways. Historian and philosopher Brook Ziporyn has described a form of holism which "defines 'parts' and 'wholes' in such a way that the parts in a whole obtain their meaning from their contextualization in that whole and are altered, in all aspects of their being, by their relationship with the other parts."[220] Ziporyn suggests that early Greek philosophers looked to mathematics as a model to understand metaphysical questions. This meant that they understood objects in the universe to be quantified, discrete, and mutually exclusive. In contrast, Chinese thinking has been motivated by "social and personal ethical questions" so that "the way *humans* interact is the model for how *things* interact." This has led to a "pervasive Chinese holism" in which objects in the universe are understood to be reciprocal, inclusive, and mutually influential.[221] Every "thing" in the universe is a part that cannot be defined in isolation, but rather can only be understood in relation to other parts and to the whole.

Nee's Christian commitments obviously kept him from going down the paths of some of the stronger and more radical forms of Chinese holism, such as Buddhists who claimed that "there is no devil besides the Buddha and no Buddha besides the devil."[222] Nevertheless, by emphasizing the distinction between soul and spirit, he still ended up making iconoclastic claims about holism and value that had important parallels in Chinese thought. One of the implications of a holistic philosophy is that it may upset obvious or commonplace understandings of value. If, in a holistic universe, every "thing" is defined in relation to other things, it is hard to evaluate discrete "good" and "evil" people, actions, events, or ideas, since their "goodness" or "evil" are dynamically and relatively defined in relation to other things, which are again defined in relation to other things in a chain of infinite progression.

In this light, Nee's claim that the soul included the mind, emotion, and will but that the spirit transcended the soul took on a striking significance. It is important to remember that for Nee, the point was that in the eyes of God, all actions taken by the independent soul were ultimately sinful or unethical. Thus, on some level, all reason and analysis, pleasure and suffering, and every exercise of the free will that was not instigated by the spirit was fundamentally equal and undifferentiated. The best of actions and the worst of them, the wisest and the most foolish, so long as they were undertaken independent of God, were equally meaningless.

[220] Ziporyn, *Evil and/or/as The Good*, 28.
[221] Ziporyn, *Evil and/or/as The Good*, 42–44.
[222] Ziporyn, *Evil and/or/as The Good*, 344.

Conversely, so long as people acted from their union with God in the human spirit, actions that seemed good or evil, wise or foolish, ecstatic or devastating, could all be understood as fulfilling God's will. Nee was not arguing for a completely unbounded antinomianism, since he believed that God would always work according to the Bible, but he still opened up a wide space for radical inversions of value. His experiences at Fuzhou are a helpful example. No matter how right or wrong Leland Wang's arguments may have been, God's command was for Nee to suffer in silence. As painful and unjustified as Nee's excommunication was, it too was God's choice.

On the positive side, Nee argued that a Christian should "allow the Holy Spirit to operate in his spirit." Such a spiritual Christian "allows the life that the Holy Spirit gives him to supply him with the power to do everything that is necessary for his conduct and his humanity." In contrast, the soulish Christian was still "acting according to his own tastes," trying to serve God according to his "natural intelligence, and with his own numerous and very wise arrangements." In Nee's view, the way of the spirit was in some ways *easier* since it required less effort and planning.[223]

Nee thus drew a sharp contrast between the spiritual Christian's simple channeling of God's power and the soulish Christian's preoccupation with busy artifice and hard work. This contrast suggests the second way in which the content of *The Spiritual Person* echoed Chinese religious concerns, that is, in its invocation of the concept of effortlessness, or *wuwei*. *Wuwei* is difficult to translate, but it stands at the heart of Daoist ethics. The first term, *wu* means simply "no," "not," or "there is not." The second term, *wei*, has a wide semantic field encompassing action, intention, and artificiality, among many other meanings.

In classical Daoist thought, the *wuwei* of the universe manifests itself in "spontaneous patterns, routines, cycles, rhythms, and habits of nature," while the Daoist sage "makes it possible for the spontaneous *wu-wei* forces of the *tao*, [the ineffable "Way" that underlies reality,] to work their way in human affairs. The sage himself sees the human world from the point of view of the *tao*. He removes the obstacles to the free operation of the *tao*." Daoist virtue, then, consists not in prohibiting desires, but allowing the universe a thoroughfare through human channels.[224]

The analogy to Nee's thought is clear. By focusing intently on the distinction between soul and spirit, Nee wanted to allow space for a kind of effortless, spontaneous Christian life. His thought was deeply mystical, but it was also opposed to many forms of asceticism in the sense of rigorous spiritual disciplines or the harsh treatment of the body and soul. The soulish Christian might exert

---

[223] NTSWJ 12, 163–164.
[224] Schwartz, *The World of Thought*, 202.

strenuous effort on God's behalf and have many good ideas for Christian service, but Nee idealized instead the "spiritual Christians" who simply recognized that the sinful "old human" was already crucified and that the way was clear for them to allow the Holy Spirit to work in their human spirits. Thus, God would have his way in human affairs through Christians who were, in some ways, passive channels—active only in their consecration, the act of giving themselves to God.

While *wuwei* is strongly associated with Daoism, it is important to recognize that the idea had broad appeal and deep roots in much of Chinese philosophical and religious thought. One of the most famous passages of Confucius's *Analects* reports, "The Master said, 'At fifteen, I had my mind bent on learning. At thirty, I stood firm. At forty, I had no doubts. At fifty, I knew the decrees of Heaven. At sixty, my ear was an obedient organ for the reception of truth. At seventy, I could follow what my heart desired, without transgressing what was right.'"[225] Many Chinese of every religious and philosophical persuasion, including those who had little intentional religion or philosophy at all, prized the idea of a natural sage.

One of Nee's greatest accomplishments was to craft Christian doctrines in forms that would appeal to Chinese audiences without actually drawing from the content of other religions or teachings. Nee's ideas had many points of contact with classic Chinese thought, but it is unclear to what extent he knew or directly used these materials. In his childhood, he had received at least the basic grounding in the classics that was common to nearly all educated Chinese of his generation, but beyond that, he almost never cited indigenous Chinese traditions approvingly, and certainly not as sources for his own writings.[226] Still, Nee successfully drew Chinese audiences while presenting himself as a teacher of purely Christian doctrines based only on the Bible. Part of the enduring appeal of Nee's biblical exposition in the Chinese-speaking world is that his doctrines fulfilled certain cultural expectations with which they were well acquainted.

The Spiritual Person

Throughout his life, Nee received hundreds of letters from his followers. They are universally respectful, and some of them seemed to refer to the classic Chinese relationship between a master and his disciples. Nee's correspondents addressed him as "brother" or "elder brother" and signed off as "little sisters" or "little brothers" in Christ. For some of Nee's followers, the justification for

---

[225] *Analects*, Book 1, chapter 2, accessed on December 8, 2016, at http://china.usc.edu/confucius-analects-2

[226] Kinnear, *Against the Tide*, 35–36.

their religious beliefs was probably their confidence in Nee's personal, spiritual maturity.

The fact that a following could so rapidly and reverently coalesce around a teacher of mystical doctrines suggests some of the practical results that followed from Nee's decision to write a detailed, spiritual itinerary. In a culture that embraced both complex ethical teachings and literary accomplishment, an immense mystical and devotional treatise held special attraction. Those who propounded such teachings were usually embodied in the figure of the sage-teacher.

In later years, Nee and his co-workers repeatedly had to repudiate the concept that Nee was the master of a new Christian society.[227] The origins of these myths certainly had something to do with Nee's experiences during this period of his life in the mid- to late 1920s. If Nee's readers were culturally primed to look for a charismatic sage, Nee's personal history at this juncture seemed ready to oblige. The later issues of The Christian and the final sections of The Spiritual Person were written under dramatic circumstances.

By 1928, Nee had been sick for years and his health was rapidly declining. With the printing of The Spiritual Person in the fall of that year, he had ostensibly discharged his commission from God. In his own testimony, he suggests that "After the publication of the book, I prayed in God's presence, 'And now, let your servant die in peace!'" Initially, it seemed that God might grant his request. Nee writes that he had become "as withered as a skeleton" and that the "experienced nurse" who attended him was sure that he had only "three or four more days," weeping whenever she saw him and confiding to others that he was the most pathetic case she had ever seen. One friend even "telegraphed churches in various places, saying there was no hope for [Nee], and there was no further need to pray for [him]."[228]

Still, Nee and some of the co-workers who had begun to gather around him in Shanghai had not completely lost hope. Perhaps a miracle was still possible. One day, with no other possible means for healing, Nee turned again to God, asking for a reason for his death. Nee then confessed his sins, fearing that some hidden mistake might be the cause for his punishment by sickness. Finally, recognizing his desperate state, he admitted his lack of faith. Nee then devoted himself to fasting and praying, eating nothing from the morning until three in the afternoon. At the same time, his co-workers gathered in the home of Ruth Li to pray. Unexpectedly, as Nee was alone in his room, God answered. Nee writes:

[227] NTSWJ 25, 199; NTSWJ 26, 49–50.
[228] NTSWJ 26, 245.

As I prayed to God and asked him for faith, he gave me a word, which I will never forget in all my life. The first phrase: "The righteous shall live by faith" (Rom 1:17). The second phrase: "Stand by faith" (2 Cor 1:24). The third phrase: "Walk by faith" (2 Cor 5:7). These few phrases caused me to be filled with joy because the Bible says, "All things are possible to the one who believes." (Mark 9:23). So I thanked and praised God because he had already given me a word. I believed that God had already healed me.[229]

Nee's faith in divine healing was immediately tested—if he believed the message, he should rise out of bed. He struggled mightily to do so, "sweating so much that it was like I had been soaked in the rain." Nevertheless, he stood and "put on the clothes that I had not worn for a hundred and seventy-six days." In a cold sweat, he managed to get completely dressed. God then told him to go downstairs to the home of Ruth Li where "a group of brothers and sisters had been fasting and praying regarding my sickness for two or three days." When the astounded group of "seven or eight brothers and sisters" opened the door, they were "speechless and motionless." Nee recalls that "Everybody sat quietly for about an hour, as if God appeared among people." That very day, the small Christian group rented a car to visit "the famous woman preacher, Dora Yu" who was "extremely amazed, for she had recently received news that I was about to die."[230]

The shadow of death had galvanized Nee's writing of *The Spiritual Person*. Now, however, the threat of darkness was suddenly and miraculously dispersed by the apparent hand of God. In the eyes of the faithful, God had dramatically affirmed Nee's message and his faithfulness, and the small group of Shanghai Christians and the scattered congregations around China that had been following Nee now treated him as if he "had been raised from the dead."[231] They believed that they had external confirmation of God's approval of their "older brother."

[229] NTSWJ 26, 246.
[230] NTSWJ 26, 246–248.
[231] NTSWJ 26, 248.

4

The Nanjing Decade

After Watchman Nee's miraculous healing from tuberculosis in the fall of 1928, he set about employing his time and energy with characteristic determination. Nee recalls that during the very week of his recovery, he "spoke for three hours from the platform on the Lord's day."[232] Over the next ten years, as China enjoyed a period of relative peace, Nee's activities and following would also expand at an impressive rate. During these years, by publishing, holding conferences, and visiting different congregations, Nee laid the foundations for a cohesive, self-propagating cluster of local congregations that had a strong sense of group identity.

Nee's co-workers easily imbibed and transmitted the pithy and powerful summary of his message as he formulated it in these years, that is, the supremacy of Christ. In the name of Christ, Nee's followers established congregations throughout China, mostly without Nee's direct oversight. At the same time, Nee fueled this grassroots participation by formulating a theology of overcoming in which Christian fidelity and activity would have significant stakes in the age to come. The ability of Nee's co-workers and their congregations to cooperate and expand their movement without formal, central direction would prove to be a critical factor in their future survival.

By 1928, Nee had already been in Shanghai for almost two years. Although his sickness had obviously limited his ability to engage in practical church leadership, he still had managed to gather an impressive amount of support while continuing to publish *The Christian* and writing *The Spiritual Person*. Nee was never in particularly robust health, suffering from a chronic case of angina pectoris, . which caused him chest pain and fatigue throughout his life. Nevertheless, he was no longer under the immediate threat of death, and with his newfound strength, he began to work on his vision of the "local churches" in earnest.

Unfortunately, few detailed records of his practical efforts remain. Although some of the congregations that followed Nee may have kept more careful records, Nee himself did not keep church membership lists. Nee may have never forgotten his critique of the Methodist's "book of life," and one of his central definitions of a sectarian group was that "it does not include all regenerated

---

[232] NTSWJ 26, 248.

The Spiritual Person. Paul H B Chang, Oxford University Press. © Oxford University Press 2026.
DOI: 10.1093/9780197793664.003.0005

believers."[233] In other words, Nee continued to insist that whatever visible congregation he was a part of was inseparable from all other regenerated believers, that is, all true Christians. Thus, membership lists were irrelevant and divisive.

Despite the lack of records, a general sketch of Nee's work and following can be made. By 1928, the year of *The Spiritual Person*'s first printing, Nee and his Shanghai co-workers had already attracted enough congregants and financial support to make designated physical premises both necessary and possible. In January of that year, they rented a building on Wendeli Lane off of Hardoon Road in Shanghai's International Settlement. Not long afterward, the group purchased both that property and an adjacent one, giving them space and freedom to modify the buildings to suit their purposes. Thus, a few hundred could gather on the ground floor to listen to preaching while the upstairs rooms could be used for hospitality and business, including offices for church affairs and publications.[234]

It is difficult to trace the state of Nee's supporters and followers around the country leading up to 1927, but clues are scattered throughout issues of *The Christian*. Some issues of the periodical contained a section in which Nee answered questions sent in from his subscribers and readers. Although the so-called Question and Answer Box cannot give a comprehensive picture, analyzing the letters can still give some sense for the minimum reach of Nee's work and the nature of his following.[235]

Between 1925 and 1927, during the roughly two-year run of *The Christian*, Nee received letters from at least nine Chinese provinces: Anhui, Fujian, Guangdong, Henan, Jiangsu, Jiangxi, Rehe, Shandong, and Zhejiang. In addition, Nee received letters from Beijing, Shanghai, and Singapore. Even if one assumes that all correspondents of the same surname from the same place are, in fact, the same person, Nee still received letters from almost fifty different writers spread throughout those different locations.[236] Nee was thus reaching an

---

[233] NTSWJ 7, 195–196.

[234] Kinnear, *Against the Tide*, 133. The property was eventually expanded to include five consecutive lots (197–198).

[235] The "Question and Answer Box" was supposed to appear in every other issue, but it appeared on a more infrequent, irregular schedule. Even when the section was printed, it was not consistently edited. Usually, correspondents were listed only by their surname. Occasionally, a full name was given, at other times, the correspondents remained anonymous. Finally, the feature was most inconsistent with regard to locations. Sometimes the locations were left off altogether. Mostly, however, the name of one place was offered. This name could refer to a province, county, city, or even village. Generic names such as "Feng Village" have made it nearly impossible to trace the specific place. Thus, Nee's following may have been larger and more extensive than the feature indicates, but at least a rough approximation of Nee's influence can be ascertained.

[236] The layout of the publication suggests that longer letters from one person with multiple questions were often broken into smaller parts so that each question could be addressed in turn. Nevertheless, if we do not assume that each surname from each location is the same person, then Nee may have corresponded with around two hundred different people, not including the many anonymous questions.

engaged audience in a significant number of large Chinese provinces and important cities.

These scattered writers varied widely in their understanding of Nee's message. While some of the writers were evidently quite familiar with the Bible, Nee's theology, and other Christian doctrines, other writers were confused regarding even Nee's basic teachings concerning church administration, Bible interpretation, or appropriate Christian responses to social, political, and religious trends.

Despite these differences, the writers were more uniform in terms of their identification with Nee, and implicitly, with each other. The pages of *The Christian* show the birth of something akin to a fellowship of churches or a Christian movement. Although the writers did not know each other, except by reading one another's letters, the writers all agreed with Nee about the primacy of the Bible in evaluating Christian claims and practices. They were also tacitly convinced that Nee offered the most faithful biblical interpretations, and they proved this again and again by asking him to solve exegetical questions and by requesting his opinion of other Christian groups and teachings. In particular, they frequently wanted him to enumerate ways in which the beliefs or practices of other Christians were unbiblical. By reading one another's letters and sharing in their correspondence with Nee, individual writers could see that there were many more throughout China who thought as they did, although at this stage there was little evidence of association or direct communication with one another.

This set of letters can be usefully contrasted to another set of letters that were sent about ten years later. Between 1937 and 1939, Nee published *The Open Door*, which was meant to be a special, temporary publication for helping different churches and individuals stay in contact during the Second Sino-Japanese War, when many were forced to flee or relocate. If, in the mid-1920s, the different correspondents to *The Christian* were unknown to each other, by the mid-1930s, they wanted to keep track of each other by name. In the very first issue, twenty-four different "co-workers" or full-time ministers were named and the details of their travel plans and addresses were shared. In subsequent issues, dozens of further names were supplied in a flurry of letters sent across China.

In two years and eighteen issues of *The Open Door*, all the original provinces and cities that had sent letters to *The Christian* were represented again. In addition, the editors received letters from the following additional provinces: Gansu, Guangxi, Guizhou, Heilongjiang, Hubei, Hunan, Inner Mongolia (then Suiyuan), Jilin, Liaoning (then Fengtian), Shanxi, Sha'anxi, Sichuan, Tibet (then Xikang), and Yunnan. Cities such as Hong Kong, Macao, and Tianjin were now represented, as were various parts of Indonesia, Malaysia, and the Philippines. In *The Open Door*'s last issue of September 1939, the editors even published a letter from Thailand written by two women who called themselves "useless children" and "weak sisters in the Lord," but had nonetheless managed to convert a group of formerly devout Buddhists.[237]

Even without detailed records, it is obvious that the ten years between 1927 and 1937 were pivotal and productive ones. In 1924, when Nee had first received his vision of local churches throughout China, he was about to be expelled from the only congregation to which he had ever belonged. By only about fifteen years later, his vision had been significantly realized, and, in some ways, exceeded, with the robust representation of churches beyond China in various Southeast Asian countries. Nee had gone from a solitary, transient preacher to a recognized leader of dozens of co-workers and congregations, who were working at a rapid pace to spread their message even in the face of a devastating war.

Historically, Nee's completion of *The Spiritual Person* in 1927 roughly coincided with the beginning of what has become known as the "Nanjing Decade." This was a short period of stability inaugurated by the Northern Expedition, Chiang Kai-shek's successful military campaign. Chiang's defeat of various warlords and the rival Beiyang Government meant that Northern and Southern China were united under a common central authority as they had not been since the waning years of the Qing Empire. Although the benefits of peace were unevenly shared, much of China enjoyed a period of relative calm. Nee's recovery from tuberculosis and redoubled efforts could hardly have been better timed. Both Nee's publications and his traveling co-workers circulated with ease. Meanwhile, the congregations that used his writings could study and practice his teachings, increase their numbers, and solidify their sense of common identity.

The Case of Witness Lee

The story of one individual helps to illuminate the way in which Nee's interested correspondents in 1927 became his dedicated co-workers by 1937. In many ways, the life of Witness Lee (1905–1997) was a mirror image of Nee's own. Lee was born just two years after Nee in the city of Yantai in the northern province of Shandong. Yantai, like Fuzhou, was a coastal city with a long history of interaction with foreigners. Like Nee, Lee was a third-generation Christian. Lee's maternal grandfather had been converted by the Southern Baptist mission in China, but Lee considered himself to be a nominal Christian throughout his childhood. He attended Sunday School but had not been baptized. Lee enrolled in postsecondary education at a mission school, and, in 1925, while he was still a teenaged college student, he was converted by an itinerant female evangelist,

---

[237] NTSWJ 32, 364–365.

Peace Wang (Wang Peizhen, 1899–1969), who would go on to become one of Nee's most loyal and capable co-workers.

Lee himself would eventually play a pivotal role in preserving and expanding on Nee's legacy. While a full accounting of Lee's life and work merits its own monograph, in brief, Lee helped Nee to lead the Chinese and overseas congregations for decades. After Nee's imprisonment, Lee went on to establish Christian communities inspired by Nee's writings in Taiwan, the United States, and around the world. Lee published Nee's works wherever he went, while adding his own voluminous writings, which built on the core of Nee's teachings while expanding on new topics. Toward the end of his long life, Lee completed an enormous commentary on every book in the Bible and broached new theological ground in his interpretations of the New Jerusalem and Christian deification.

In the early 1920s, Lee was just a young Christian in the small world of Chinese Protestantism. He became aware of Nee almost immediately. Soon after a dynamic experience of salvation, Lee was hungry for biblical knowledge and Christian teaching. He subscribed to a Christian periodical and voraciously read every article of every issue. He writes: "As I read, I frequently noticed articles under the by-line of Watchman Nee. It was obvious that those articles were the most outstanding ones on biblical truths. They were the best in the whole paper. The more I read them, the more I enjoyed reading them. From the way this writer addressed his readers, I imagined he was an aged Christian teacher, perhaps over sixty years of age."

When the paper posted the announcement that Nee would be publishing his own paper, *The Christian*, Lee subscribed immediately and frequently read each sizable issue on the same day it was delivered. He ordered everything else Nee published and eventually began to write to Nee. The "Question and Answer Boxes" of *The Christian* record some of this correspondence, suggesting that Nee found Lee's questions interesting enough to print.

Although Lee was worshipping with the Chinese Independent Church, reading Nee's works caused him to be "through with denominations." When a like-minded friend from the same church was transferred to Shanghai on business, Lee encouraged him to join Nee's congregation. Years later, the friend would become one of the elders in Nee's Shanghai congregation. Meanwhile, Lee remained in Yantai, although he wanted to visit Shanghai and listen to Nee's preaching directly. By the end of 1927, when the Chinese Independent Church elected Lee to be a member of its board, he could stand the contradiction no longer. He "asked them to remove my name from their 'book of life,'" and he "began to meet regularly with the [local] Brethren Assembly, attending all their seven weekly meetings."[238]

---

[238] Lee, *Seer of the Divine Revelation*, 285–286.

In 1931, Lee registered to attend one of Nee's conferences in Shanghai, hoping to finally meet Nee face to face. Unfortunately, the outbreak of hostilities with Japan kept Lee from leaving the province. Lee had left his former denomination on good terms, however, and through them, he was finally able to arrange a meeting with Nee. During the summer of the next year, Lee convinced the Chinese Independent Church to invite Nee to visit and preach to their congregation. Lee appears to have been thoroughly impressed by Nee's behavior and influence. As an elderly man, Lee recounted wistfully:

> My time with Watchman during those days deeply impressed me with the sweetness, loveliness, attractiveness, and newness of the Lord. Those days provided a new start for me in following the Lord and caused me to have a basic turn from knowledge to life. Because of those days with Watchman Nee, I began to have fellowship with the Lord in a more intimate way. The Lord became more precious to me. That experience was even greater than my experience of salvation. Those days with Watchman affected my pathway in the Lord throughout all the following fifty-nine years, since 1932. For eternity I can never forget those days! What a mercy and a grace it was to me.[239]

For Lee, the visit highlighted the contrast between his Brethren congregation's emphasis on "the accuracy of biblical knowledge" and Nee's teaching concerning "the necessity of life." Lee concluded that although the Brethren were knowledgeable teachers of sound, biblical doctrines, Nee's living, fresh relationship with Christ suggested an even deeper mastery of Christian teachings. For Lee, Nee not only taught but also personally epitomized biblical theology, suggesting a "basic turn from knowledge to life."

Nee had a similar effect on others. A member of the church's board came to Lee's home during the very evening of Nee's departure to ask for help on behalf of "another believer in distress." When Lee took him aside for fellowship, the man pleaded with Lee to baptize him that very night in the sea. Lee acquiesced; they started a meeting in Lee's own home, and a congregation quickly formed.[240] Some of Nee's followers later saw 1932 as an important landmark in the spread of Nee's message, beginning in Fuzhou in 1924, moving to Shanghai in 1928, and coming to Northern China in 1932.[241]

Lee wrote again to Nee, informing him of recent events, and Nee returned to Yantai in April of the following year to "confirm and strengthen" the new congregation, preaching both in their meeting hall and to denominational Christians in

---

[239]　Lee, *Seer of the Divine Revelation*, 288–289.
[240]　Lee, *Seer of the Divine Revelation*, 288–289.
[241]　Kinnear, *Against the Tide*, 163.

the auditorium of the Chinese Independent Church. Lee felt called to become a full-time minister, but he struggled to muster the faith to give up his well-paying job, which supported both his growing family and the church. Nevertheless, in a moment of crisis, he finally conceded his future to God and turned in his letter of resignation. Lee then engaged in a preaching tour, returning to find a letter from Nee, dated from the very time Lee had been struggling most intensely with God over his future. In it, Nee wrote simply, "Brother Witness, as for your future, I feel that you should serve the Lord with your full time. How do you feel? May the Lord lead you."[242]

Lee immediately felt that he had to go in person to Shanghai to hear the story from Nee. There, Nee related that he had written the letter while he was on the Mediterranean, returning to China from a trip to Europe. As he prayed for God's work in China, he "felt he should write [Lee] a note telling me that I should spend my full time serving the Lord." Right away, Lee was "fully convinced that [Nee] was a person wholly with the Lord. Otherwise, how could I be thousands of miles away struggling with the Lord and he be on the Mediterranean Sea receiving a burden to write me concerning this matter at the very instant God was dealing with me?" Lee concluded: "[Watchman] did not need to ask me to work with him; I had already made the decision. I had to follow him and work with him."[243]

Lee ended up staying in Shanghai from October 1933 to February 1934. Nee himself was just turning thirty years old, but he was already filling the role he had seen Barber play, that is, by serving as a spiritual mentor to younger Christians and a bridge to key Western Christian teachings. Under Nee's tutelage, Lee began to understand church history and the Bible from Nee's particular perspective, a combination of Brethren and Keswick themes that emphasized the importance of both the church and the divine life in the human spirit. Just as years before, Barber had pointed him in the direction of Jessie Penn-Lewis and other spiritual writings, Nee now introduced Lee to his preferred biblical scholars and Brethren exegetes.[244]

As Lee proved to be a capable teacher in his own right, Nee entrusted him with further responsibilities in both publication and preaching. When the Third Overcomer Conference was held in Shanghai in January 1934, Lee was readily at hand, meeting other Christians who had come from across China to participate. On the Sunday preceding the conference, when many expected to hear Nee speak, he was unexpectedly absent. Instead, Lee was given a short note the same morning, asking him to preach in Nee's place. By February of that year, Nee and

---

[242] Lee, *Seer of the Divine Revelation*, 291.
[243] Lee, *Seer of the Divine Revelation*, 292.
[244] Nee recommended textual critic Henry Alford's *New Testament for English Readers* and Brethren leader John Nelson Darby's *Synopsis of the Bible*.

the other Shanghai co-workers asked Lee to move his family to Shanghai to become one of their number. Lee agreed, and for the next fifteen years, as he traveled across China to establish new congregations and strengthen existing ones, he understood his work with Nee to be part of the "one flow and one current of the Lord's work in China."[245]

The Formation of a Fellowship

Lee's narrative is especially dramatic and striking. He rapidly earned Nee's confidence and proved himself to be an outstanding leader even in Shanghai, where Nee's most trusted supporters lived and worked with him. Although the particular details may have varied, Lee's story still exemplifies the path taken by many Christians who were barely learning Nee's name in the 1920s but who would, over the course of a decade, find themselves increasingly drawn to associate with the like-minded churches and fellow Christians who also followed Nee's teachings.

As a sign of the group's growing influence and cohesiveness, outsiders began to give Nee's followers various names. Because of the popularity of *The Christian*, some referred to the group as "The Christian Assembly." Others took their cues from the particular, nondescript names Nee's followers used for their buildings and called the congregations the "Assembly Hall" or "Meeting Place" (*juhuisuo/ juhuichu*) churches. In 1927, Nee and some of his publication team had translated and printed a small hymn book for use during congregational worship. Many of the songs within the pamphlet and its title were translated from a Plymouth Brethren work called *Hymns for the Little Flock*. It was a memorable title, and the churches that followed Nee's teachings soon gained another nickname as the "Little Flock." Nee was horrified by the development and quickly struck the words "Little Flock" from the title of the hymnal.[246] Neither he nor those within his movement would refer to themselves by any particular name at all, since a separate name was one of Nee's major criteria for discerning sectarianism. Nevertheless, for many outsiders, the moniker stuck.

While the expansion of the Little Flock Christian assemblies was impressive, their initial rate of growth was outpaced by that of the True Jesus Church, which was probably the fastest-growing Christian movement in China. In 1922, only five years after its founding, the True Jesus Church already claimed a membership of ten thousand. The True Jesus Church and the Christian Assemblies were the only two indigenous Chinese churches to gain a true national following. As

---

[245] Lee, *Seer of the Divine Revelation*, 298.
[246] NTSWJ 18, 93–95. Kinnear, *Against the Tide*, 142–143.

they fought to establish themselves and define their identities, their differences and similarities illuminated both the Chinese Christian landscape and the surprising, malleable forms that global Christianities could take.

Like the Christian Assemblies, the True Jesus Church traced its founding to a native Chinese Christian and maintained a scrupulous distance from both Western denominations and the Sino-Foreign Protestant establishment. Also like the Christian Assemblies, the True Jesus Church combined an Adventist eschatology with a focus on evangelism and mission, charging its adherents to spread the message in the face of Christ's soon return and the end of the age. The combination of these factors proved to be a potent brew, galvanizing average Chinese citizens from all walks of life to devote much of their time, energy, and money to Christian purposes. Both the True Jesus Church and the Little Flock quickly broke free from their local bases of support to cross provincial and even national boundaries.

Two of Nee's published correspondents in *The Christian* sought Nee's counsel on the True Jesus Church. Nee responded that it was necessary to "speak the truth in love," since by his estimation, the True Jesus Church was "a heretical organization."[247] Nee does not seem to have been aware of the True Jesus Church's unitarianism, which, for him, would have been further evidence of heresy. Instead, he condemned their "very many errors," including "confusion regarding the great truth of salvation."[248] To Nee, this ignorance of redemptive atonement and salvation by faith meant that "They give up the salvation of the cross and do not preach it."[249]

Instead, Nee rather polemically argued that True Jesus followers "focus on the Holy Spirit, but what they receive *are actually* evil spirits."[250] For support, Nee referred to 1 John 4:1–3, in which the writer of the epistle urged his listeners to discern between spirits that were from God and "the spirit of the antichrist."[251] Nee prefaced all his remarks by demurring that "we should not criticize others, but for the sake of true teaching, we must reject heresy." Still, he could not refrain from pointing out that the True Jesus Church's "Biblical exposition is an incoherent jumble of false analogies and groundless suppositions pulled out of thin air, which are not even worth laughing at by those with knowledge."[252]

To be sure, Nee's theological differences with the True Jesus Church were legion. Besides their unitarian conception of God, the True Jesus Church also held to Sabbath observance and worship. The group drew both many of its members

---

[247] NTSWJ 7, 122.
[248] NTSWJ 7, 182.
[249] NTSWJ 7, 122.
[250] NTSWJ 7, 122. Emphasis in the original.
[251] NTSWJ 7, 123 and 182–183.
[252] NTSWJ 7, 122–123.

and a number of its key leaders from the relatively small but influential Seventh-Day Adventist denomination. The True Jesus Church combined this Adventist heritage with a heavy Pentecostal emphasis on baptism by the Spirit and glosso-lalia, or speaking in unknown tongues.

Nee's accusation that True Jesus Christians "give up the salvation of the cross," and his denunciation of True Jesus teachings as "confusion regarding the great truth of salvation," probably had to do with the True Jesus Church's confident exclusivism. They were sure that so-called Christians outside of their group, who had not received their own salvific rites of baptism and tongue-speaking, were destined for hell.

True Jesus theology was a creative amalgam of many existing Christian themes, including Adventist eschatology and Sabbatarianism, Oneness Pentecostal conceptions of God, Spirit-baptism, and glossolalia, and some-thing akin to Tridentine Roman Catholicism, with its emphasis on the salvific nature of sacraments, performed correctly, under the auspices of the one, true church. Each of these commitments could be supported with biblical texts, something that was of paramount importance to both the True Jesus Church and the Christian Assembly. In the West, however, such disparate groups used very different rationales to justify their theological emphases. The Roman Catholic emphasis on sacramental rites, for instance, was based upon the church's careful custodianship of tradition, something to which the True Jesus Church paid little attention.

Instead, as was the case with many other global Christian groups, the True Jesus Church argued that the primacy and immediacy of the Holy Spirit superseded all other forms of authority. The fact that adherents directly interacted with the Holy Spirit seemed to herald a return to the apostolic age and shrank the rele-vance of the intervening years of the Christian tradition. The unmediated guid-ance of the Spirit also seemed to minimize the importance of ordained pastors, formal theological education, and vested institutions. With the gatekeepers of Christian authority thus bypassed, ordinary believers were empowered to pick and choose from virtually any Christian teaching that appealed to them, supporting their claims with what Nee disparagingly called "an incoherent jumble of false analogies and groundless suppositions." Theologian Harvey Cox has more charitably referred to the resulting beliefs as "spiritual bricolage."[253]

While theological differences between the two groups were extensive, the dis-crepancy in their general attitude and outlook may have been just as significant. Nee largely drew from Westerners to critique other Western doctrines. As a re-sult, he was selective in his critiques of other Christians, attempting to carefully

---

[253] Harvey Cox, *Fire from Heaven: The Rise of Pentecostal Spirituality and the Reshaping of Religion in the Twenty-First Century* (Reading, MA: Addison-Wesley Publishing, 1995), 305.

discern the specific doctrines and practices that should be accepted and opposed. In part, his attempt to "de-Westernize" Christianity came from what he felt were the best resources *within* the Western tradition—other reformers who had decried the problems of the church.

The True Jesus Church embraced a much more aggressive brand of nationalism. When one Western missionary rebuked a True Jesus leader for "stealing the sheep," the Chinese man quickly retorted, "Whichever one of you is a foreign sheep can go back with [the missionary]!"[254] Similarly, when True Jesus representatives were invited to the National Christian Conference of 1922, they took the opportunity to harangue the gathered Christian leaders to their faces. Even though about half of the Conference was composed of Chinese nationals, the True Jesus Church's delegation accused them of "being used by the imperialists as the vanguard of their invasion."[255]

In contrast, although Nee attacked the denominational and clerical system and considered that most Christians were tragically lacking in true spiritual experiences, he went out of his way to embrace them *as Christians*. For instance, he argued that "To speak of [ourselves as being] the church in Shanghai, one must include all of the believers [in Shanghai], otherwise, [we cannot be] counted as the church in Shanghai."[256] Indeed, because the basis of his arguments was an appeal against sectarianism, Nee repeatedly insisted that all true Christians were united in Christ's one body.

The foreign missionaries who eventually left their denominations to follow Nee were probably not welcome, nor did any appear to seek membership, in the True Jesus Church. In the future, modern-day descendants of the Little Flock would be much more successful at gaining indigenous leaders and followers *outside* of China, where Nee and his successors' ability to adopt a more recognizably international, evangelical language has paid dividends.

The difference in attitudes also affected the cohesion of the groups as a whole. Once the True Jesus Church unleashed the critical power of direct spiritual visions against other Christian groups, it was hard to keep the process from replicating itself. Within two decades, at least fifteen splinter groups broke off with their own charismatic leaders and new revelations from God.[257] In contrast, Little Flock churches also broke into dissenting divisions, but because of their ideal of church unity, they did so at a much slower rate and with more subdued rhetoric.

For the True Jesus Church, however, the nature of their movement had significant payoffs. The fierce rejection of all other Christian groups harnessed an

[254] Lian, *Redeemed by Fire*, 54.
[255] Lian, *Redeemed by Fire*, 58.
[256] NTSWJ 22, 45.
[257] Lian, *Redeemed by Fire*, 62.

explosive amount of religious power and authority. By teaching its members that they alone held the rites and teachings that could lead to salvation, the True Jesus Church condemned other so-called Christians to hell and suggested that they belonged to the devil.[258]

Both True Jesus adherents and Little Flock followers frequently mentioned their uncertainty about salvation as a major impetus that drove them to seek new Christian groups and teachings.[259] This fact suggests that among Chinese Christians, there was a significant amount of confusion over how Christians could know that they were saved and what their eternal destinies would be. This confusion may have been the result of the multiplicity of different denominations, each with its own perspective on Christian salvation, but it may have also been an expression of popular Chinese religiosity, which has, throughout the centuries of modern Chinese history, given rise to repeated grassroots expressions of redemptionist and salvationist societies.[260] On this subject, as on so many others, Nee selectively appropriated a distinctive, minority school of Western Christian thought and used it as a corrective to more commonly held beliefs. Once again, the abstruse nature of his thoughts and his subtle, involved exegesis may not have been an obstacle to, but rather, a further impetus for his ideas' popularity in the Chinese context.

Nee's Theology of Salvation

The different Christian groups that participated in the Anglo-American evangelical movement can be divided in many different ways. By the nineteenth century, one of the most significant theological divisions was the distinction between those who held to a Wesleyan or Arminian soteriology as opposed to those who held to a Calvinist or Reformed soteriology. These two camps disagreed over the possibility of Christians losing their eternal salvation. While Arminians argued that certain sins were grievous enough to entail the possibility of even a converted person experiencing damnation, Reformed theology held that the eternal bliss of the elect was secure and that no human action could thwart God's designation once a person had become a true Christian.

One of the reasons the division persisted was that, in a deeply biblical culture, both sides were able to marshal copious scriptural references to prove their

---

[258]   Lian, *Redeemed by Fire*, 49.

[259]   Inouye, *China and the True Jesus*, 118.

[260]   While Prasenjit Duara coined the term "redemptive society" in *Sovereignty and Authenticity*, the importance of such groups and their interest in questions of salvation have been long noted by many scholars of Chinese modernity. The White Lotus and the Boxers are two well-known examples. In *Redeemed by Fire*, Lian Xi argues that much of Chinese Protestantism during the Republican Era followed these established patterns of popular Chinese religion.

points. At different times in the biblical narratives, Jesus and the apostles made statements that could be taken to support either claim. For instance, Jesus famously enjoins his followers to take the narrow gate since the broad way will lead to destruction, but he also assures his disciples that they are in his and in his father's hands, so that no one can snatch them out.[261] Similarly, Paul both speaks of struggling to win God's approval and also exults that nothing can possibly separate him from the love of God.[262]

Nee believed that the concept of the "millennium," as introduced in the book of Revelation, opened the door to a third way that harmonized the apparent discrepancy. Two of the verses in the passage on the millennium mention something called "the first resurrection." Those who take part in the first resurrection are "blessed and holy," and "over these the second death has no authority." Like much of the book of Revelation, these passages are obscure and can be interpreted in many different ways. Nee chose to connect the first resurrection to Paul's use of the phrase "out-resurrection" in Philippians 3:11, where the apostle hopes to "arrive at the out-resurrection from the dead."

Although most English versions of the Bible translate the Philippians passage simply as "resurrection," Nee was attuned to the fact that the Greek noun for resurrection, *anastasia*, in this case, carries the unique prefix "*ex.*" Nee pointed out that Paul had already argued at length earlier in his Philippian letter that he wanted to live and not die (1:23–25).[263] Furthermore, in Nee's view, the Bible taught that *all* human beings, regardless of whether they were saved or damned, good or evil, would be resurrected from the dead for the final judgment. Thus, if Paul was hoping to attain this "out-resurrection," it must refer to something other than the common or general resurrection of the dead; it must be a resurrection that could be experienced even by the living.

Here, Nee believed that the passages in Revelation could be helpful. Those who attained to the first resurrection, or the out-resurrection, were freed from "the second death," which, in Nee's mind, "does not mean to die, but rather to go to a place and suffer."[264] This place of suffering was reserved for Christians who had genuinely received the life of God, but who had also lived sinful human lives. The existence of a third option negotiated the stark dichotomy between eternal life and damnation. According to Nee, when Paul spoke of his hope to attain the out-resurrection, he meant to avoid the possibility of eschatological suffering and instead receive the reward of becoming one of the "priests of God and of Christ" to "reign with him for a thousand years."[265] The millennium thus

---

261 Matthew 7:13; John 10:28–29.
262 1 Corinthians 9:24–27; Romans 8:31–39.
263 NTSWJ 16, 203.
264 NTSWJ 16, 203.
265 Revelation 20:6.

functioned as a time of both reward and punishment. Those Christians who fought the good fight could expect a glorious period of joy, while those who did not meet God's standard would spend those thousand years suffering instead.

A few years later, in 1931, Nee dwelt on a parable in the gospel of Matthew to expand on the question of reward and punishment for Christians. In the first parable, there were ten virgins. Five were prudent, taking oil in vessels to supplement their lamps and five were foolish, neglecting to do so. They all fell asleep, and at midnight, they were awakened to meet the bridegroom. The wise were able to light their lamps again, meet the groom, and enter the wedding feast. The foolish had to scramble to buy oil, and as they were doing so, the door was shut, and they were not allowed to participate in the feast.

Nee argued that in the parable of the virgins, the entire group of ten virgins must all be genuine believers. They are all called virgins, which suggests they "were different in their behavior but not in their nature."[266] Furthermore, the judgment in this parable takes place after they had all "fallen asleep," a common biblical trope implying death. The parable thus suggested that a Christian could undergo variable rewards or punishments *after their death*. Nee argued that, as Christians, all the virgins in the parable had their ultimate destiny secured. Their different behaviors during their lifetime, however, affected their experience of the coming millennium, an intervening space of one thousand years before the advent of timeless eternity. For Nee, a proper understanding of the human spirit helped illuminate the obscure parable.

All the virgins in the parable had oil in their lamps, but the five prudent virgins also had oil in their vessels. For Nee, these suggested "two kinds of oil." The "oil in the lamp" pointed only to the Holy Spirit's *initial* union with the human spirit in regeneration, since the Bible states that "The spirit of man is the lamp of Jehovah."[267] This oil was to secure eternal salvation. The oil in the vessel, however, suggested not only the Spirit's presence but also a certain fullness: that is, the extra oil. Thus, "God's intention is for us to be filled with and full of oil. He does not only ask that we have oil in the lamp. A student's final goal in studying is not just to pass the examination (salvation) but to receive full marks."[268]

To be full of the Holy Spirit was to reach the actual goal, to come up to God's standard in God's "examination." Such excellence would have its reward. In the parable, the prudent virgins who had oil in their vessels were welcomed into the wedding feast. The foolish virgins, however, would also face consequences for their lack. Nee wrote:

---

[266] NTSWJ 15, 285.
[267] NTSWJ 15, 287.
[268] NTSWJ 15, 287.

After resurrection, some will enjoy happiness, while others will undergo suffering. For example, if a Christian's temper is not remedied while they are alive, it will not be remedied in death either. The rich man's avarice, pride, and selfishness [in the parable of Lazarus] were still there after death, they were unchanged. Death cannot make a person holy, or else everyone would be holy because everyone dies once.[269]

Nee's anthropology thus spilled into eschatological and soteriological implications. The fact that the human spirit was the point of regeneration meant that Christians could all be assured of eternal life. The variation in human souls, however, and the persistence of sins and failures in Christian souls would have repercussions after death. Sooner or later, God's standard of holiness would be met by all, and death was not the end. Christ's return would inaugurate a millennial kingdom, so named because it spanned one thousand years. During this period, the Christians who were victorious and filled in spirit would be rewarded with "the bliss of enjoyment" in that kingdom, which was likened to a wedding feast in the parable of the virgins.[270] Christians who had failed to lead a spiritual life would spend the thousand years making up for their soulish deficiencies in the place Matthew refers to as "outer darkness." Even this phrase, Nee suggested, showed that something of a third destiny was available to Christians, arguing that "The New Testament never says that hell is in the outer darkness. Hell is not darkness, instead, it has fire."[271]

Nee's Keswick predecessors had tried to negotiate the gap between Reformed doctrine and the Wesleyan emphasis on practical holiness. They frequently enjoined their hearers to come up to God's standard of holiness. In fact, the perceived gap between the Bible's teaching regarding sanctified living and the average Christian's experience of the same was part of the Keswick Convention's raison d'etre. When they were accused of introducing Wesleyan perfectionism, however, Keswick teachers defended themselves with classic Reformed doctrines on the persistence of sin and the perseverance of the saints. They scrupulously avoided any suggestion that sin could be eradicated or that a lack of holiness might cause a Christian to lose the security of their salvation. Deprived of future rewards and punishments, holiness in daily life had to be its own reward.

Nee's introduction of a thousand-year period of either suffering or bliss introduced a further, stark incentive for Christians to live properly. Although Nee avoided going as far as the Arminian position by precluding the possibility of

---

[269] NTSWJ 15, 292. The reference is to the story of Lazarus and the rich man in Luke 16, in which a beggar named Lazarus and a rich man both die. The rich man is tormented after his death for his greed and neglect of the poor while Lazarus rests "in Abraham's bosom."
[270] NTSWJ 15, 293.
[271] NTSWJ 15, 308.

eternal damnation for the truly converted, Christians who followed his teachings still had to think about a serious, potentially thousand-year-long consequence for their actions. Although this creative position seemed to break the deadlock between Reformed and Arminian notions of salvation, it depended upon a startling concept.

A large measure of the initial appeal of the sixteenth-century Reformation had been the denial of the Catholic notion of purgatory. One scholar of the period has argued that purgatory was "one of the most successful and long-lasting theological ideas in the Western Church" and that the success or failure of the Reformation can be significantly correlated to local emphases on purgatory.[272] By freeing Western consciences from the terror of purgative flames or the need to pray for the suffering dead, Reformers harnessed a powerful psychological energy and attracted many Christians to their message. Since that time, few, if any Protestants had dared to broach the idea that Christians could still suffer for their sins after their deaths.

To be clear, Nee's concept of the thousand-year kingdom as a reward and punishment differed in critical ways from the Catholic notion of purgatory. For Nee, the period of time was fixed, whereas for Catholic theology, the period of purgation was undefined. Likewise, for Nee, the bliss and suffering depended only upon an individual's own actions and readiness—the fullness of oil in their own vessel—whereas for Catholics, the church and the "intricate industry of prayer" for the dead had an effect.[273] Nevertheless, like Catholics, Nee saw something of a middle road between the stark evangelical alternative presented by Reformed and Wesleyan doctrines. Sin could have real and lasting effects that went beyond the span of a human lifetime, but Christians had no need to fear eternal torment or annihilation.

Nee was not the initiator of this novel idea. In his *Study on Revelation*, Nee referenced Robert Govett (1813–1901) a number of times.[274] In a conference given in 1934, Nee explicitly lauded Govett for being the first to "see the problem of Christians gaining a reward." In Nee's understanding, Govett discovered that "although people are saved by faith, nevertheless, before God, they gain a reward based on their actions." Furthermore, Govett had also taught Nee the idea that "there is a possibility that Christians will be excluded from the millennial kingdom."[275] Govett's published works, which are still being printed today, claim that "eternal life is God's unconditional gift to believers" even while their "participation in the kingdom of Christ is conditional on their conduct, as good or evil."[276]

---

[272] Diarmaid MacCulloch, *The Reformation* (New York: Penguin Books, 2003), 13.

[273] MacCulloch, *The Reformation*, 13.

[274] For some examples, see NTSWJ 16, 39, 43, 52, 67.

[275] NTSWJ 11, 158–159.

[276] Robert Govett, *Entrance into the Kingdom or Reward According to Works* (Miami Springs, FL: Conley & Schoettle Publishing Co., 1978), 1.

Govett's position, however, was deeply idiosyncratic, and the Christian Assembly was probably the largest contemporary group that espoused his beliefs. Govett was also the first pastor of Surrey Chapel, the congregation to which Barber belonged. When she left the Church of England, Barber was baptized by immersion by Govett's successor, and Surrey Chapel supported her final mission to China, during which she contacted Nee. Thus, although Nee never explicitly credited Barber with introducing him to the writings of Govett, it is almost certain that this was the case. The fact that these Surrey teachings sharply distinguished Barber from other Western missionaries, and their legacy flourished in China while virtually disappearing from the West, is another surprising irony of Christianity's simultaneous progression and recession around the world.

The Glory of the Church and the Overcomers

The idea of a thousand-year period of either reward or punishment for saved Christians had startling implications for the individual believer. Nee pushed these implications further, expanding them to the church as a whole, and arriving at a synthesis between Surrey soteriology, Keswick spirituality, and Brethren ecclesiology that may be his most significant contribution to the history of Christian thought, in some ways even more novel and certainly more far-reaching in scope than Nee's teachings on the human spirit.

On a collective level, Nee taught that God's children living up to the biblical standard could literally define the epoch and the course of human history. He had a suitably impressive name for these Christians who would fulfill God's plan: the overcomers, literally, "the victorious ones" (Chinese: 得胜者).[277] According to Nee's understanding, these overcomers offered a further solution to thorny theological problems that had long troubled evangelical Christians.

Evangelicals held that the true church was composed of all born-again or regenerated Christians. These Christians could be found in any number of denominations; however, sometimes side by side with "nominal" Christians who were, by this definition, not true Christians at all. Thus, the church was amorphous, invisibly spread throughout visible congregations.

As early as the Fuzhou years, Nee had offered his understanding of the local churches as a more visible manifestation of the invisible church of the regenerated that all evangelicals believed was the "one, holy, and Catholic"

---

[277] The English term "overcomer" had been used by Jessie Penn-Lewis, but Nee's use of it was distinct. Tellingly, Penn-Lewis tended to speak of overcomer in the singular, emphasizing individual Christian victory, whereas Nee preferred the plural, overcomers as an ecclesial community.

church of Christ.[278] After years of theological reflection, however, he focused even more keenly on the inherent contradictions of the invisible church. Nee argued that if God's goal was to "testify to His Son's victory," then "all failing believers hinder God's work."[279] If God's goal was not simply visibility or testimony, but victory, then the fractured, compromised status of the visible church was even more problematic. Nee wrote:

> Satan cannot overcome the individual Christ, but he can shame the individual Christ by means of the corporate Christ. The defeat of the body is the defeat of the head. The defeat of a single member is the defeat of the body. We are the continuation of Christ. We are the extension of Christ, (Isa 53:10) just as we were the extension of Adam. God leaves us on the earth so that we can accomplish his eternal plan, achieve his eternal purpose.[280]

Anthropologists have suggested that the culture of the Sinosphere is attuned to shame in ways that Western culture may not be.[281] It is hard not to see something of that tendency here, as Nee argued that the failure of individual members reflected not only on themselves but also on the whole body of Christ and on Christ himself, the head of the body. For Nee then, glory was partially defined in relation to shame. The failure of Christians was a shame (*xiuru*, 羞辱) to Christ, but their holy living glorified God and shamed Satan instead. A sensitivity to shame may help to explain Nee's deep concern that God should have some kind of vindication, an open triumph over Satan that proved Christ's victory in the invisible realm.

For Nee, the possibility of God's being shamed presented an obvious conundrum. He combined the pessimistic assessments of both Keswick and the Brethren regarding the state of Christianity. From his Keswick sources, he drew the conclusion that many, if not most, Christians were living defeated, compromised Christian lives. From his Brethren sources, he concluded that the visible church was ruined by division and impurity. From both sources, he learned that Christians and churches had become too deeply entangled with "the world"—the corrupting tide of popular culture, society, and politics. If God and

---

[278] Carter, *Anglican Evangelicals*, 9.
[279] NTSWJ 11, 118. Nee uses a Chinese expression that literally means to dismantle the stage someone is on, something akin to pulling the rug out from under them.
[280] NTSWJ 11, 119.
[281] The classic study on this point is Ruth Benedict's *The Chrysanthemum and the Sword* (Boston, MA: Houghton Mifflin, 1946). Since then, the claim has been frequently contested and qualified in the academic literature. Still, the fact stands that one of Nee's key contributions to ecclesiology vis-à-vis his Western interlocutors relies on a sensitive awareness of God's potential shame. It also relies on a holistic integration between the "individual Christ" and the "corporate Christ (團體基督)."

Satan were fighting for visible victory and shame, it seemed that Satan, rather than God, was prevailing.

Nee relied on the Keswick distinction between "average" and "normal" Christians to argue that the common condition of average Christians was not normal: that is, it did not meet God's standard as outlined in the Bible.[282] Nee began to see these "normal," victorious Christians as the focal point of God's work on earth. God did not merely want an invisible church of true believers spread throughout many mixed congregations, as most evangelicals and Keswick writers affirmed, nor a small group of congregations that could maintain a pure testimony, as was the purpose of the Brethren assemblies. Instead, Nee argued for some combination of the two, believing that God would somehow gain a group of overcomers to represent the whole body of Christians in victory before Christ returned in glory to reclaim the earth. Some of the overcomers would offer a visible testimony in local churches, while others would be invisibly distributed in Christian congregations around the world and throughout history.

On this historical register, Nee now saw the overcomers as the main characters in God's plan of salvation, revising the timeline of dispensations he had inherited from the Brethren. Nee agreed with the Brethren that human history could be divided into dispensations or periods of time in which God dealt with humanity under certain arrangements. Thus, the Brethren and Nee both taught that God governed humanity directly in the case of Adam and Eve before the fall, then according to the law in the age of Moses, and later through grace after Jesus's incarnation. In this scheme, the transition between dispensations was critical. John Nelson Darby had focused on the "awful apostasy" that marked human failure at the end of each age, which required a new dispensation.[283] Nee now argued that the dispensations changed because of the positive testimony of the overcomers. Thus, in the contemporary era, Nee believed that the overcomers would represent the church "in the end times," allowing God to claim victory and end the current dispensation by ushering in Christ's second coming.[284]

Problems of the Church

The boldness of Nee's departures from standard Brethren teachings was the result of a growing disaffection. In 1929, Nee's extensive book-buying from a London publisher had resulted in his becoming acquainted with the publisher's friend, a Brethren minister named George Ware. Ware and Nee corresponded

[282] Melvin Dieter et al., *Five Views on Sanctification* (Grand Rapids, MI: 2011), offers a Keswick view on sanctification centered on the distinction between average and normal.
[283] Kelly, *Collected Writings, Ecclesiastical*, 174, 180.
[284] NTSWJ 11, 144.

for about a year, and the Brethren fellowship to which Ware belonged became quite excited about the "existence of this work of God in China."[285] One of their number, a British engineer by the name of Charles Barlow, was delegated to Shanghai by his employer. The Brethren took the opportunity to ask Barlow to visit Nee and to learn more about the nature of Nee's work.

Barlow was deeply impressed with what he saw, writing back that "Some of these dear brethren are very sincere and thirsting for truth." He added that "Watchman Nee is undoubtedly the outstanding man among them. He is far beyond all the rest. He is only 28, but has had a good education and is possessed of marked ability. He is a hard worker and reads much. He is, too, a great student of J. N. Darby, and has evidently been greatly helped by his writings."[286] When Barlow returned in person, his reports created a stir and the Brethren ended up sending a significant delegation to the Shanghai congregation in the fall of 1932. After two weeks of careful observation, the visitors decided to take communion with the Chinese congregations, a significant act for a group of so-called Closed or Exclusive Brethren. In essence, the Brethren agreed that the Shanghai congregation was based on the same principles as their own gathering and could be completely identified with one another.[287]

Excitedly, the Brethen extended an invitation for Nee to return the visit in the coming year, and in June of 1933, Nee made his first visit to the West, visiting Brethren congregations in Great Britain, the United States, and Canada. His talks on this tour were well received by many, but Nee was beginning to have misgivings. He was bothered by the Brethren's spiritual pride, hearing them boast on several occasions that they had the highest spiritual revelation of any Christian group. Once, after listening to a long doctrinal discussion, he apparently chided his audience that all their knowledge of the truth would not help them much in China, suggesting that "if when the need arose you could not cast out a demon!" He also confided later to Barlow that "his people" had "wonderful light, but oh so little faith."[288]

During his trip, Nee also went alone to the Christian Fellowship Center, an independent evangelical church that was being led by Theodore Austin-Sparks, a former Baptist minister and a fellow student of Penn-Lewis's teachings. Nee had subscribed to Austin-Sparks's periodical, *A Witness and a Testimony*, and had found his teachings deeply congenial. Like Nee, Austin-Sparks had pushed Penn-Lewis's emphasis on the individual Christian's inner, spiritual life toward a more corporate dimension. Also like Nee, Austin-Sparks accepted many of the

[285] A. J. Gardiner, *The Recovery and Maintenance of the Truth* (London: Stow Hill Bible and Tract Depot, 1951), 216.

[286] Kinnear, *Against the Tide*, 140–141.

[287] Kinnear, *Against the Tide*, 147–149.

[288] Kinnear, *Against the Tide*, 152.

Brethren's criticisms of the church, but he did so with more of an ecumenical emphasis on the positive aspects of the church. In a 1933 issue of *A Witness and a Testimony*, Austin-Sparks wrote that he had seen that "denominationalism, sectarianism, and all divisions which are of earth" contradicted "the truth of the universality of Christ, and the heavenly nature and vocation of 'the Church, which is His Body.'" Thus, he felt that "the Lord was leading us out from such and calling us into the spiritual, universal, heavenly ministry of His Son in relation to the *whole* Body as here on the earth."[289]

It was probably fitting then that Nee's decision to take communion at the Christian Fellowship Center ended up scandalizing his Brethren hosts and cutting him off from their fellowship. The Exclusive Brethren were zealous about maintaining a Christian principle that has become known as double separation. According to this principle, congregations must excommunicate not only apostate Christians but also all those who had some kind of fellowship or communion with apostate groups, even if those persons were not themselves apostate. After hearing about Nee's decision to associate with the Christian Fellowship Center, the Brethren leaders demanded an explanation. Nee demurred, writing back to one correspondent that he was still "waiting for light" and would like to consult with other leaders in the Shanghai congregation.

Over the next two years, Nee and the Shanghai elders and co-workers continued to correspond with leaders in the Brethren movement. It eventually became clear to both parties that there were fundamental differences between the two groups. Finally, in July 1935, Nee, Witness Lee, and several of the other Shanghai leaders sent a long letter to the Brethren. It suggested that only "moral corruption" and "heresy regarding the person of Christ" disqualified a person from receiving communion. Otherwise, "as for who can truly have fellowship, this is for the Holy Spirit to decide, and it is not for us to say." It then accused the Brethren of using artificial, human means to interfere with the Spirit's direct guidance in these matters, the very grounds upon which Darby had rejected the clerical system.[290]

The Brethren were incensed. They wrote back that they had "judged before the Lord that we must entirely repudiate, as not being of God, the principles you set out as governing fellowship, and that since you identify yourselves with these principles, we are unable to walk with you, or to receive from or commend to you. This, of course, applies also to all those maintaining links of fellowship with you."[291]

[289] T. Austin-Sparks, "Editorial," *A Witness and a Testimony*, January–February, 1933, 2.
[290] NTSWJ 26, 186–189.
[291] Gordon Rainbow, "The China Episode, 1932–1935," accessed on September 5, 2025, at www.mybrethren.org/history/hy29chin.htm

Lee later clarified that the Shanghai congregation's decision signified a determination to forge a new path that represented their special sense of commission, writing that "In our consideration, we realized that we could neither follow the way of the Brethren nor follow the way of Brother Austin-Sparks. The way of the Brethren was exclusive, and the way of Brother Austin-Sparks was without practicality."[292]

Nee's writings reveal his attempt to avoid the extremes of the Brethren and the Keswick teachers. Nee conceived of actual, local churches that would faithfully represent both the criticisms of the Brethren and the mystical spirituality of Penn-Lewis and Austin-Sparks. There was a definite tension in Nee's thought between his belief that Christians should leave denominations and other unbiblical sects and his equally strong convictions that Christians should testify to the unity of Christ through their communal life. In Nee's mind, this contradiction was resolved when a congregation did not claim to be the "local church" but simply to "stand on the ground of the church." They did not claim to represent the church exclusively but only to be standing on the right ground: the foundation of the undivided, unsectarian Christ.[293]

This was a subtle distinction, and it seems that many of Nee's followers did not entirely understand it. In a letter to his co-workers that was written in 1935, Nee bemoaned the poor response to his "Overcomer Conference." He wrote that during the conference, "we saw what God's center is and how Christ should have the first place in all things." The gist of the message seemed to have been missed by Nee's associates—the leaders in the very congregations that read his ministry and sent representatives to his conferences. Nee continued, "Unfortunately, however, in the last two years, we have not seen greater loyalty, faith, and love toward Christ . . . Instead, we see that leaving the denominations, church meeting arrangements, baptism by immersion, and head coverings have become the center of the truth among us." Exasperated, Nee rhetorically asked, "Have we no other testimony other than these outward matters?"[294]

At the end of his letter, Nee admitted to the difficulty of following the path that God had revealed during the Overcomer Conference. He suggested that "If we do not have faith nor obedience, or know by experience what overcoming, filling, forsaking the self, and warfare are, how can we testify on Christ's behalf in these matters? Then we can only choose easy things, like leaving the denominations, etc., to be our testimony!" This was especially true because the outward messages were so "very effective" in causing "many people [to be] moved to obey the Lord

---

[292] Witness Lee, *History of the Church*, 102.
[293] NTSWJ 22, 88–93.
[294] NTSWJ 26, 198.

and walk in the way because they know the denominations are wrong, so they leave them and break bread with us."[295]

Some of Nee's co-workers may have avoided the difficult work of understanding his more abstract teachings on overcomers, the ground of church, and the spiritual life. As the True Jesus Church had found, it was much easier to win fellow Christians with a bold, critical message that denominations were unbiblical. Thus, Nee proposed something of a moratorium, concluding,

> Therefore, *I ask you brothers, to resolutely determine to refuse to discuss questions like leaving the denominations with anybody who has not yet completely consecrated themselves to God and begun to walk the way of the cross.* We can only speak of such outward matters with those who are already living in the will of God. At all costs, we must avoid making *The Assembly Life* [Nee's book on the organization of the church] an advertising product for outsiders. We must remember that our goal is not to build up our own church, but to gain a benefit for God. What is the real need of people today? Is it life? Or is it fellowship (on the ground of the church)? Brothers, we must come to ourselves.
>
> As for the brothers who have already come among us, we should not look down on them. Even less should we treat them harshly. We should remember that our own spiritual situation is only so much, how can we be overcritical of them? Now all we can do is to earnestly pursue deeper experiences, so that we can serve them with a loving heart. Their future spiritual training will be set by how we pursue today.[296]

This open letter offers fascinating insight into Nee's thinking as both a Christian teacher and a church leader. In it, Nee's main concern seemed to be too *much* success in gaining a following. Rather than reveling in the numbers joining his movement, he worried that the purity and standard of his vision would be diluted by the loud pronouncement of some of his simpler, more concrete criticisms. Of course, it is hard to know how many of Nee's followers actually took up his calling to deal with the harder and deeper matters.

Teaching people to "walk in the way of the cross" in "faith and obedience" was certainly more demanding than simply taking up the banner of Nee's biblical practices and teachings to draw followers away from the denominations. The latter option was certainly more accessible. Nee seemed to recognize this fact when he concedes that "We should not despise the brothers who are already among us." As the central figure in a growing circle, he had to maintain a careful balance. His qualified response to what he perceived to be the Brethren's

[295] NTSWJ 26, 201–202.
[296] NTSWJ 26, 204, emphasis in the original.

sectarianism meant that he could not push people away or expel them for a lack of spirituality. At the same time, he had to guard against the possibility of sectarianism among his own followers, whether from those who were enthusiastically poaching members from existing denominations or from those who were tempted to despise the superficial and unspiritual among the assemblies.

Christ as Everything: Watchman Nee's Self-Definition

Nee attempted to thread this needle by formulating a definition of himself and his followers that was both ecumenical and demanding. During the earlier Overcomer Conference of January 1934, Nee had shared a message that was aptly titled, "What are We?" In it, Nee averred that "We are not some thing. We are not a new denomination, and we are not a new religious group, or a new movement, a new organization. We are not here to join a certain group or to create a new group." Thus far, he could have been articulating a standard Brethren self-description of their own group, mostly defined by negative statements. Nee continued, however, by arguing that God had given them "a special calling and commission."[297]

Nee emphasized a strange and particular phrase from 2 Peter 1:12, the "present truth," which Nee thought could "also be called the 'up-to-date truth.'" In keeping with his deep regard for biblical wisdom as unlimited and all-encompassing, Nee explained that "All the truths are actually in the Bible." The problem was simply that "because of human ignorance, human unfaithfulness, human neglect, human disobedience, many of these truths were buried in the Bible, and hidden from humankind." In the course of history, God had intervened and "allowed humanity to discover particular truths in particular ages," to address the contemporary need. Progressively then, throughout many generations, God had lifted the veil of ignorance. The "present truth" was God's timeless biblical message brought out for a specific moment in time.[298]

In Nee's understanding of Christian history, certain figures and groups had recovered and represented the "present truths." Reflecting his nineteenth-century Anglo-American evangelical sources, Nee admitted that even though there were recoveries before the sixteenth century, the most significant had begun with the Protestant Reformation. Thus, in rather rapid succession, Nee covered Luther, the Anabaptists, the Pietists, the Moravian Brethren, Roman Catholic Quietists,

---

[297] NTSWJ 11, 149. It is also possible to translate Nee's opening phrase as "We are not anything (我們並不是甚麼)."
[298] NTSWJ 11, 150.

Methodism, the Brethren, the Holiness and Keswick teachers, Penn-Lewis, the Welsh Revival, and the Azusa Street Revival.

Nee acknowledged that there was no direct, visible, or institutional link between these heterogeneous groups, but he claimed that they represented the invisible work of the Spirit, a history of the unbroken chain of overcomers that God had produced in scattered times and places throughout the church age.[299] For Nee, these truths culminated in a recent revelation. Nee wrote that "it was only in 1934 that we realized that Christ is the centrality of everything to God. Christ is God's centrality, and he is God's universality. Nothing of God's plan is apart from Christ."[300]

If Nee had wanted to distinguish his "special calling and commission," he could have chosen any one of his distinctive ideas. Instead, he trained aspiring overcomers to focus on one of his most recent "discoveries," which was also a claim that was so common as to be almost unobjectionable to any Christian: that is, the supremacy of Christ. Jesus-centered devotion cut across many of the enormous divisions that marked contemporary Christianities: liberal and conservative, elite and popular, Chinese and Western. Even some roughly contemporary Buddhist scholars like Zhang Chunyi (1871–1955) praised Jesus, claiming that "Christ is originally a bodhisattva" who "taught people to eliminate the three poisons—craving, ill will, and delusion—with all their soul and strength."[301]

Nee had a particular understanding of Christo-centrism, however, that differentiated his ideas from those of the general Christian and non-Christian milieu. Nee began the Third Overcomer Conference with a set of seven messages on "God's Center or the Centrality and Universality of Christ."[302] In those messages, he argues that "All of God's truths have an organization, they can be apprehended. God's truths have a center, everything else is subsidiary." Nee suggested that many different teachings, including some that could be ascribed to him, were of only secondary importance. Among these peripheral teachings were "baptism, speaking in tongues, leaving denominations, sanctification, keeping the Sabbath." Nee suggests that these different doctrines and practices were generally based on people's "own inclinations and the needs in their environment." But God himself has a need and a central work.[303]

---

[299] Nee was building here on Brethren historiography, as in Edmund Broadbent's *The Pilgrim Church* (Oxford: Oxford City Press, 2019).

[300] NTSWJ 11, 165–166.

[301] Lan Pan-chiu and So Yuen-tai's "Mahayana Interpretation of Christianity: A Case Study of Zhang Chunyi (1871–1955)" *Buddhist-Christian Studies* 27 (2007), 78. Zhang was publishing his works in Shanghai at almost exactly the same time at Nee, his *Zhongguo Jidujiao* (Chinese Christianity) was reprinted in Shanghai in 1927. Lan and So, "Mahayana Interpretation," 85.

[302] NTSWJ 11, 87.

[303] NTSWJ 11, 87–88.

This central work was to unite the believer to Christ. This union was so complete that it was incorrect to claim that "I draw power from Christ to help me be a human being." Instead, a Christian should say that "It is Christ who is the human being *for me*." In this case, it was telling that Nee did not use the usual Chinese word for "Christian" (*Jidutu*, 基督徒), which could be translated as a follower or disciple of Christ. Instead, he preferred *Jiduren* (基督人), which can be translated "Christ-person" or "Christ-human," perhaps because the term indicates a personal blending of the two parties.[304]

Nee explained this possibility by building once again on the distinction between the soul and the spirit. He argued that Christians must reject their souls to live by their spirits. This was equivalent to rejecting everything that was independent or separate from Christ and choosing to live by the part that was entirely united with Christ. Thus, the flip side of Nee's transcendent mysticism was the demanding road of the cross. Nee put the two sides directly in juxtaposition.

> Victory is Christ! Patience is Christ! What we need is not patience, gentleness, love, but Christ. Christ wants to take the first place in all things. Christ lives out patience, gentleness, and love from within us. We human beings, apart from death, are not worthy of anything. We are only worthy to die. When God created Adam, he gave Adam his will and told him to obey. God's new creation of us is not that way. Instead, God puts us in the place of death, and God himself lives out his will from within us. We should not only see a substitutionary Savior on Mount Golgotha. Even more, we should see that within us is the Lord who will live for us.[305]

When Nee argued that Christ should have the first place in all things, he was not simply returning to well-worn Christian teachings about devotion to Jesus. He was arguing for a human experience in which Christ initiated and encompassed everything through spiritual union. The human role was to embrace death and total self-abnegation. "We must know the self thoroughly," Nee writes, accepting that "the self deserves only to die," and embracing the fact that "the self must come to an end." In this way, Christ really gained the first place because everything was initiated by Christ from the human spirit.

According to Nee, the human self was put to death. Even though the Christian cooperated with Christ in every action, Christ shared in the agency and gained all the credit for every good work. Nee's preferred translation of Christ's prominence was *jü shouwei* (居首位), to occupy, or reside in the first place. In

---

[304] NTSWJ 11, 105.
[305] NTSWJ 11, 106. Nee's first declaration can also be translated "Overcoming is Christ!"

normative Christian thought and action, Christ was the first mover through the point of union in the human spirit.

For Nee, the final implication of Christ's centrality was that Christian work and messages must be entirely governed by this rule. In other words, he wanted all Christian ministry to be judged by the standard of his particular understanding of Christ. This included his own previous and future work. Christ's superiority, he had now concluded, was the center of all of God's "systematic and interrelated" truths. Thus, *The Spiritual Person*, with its emphasis on distinguishing the soul and the spirit, was important because true spirituality was what allowed Christ to live through the Christian and gain glory. The overcomers were the collective expression of this same Christ, allowing Christ to gain victory on the scale of the church and to incite Christ's second coming.

The significance of "What are We" is that it is the only place in Nee's entire corpus where he directly defined himself, his followers, and his work at a higher level of metanarrative. On a sociological level, Nee's followers often seemed to act as a denomination, and a sectarian, cohesive one at that. They recognized one another, they revered Nee's teachings, and their services and activities were similar. Nee's followers, however, consistently refused denominational identity because of their rejection of group names and formal organizations. It is therefore especially instructive to consider the boundaries of the "we" that Nee had in mind in his self-definition.

Nee taught that "concerning the church, we have to hold fast what we see today." He also argued that the testimony of the preeminence of Christ "is today in America, England, France, Spain, and even Africa. It is everywhere. But the numbers are few, and from an external perspective, they are extremely poor. We need to pray for these places."[306] Both Nee and his followers rejected a separate identity for their group because they wanted to include others as part of the same movement. Just as the early Brethren saw themselves as catholic but not Roman, Nee and his followers wanted to embrace Christians throughout the world, even those who had never heard of Nee or his teachings, and even if they were "extremely poor."

In the end, Nee used a common argument regarding the supremacy of Christ in an uncommon way. He argued that the world was short of sanctified believers who could show the evidence of Christ's living within them. Nonetheless, Nee was willing to point to specific countries and people, suggesting that the testimony he had in mind had a certain tangibility. Given his ongoing dispute with the Brethren, Nee's quotation seemed pointedly to suggest that the Christian Assemblies played a central role in bolstering the numbers and condition of

[306] NTSWJ 11, 168.

those who would uphold this Christo-centric witness. He asked his Chinese audiences to pray for fellow small congregations, scattered throughout the globe.

Nee thus taught his audience that they could be the active center of God's work in the world, not marginalized occupants of a mission field. The vibrancy and power of Nee's revelations and the growing strength of those gathered around him seemed to suggest a radical recentering of God's work, as did the short history Nee provided, which ran through Europe and North America only to conclude in China.

Nee's claims depended on at least one critical assumption that was shared by mainstream Chinese patriots in his era. China could be at the center of history. For Nee, however, unlike for most of his countrymen, China's prominent role would not take place in the visible history of world affairs but in the mostly invisible realm of God's work. Witness Lee recalled that Nee believed that "the Lord was forced to come to China, because, as far as the practice of the church life was concerned, China was still virgin soil, whereas the United States and Europe had been spoiled."[307]

Thus, while other Chinese worked toward China's military or political resurgence, Nee argued for China's importance to the spiritual progress of humanity. Christians in China were now charged with "calling out to God's children to return to God's central commission." Their relatively small numbers were only to be expected. Although they were dwarfed by both the global church and by the overwhelmingly non-Christian Chinese populace, this only made them similar to many of the other groups that Nee had designated as his spiritual lineage, groups like the Anabaptists, Quietist Catholics, and the Plymouth Brethren. Like these groups, and like John the Baptist, they would be a "voice in the wilderness."[308] Once again, God's testimony would be carried forward by a determined minority of reformers.

In the end, one of the most interesting tensions in Nee's thought was the question of the relationship between these visible groups of reformers and the overcomers. Nee's desire to admit all who were not openly sinful or heretical meant that he refused to form a special fellowship composed only of overcomers. The Little Flock churches would be open to all, including weaker Christians who were obviously struggling in their Christian lives. At the same time, Nee's prophetic interpretation of the seven churches in Revelation indicated that overcomers were to be found in every kind of Christian group, even ostensibly apostate ones like the Roman Catholic Church and denominational Protestantism. In terms of the individual Christian's reward and punishment,

---

[307] Witness Lee, *The Genuine Ground of Oneness* (Anaheim, CA: Living Stream Ministry, 1979), 135.
[308] NTSWJ 11, 166–167.

overcoming was all that mattered. In terms of God's interests, however, a group of overcoming believers still had to maintain a visible, corporate testimony of the one, pure church. This was the basis of Nee's disagreement with Austin-Sparks, whose view of the church "was without practicality."[309]

For his part, Nee could be exceedingly practical in thinking about the visible organization of the church. Many of his works during this period dealt with the finer points of defining church offices, the kinds of meetings a local church should have, their proper arrangements, and other quotidian details of actual congregational life. It could be hard for his followers to see how his teachings on the best way to conduct Bible study meetings were related to the supremacy of Christ. Nevertheless, in the very message in which he insisted on Christ's preeminence, Nee also averred that "Our work today is to return to the ground of the church as it is found in the Bible," adding that "All of God's truths take the church as the starting point."[310]

One of the ways Nee tried to square this circle was to return to the mysterious, unitive relationship between Christ and the church. Any interest in the church could also be understood as an interest in Christ. As Nee explained, "The Lord Jesus and the church are *Christ* (1 Cor. 12:12). When the individual Christ and the church are joined, they become the *corporate Christ.*" As his followers met in homes and the nondescript "assembly halls" they favored, their "living and testimony should display Christ, display his life, his victory, and his glory."[311]

Even if the local churches included many average Christians, Nee still believed that, in some way, the churches reflected the high standards he had crafted from Keswick and Brethren teachings. For him, Christ's victory could only be shown by Christians who were utterly selfless, and this selflessness could only be proven by living in unity and purity in mixed congregations of local churches in every city. Thus, he could argue for both Christ's supremacy and the "ground of the church as it is found in the Bible" as the "starting point" of all truth.

In the end, Nee was left with an uncertain answer to the question he posed at the outset—"What are we?" Of course, since he refused to call himself, his co-workers, and his followers a denomination, sect, movement, organization, or even a thing, this difficulty with self-definition is perhaps not surprising. Nee's strongest rhetorical points were on the supremacy of Christ, but many other ministers and Christian groups also spoke in much the same way. The distinction between Nee and those Christians remained in the subtext, the arguments about how the supremacy of Christ had to be upheld through the Bible, the self, the human spirit, and the nature of the church that Nee had already explained to

---

[309] Lee, *The History of the Church and the Local Churches*, 102.
[310] NTSWJ 11, 167.
[311] NTSWJ 26, 184.

his audience. Although he preferred to march under the ecumenical banner of Christ, Nee and his audience were distinct in their belief that, on an individual level, this Christ was found in the spirit, defined in opposition to the self, and, on a collective level, Christ was to be testified by overcomers who met on the proper ground of the church. Living in mixed congregations helped overcomers shine, reject their selves, and live in spiritual union. The combined body of overcomers would give Christ a visible testimony on the earth and allow for Jesus's second coming.

Joy and Sorrow

Around the time of the Third Overcomer Conference early in 1934, a familiar figure reappeared in Nee's life. Charity Chang, his childhood friend and first love, had finished her master's degree in Biology at the prestigious Yenching University and had come to Shanghai. Although she had previously shown no interest in Christianity, she now started coming to the meetings at Wendeli and was soon baptized. Charity's sister, Faith, acted as something of a go-between, confiding in Nee that if he proposed, her sister would accept. The two were engaged and then married on October 19, 1934, the anniversary of his own parents' marriage.[312]

Regrettably, the new couple did not have much time to enjoy wedded bliss. Charity's aunt, a wealthy woman, was infuriated by the union of her beautiful, well-educated niece to a poor preacher. She placed angry advertisements in a newspaper every day for a week. Some denominational Christians who were offended by Nee's critiques of their churches fanned the flames and circulated handbills to the Christian community to complement the newspaper advertisements. Together, they denounced Nee in vitriolic terms, accusing him of financial impropriety and hinting darkly at previous episodes of sexual immorality. Nee's biographer recalls that a missionary who received one of these papers thought it "so vile" that "I felt I needed a bath."[313]

The firestorm depressed Nee, while his confidants tried their best to comfort and encourage him. His new sister-in-law, Faith, asked rhetorically, "Does it matter what they say? You have won a wife after your own heart!"[314] Witness Lee, who had been Nee's best man, and another co-worker, Philip Luan, who had acted as the master of ceremonies at the wedding, did their best to quell the rumors with their own eyewitness testimonies. Nee himself, however, made

---

[312] Kinnear, *Against the Tide*, 164–166.

[313] Kinnear, *Against the Tide*, 166; Chen, *Meet Brother Nee*, 44–45; Lee, *Seer of the Divine Revelation*, 176–177, 308.

[314] Kinnear, *Against the Tide*, 166–167.

no public response. Once again, he showed his commitment to the painful lesson Margaret Barber had taught him, that suffering in silence was the path of the cross.

In the meantime, the Christian Assemblies continued to spread throughout China. Nee's work, *The Assembly Life*, which he feared that his co-workers were using as a "propaganda piece," was published in September 1934. In it, Nee laid out a blueprint for a kind of church practice that was faithful to the New Testament. Nee admitted that in the present day, there were no apostles in the sense of the primitive apostles with their degree of manifest holiness, power, victory, and work. Still, one could not deny that there was a "kind of person doing the work that apostles do—work such as preaching the gospel, establishing churches, etc." These unofficial apostles could appoint unofficial elders, allowing for authority and structure both locally and extra-locally.[315]

Neither the "apostles" nor the "elders" were official clergy. There was no educational requirement or formal process of ordination. Many apostles and elders even retained secular jobs to support themselves. As Nee pointed out, "In the Bible there is no worker who stops receiving wages to become a specially sponsored class. Even though Peter no longer fished, Paul still made tents."[316] Still, when finances allowed, the assemblies often opted to support their gifted members. Throughout the 1930s, the number of churches, apostles, and elders grew. The flexible, unofficial nature of these arrangements made the Christian Assemblies adaptable and able to spread quickly.

By the close of the decade in 1937, when peace was shattered by the outbreak of the Sino-Japanese War between China and Japan, there were deeply rooted congregations affiliated with Nee and his teachings throughout China. In some ways, the war years provided a special opportunity for the kinds of quick-reacting institutions that were able to respond. Both in absolute terms and relative to other Christian groups who lost vital links with their Western and missionary supporters, the congregations built around Nee's teachings gained much ground in these critical years.

To some extent, the differences in how the various Chinese Christian groups fared also came down to self-selection in the personalities of the groups' adherents. Nee once pointed out that the Western and missionary churches often gained their first converts from among their own servants and translators: that is, from people who reaped material benefits from their associations with foreigners.[317] In an age of fierce nationalism, those who were more likely to be leaders, or show independence of thought and action, were

---

[315] NTSWJ 22, 21.
[316] NTSWJ 22, 38.
[317] Kinnear, *Against the Tide*, 178–179.

also more likely to leave the established churches and to be attracted to novel messages like Nee's. During the turmoil of the war years, their initiative and courage would pay important dividends.

Late in 1937, while the bloody battle of Shanghai raged, Nee himself was in Southeast Asia, preparing for a second trip to Europe. After repeated delays, he concluded that God wanted him to "return, first do another bit of work and then resume travelling to England." Nee decided to begin a new publication, *The Open Door*. The amorphous "we" at the heart of his earlier question, "What are we?" now had "travelling workers (apostles)," to keep track of, as well as "The addresses of the meeting halls of the local churches, so that refugee brothers may find a place to go to meetings."[318]

The Open Door cemented the sense of group identity among Nee's followers and allowed for some level of organization during the chaos of the war years. Given that it was an official, institutional newsletter, it seemed to betray Nee's refusal to start another sect or institution. Thus, Nee himself admitted in the pages of *The Open Door* that he had wanted to begin such a publication some time ago, but he had "hoped that someone else would be entrusted by the Lord and would rise up to take responsibility." Since no one had done so, Nee felt compelled to take action, even while he tried to downplay the apparent institutionalization of his followers, writing, "If someone else had done this [publishing *The Open Door*] it would have belonged to the individual, as something done by grace. But if I do this, it becomes something formal, as something related to position. In order to avoid this, for years I did not dare to move."[319]

Even now, in 1937, with circumstances forcing his hand, he insisted that *The Open Door* did not signify the formation of a new denomination or congregation. He urged his readers to "Please always remember, brothers, this is a personal ministry, it is not a corporate organization."[320] Once again, however, Nee's protest contrasted with the visible facts on the ground, where their closely integrated network functioned much more coherently than many actual Chinese institutions with designated hierarchies, budgets, and operating procedures.

Although *The Open Door* was published for only two years between 1937 and 1939, it offered ample evidence of the spread and strength of Nee's following even during the turmoil of the war. At the beginning of the first issue, Nee suggested that an appropriate verse for the situation was Acts 8:4, "Those who were scattered went everywhere preaching the word." Nee suggested that God had allowed the apostolic church to experience persecution to help it fulfill its commission to preach "in Jerusalem, and in all Judea and Samaria and unto the

---

[318] NTSWJ 31, 2.
[319] NTSWJ 31, 1.
[320] NTSWJ 31, 1.

uttermost part of the earth." The early disciples were thus "preaching the word" even while they were "fleeing for refuge."[321]

Similarly, the war in China was dislodging much of the Chinese population from the coast, where fighting was heaviest. Nee urged, "Now is the time that the apostles should direct more of their labor toward the inland regions." He also urged the elders to encourage their congregations. The burden fell to average believers to spread the message with greater fervor instead of shrinking back in the face of war and chaos—"Although the apostles should move out [to preach the gospel in inland China], the disciples should also move out."[322]

Always aware of the danger that his message would become oversimplified and twisted, Nee reminded his readers, "We are not here to urge people to leave the denominations. Those who only know to emphasize leaving the denominations are not our brothers and they are not our co-workers. They are not qualified to work with us." Nevertheless, Nee affirmed that the central work of "preaching the gospel and establishing local churches" would prevail even in these times, writing that "Personally, I deeply believe that God will use this war to cause the sphere of his work in China to expand and widen. May our prayers also become deeper!"[323] As the war progressed, eventually stretching out over eight long years, Nee's and his followers' beliefs, labors, and prayers would be put fully to the test.

---

[321] NTSWJ 31, 3.
[322] NTSWJ 31, 4.
[323] NTSWJ, 31, 4.

5

The Breaking of the Outer Person

Watchman Nee managed to endure the early years of the Second Sino-Japanese War without suffering too much direct harm. One of his companions from the Fuzhou revival, Simon Meek, had established a successful work in the Philippines, and at the outbreak of hostilities with Japan, Nee had been visiting Manila at Meek's invitation.[324] By this time, any ill feelings had long been forgotten, and Meek considered himself to be, once again, one of Nee's co-workers.[325] The congregations that Meek led may have formed Nee's main base of support in the Philippines.

Nee had intended to travel to Europe from Southeast Asia, but now, as the war intensified, he decided to return home first instead. He immediately went to find Charity in Shanghai, which, at the time, was the site of the most brutal fighting in the war. When he arrived, probably around late August 1937, the National Revolutionary Army and the Imperial Japanese Army were involved in bloody, house-to-house combat through the streets of the city. The Nees' home was in the evacuated area and had been looted, but Charity was safe, staying with other sisters in the meeting hall at Wendeli, which was protected by virtue of its location in the International Settlement.[326]

Assured of her safety, Nee continued on to Hankou, where he called together as many co-workers as could come. He urged them to consider the war as an opportunity to spread the gospel and establish churches in other provinces where there had been no local testimony previously. Recognizing that many among their number had already lost their jobs and homes, Nee also established a fund for the needy to be administered through a co-worker in Hong Kong and another in Hankou, where he opened a temporary branch office of his publishing house. While the future of Shanghai was uncertain, Hankou was, for the moment, secure and centrally located.[327] Ruth Li also remained in Hankou, where she would oversee the publication of future issues of *The Open Door*, which

---

[324] Kinnear, *Against the Tide*, 181.

[325] Nee, NTSWJ 31, 6. One of Meek's early letters in February 1938 indicated that the churches were spreading rapidly throughout the Philippines as well. In October, one of Meek's preaching tours resulted in thirty-nine new local churches being established in ten different provinces. Meek's letter also indicated that businessmen (probably diasporic Chinese) were a major factor of support, both for spiritual leadership and presumably finances. NTSWJ 31, 60–61.

[326] Kinnear, *Against the Tide*, 181–182.

[327] Nee, NTSWJ 32, 78.

The Spiritual Person. Paul H B Chang, Oxford University Press. © Oxford University Press 2026.
DOI: 10.1093/9780197793664.003.0006

would coordinate the various churches' and co-workers' movements. By *The Open Door*'s third issue, printed in January 1938, demand had compelled Li to increase circulation from one to six thousand.[328] Finally, Nee left Charity, who was pregnant, in Hong Kong with his parents, where she would be safe from the ravages of war.

With things in China arranged as well as he could manage, Nee set out once again on his planned European trip. Nee's first visit to Europe had been largely initiated by his contacts with the Plymouth Brethren. Most of his time had been spent in their company, with the notable exception of his short visit to Austin-Sparks's congregation, known as the Christian Fellowship Center. Disillusioned with Brethrenism, he organized this trip around his contacts with Keswick teachers and inner-life mystics. His first destination was the Christian Fellowship Center, which became his temporary base of operations. Together, he and Austin-Sparks attended that year's Keswick Convention, in which Nee offered a memorable prayer while sharing the stage with a Japanese Christian:

> The Lord reigneth. He is reigning, and He is Lord of all. Nothing can touch his authority. It is the spiritual forces that are out to destroy the interests of the Lord in China and Japan. We do not pray for Japan. We do not pray for China. But we pray for the interests of Thy Son in China and Japan. We do not blame any man. They are only tools in the hand of the enemy of the Lord. Lord, we stand in Thy will. Lord, shatter the kingdom of darkness. Lord, the persecution of Thy Church is persecuting Thee. Amen.[329]

It was a shocking statement for a Chinese citizen during the war years. The Sino-Japanese War was a brutal, existential struggle that did not easily allow for equanimity. Propagandists from every major faction fought to control the narrative, and dehumanization along national lines was common.[330] Many Chinese adopted a patriotic stance of fierce resistance, many others simply tried to survive, and some collaborated with the Japanese invaders. In his prayer, Nee seemed to be forging a fourth option. He prayed boldly for the prosecution of *spiritual* warfare and equally boldly against identification with any national interests. He was not claiming neutrality so much as trying to reframe the entire conflict. From this perspective, nationalism was part of the problem, and the physical conflict was only a manifestation of the spiritual violence of Satan,

---

[328] Nee, NTSWJ 31, 59.

[329] *The Keswick Convention*, 1938, 246.

[330] See, for instance, Barak Kushner, *The Thought War: Japanese Imperial Propaganda* (Honolulu, HI: University of Hawai'i Press, 2006) and Chiang-tai Hung, *War and Popular Culture: Resistance in Modern China, 1937–1945* (Berkeley: University of California Press, 1994).

aimed against the church. The suffering was undeniable, but its source was invisible.

Nee's dramatic prayer was a skillful interpretation of the kind of transcendent, evangelical spirituality that inspired Keswick. These European inner-life Christians had carefully established a network of correspondence and travel through years of Keswick Conventions and other conferences. If the Brethren were exclusive and suspicious of outsiders, these Protestant devotional teachers were welcoming and friendly. Nee traveled widely, finding warm receptions in France, Germany, Norway, and Switzerland. In October, he came to Denmark, giving two messages in English that became the basis for the books *The Normal Christian Life* and *Sit, Walk, Stand*. It is possible that these manuscripts were rapidly translated and circulated among the inner-life circles that were already accustomed to sharing helpful literature. Certainly, within a few decades, there were formal printings in Danish, English, French, German, and Norwegian.

While he was in Europe, Nee received a letter from Charity, sharing the sad news of a miscarriage. Nee's personal warmth was most evident when he was with children, and the loss was a terrible blow. Nee Angus Kinnear recalls that while Nee was in England, he was known to "relax and play hide-and-seek with the children, folding himself easily out of sight into a cupboard in his long blue gown."[331] Likewise, one of Nee's sisters-in-law recalls that he always loved to spend time with his nephews and nieces. On one occasion, Nee and her son were having so much fun that the boy refused to let Nee leave their home to attend a previously scheduled co-workers' meeting. Nee promptly put the boy on his shoulders, and they went to the meeting together.[332]

Though Watchman and Charity could not know it at the time, they were never to have any children: In fact, it seems that they never conceived again. The Nees' lifelong childlessness was one of his quiet personal sufferings. He endured this along with his more public trials. Some records of his coping exist. His published works have many references to the ways in which personal tragedy could be turned to transcendence with the help of spiritual discipline.

Though Nee may have wanted to return home to comfort Charity after her miscarriage, the Shanghai co-workers charged him to remain longer in Europe to have a full discussion with Austin-Sparks on the problem, which was a continual source of difficulty—the "practical outworking of the Body of Christ."[333] In other words, their common emphasis on "the mystical 'Body' of Christ" had to be made concrete, but the details were difficult to work out.

---

[331] Kinnear, *Against the Tide*, 189.
[332] Interview with Ni Furen, June 2013.
[333] Kinnear, *Against the Tide*, 187–193.

Instead of returning at the beginning of the new year as he had planned, Nee stayed in England until May 1938, translating his own writings into English to foster a deeper conversation on ecclesiology. After months of fellowship, however, Austin-Sparks could give no satisfying answer. Nee's understanding of the principle of local churches—one church in each city—was already far more concrete than anything the British mystic cared to set down. After a brief visit to a number of congregations in North America, Nee returned to China. He would continue to forge his own path, more independent of Western influence than ever.

Excommunication and Restoration

Upon his return to China, Nee continued to care for his Shanghai congregation, which overflowed its meeting hall, even though other adjacent lots had been purchased and integrated into the complex. When a few members were moved to pray that Japanese inroads into the International Settlement would be limited, he gave his congregation a lesson in history, showing how God had used secular governments since ancient times to establish his purpose. In keeping with his own prayer at the Keswick Convention, Nee believed that Christians of every nationality must be able to stand in one accord and agree to any prayer that was uttered, warning them that "In China[,] Christians and missionaries have too much intimacy with the State. In the last European war there was much prayer that dishonored God."[334] Part of the Westernization of the gospel that Nee struggled to erase was the close relationship between the church, politics, and nationalism.

From 1939 to 1941, the church in Shanghai enjoyed something of a golden age. Safely located in the "Solitary Island" (*Gudao*) of internationally administered Shanghai, the church's physical premises and many of its members were protected from the worst ravages of war. As the war continued, Shanghai in general and the Solitary Island in particular developed a complex social ecosystem with the simultaneous rise of printed periodicals, economic uncertainty, and lavish hedonism.[335] In this contradictory environment, the church's confident message found easy publication and eager audiences, who were longing for direction and answers to the evident problems that surrounded them. The combination of Nee's growing prominence and his continued insistence on the basic invalidity of every Christian denomination made him a growing target. Perhaps

---

[334] Kinnear, *Against the Tide*, 197.
[335] Poshek Fu, *Passivity, Resistance, and Collaboration: Intellectual Choices in Occupied Shanghai, 1937–1945* (Stanford, CA: Stanford University Press, 1993), 30–48.

envious of his continued success, a number of foreign missionaries and Chinese Christians published critiques of his theology and even accusations that he was being supported by foreign funds.[336]

When the Japanese attacked Pearl Harbor in 1941, the Japanese army also took control of the International Settlement, and the Shanghai congregation's brief respite from war was ended. It soon became all too clear that Nee's sources of income were mostly indigenous. The Japanese occupation of the Chinese coast and the subsequent disruption of trade meant that many of the businesses of Nee's supporters began to falter. At this point, there were over two hundred full-time ministers, most of whom were supported by local congregations. About forty of them, however, were Nee's direct financial responsibility, since they traveled and assumed the work of apostles, without fixed ties to any specific local church. As inflation skyrocketed and financial constraints increased, many of Nee's young co-workers were pushed into desperate situations. Extreme privation, war, and fatal illnesses ravaged their ranks.

Years later, when Nee addressed a group of "those engaged in business," he pointed out the continued need to financially support the "twenty-something widows of former co-workers." In 1947, he was still haunted by the fact that he had "asked them to go out [to serve God], but not long after that, I sent them to their graves." He continued, "Among our co-workers, besides the one who contracted cholera and died, one who was killed by the Communists, and the two who died of other diseases, the rest died because of tuberculosis."[337] Disease ravaged the ranks of the young missionaries who were already weakened by physical and financial privation. Throughout the course of the war, Nee was repeatedly faced with the horrible specter of his young co-workers' deaths, due, at least in part, to his own lack of funds.

Early in 1942, Nee was presented with a startling opportunity to address his devastating dilemma. One of Nee's younger brothers, George, had earned a degree in chemistry and was a gifted researcher. George had founded *Shenghua Huaxue Zhiyaochang* (hereafter *Shenghua*, and known in English as China Biological and Chemical Laboratories), a business that manufactured and sold pharmaceuticals. Watchman recognized that, during the war years, pharmaceuticals would be a steady source of income, since they were considered necessary goods for the war effort. George was having trouble managing the administrative and financial elements of his company, and Watchman decided to work with him, devoting a certain number of hours each week to business and the rest to God, with the profits earned to be given directly to meet the churches' and co-workers' needs.

[336] Kinnear, *Against the Tide*, 199–205.
[337] Nee, NTSWJ 57, 346.

Ruth Li and a number of the Shanghai elders, however, disapproved of Nee's decision for reasons that are not entirely clear. Of course, Nee himself had spoken eloquently in the past about the need to live by faith and had also denounced the evil of commerce. Furthermore, as is often the case, problems arose in the administration of Nee's new business, and the business required more and more of his time and attention. For a spiritual man to build relationships with wealthy business partners and clients may have seemed an egregious case of backsliding, especially when set against the backdrop of a war-torn country with many co-workers who were braving extreme physical dangers to spread the testimony to rural villages.

In August 1938, while Nee was comfortably enjoying fellowship with the English congregation at the Christian Fellowship Center, Li had left Hankou to preach the gospel in rural Guizhou. Signing one of her letters from "a mountain village in Wan County," she comforted her readers, "The Lord never forgets us we are weak and cold. May we also not forget others who are weak and cold."[338] Although she referred to her spiritual condition, it is likely that her physical circumstances were similarly straitened.

Two issues later, in November 1938, Li reminded readers of Nee's original charge at the founding of *The Open Door*—that "the apostles direct their labor more towards the inland." Li, who may have been born and raised in the city of Nanjing, does not seem to have ever visited truly rural places before. She had recently learned through firsthand experience that even though the province itself might not border the sea, it might still have large and rich municipalities and counties, which were basically indistinguishable from those of littoral China. Li encouraged the co-workers to go to the truly "desolate regions" where she had seen desperate people, including coolies who broke their bodies carrying heavy loads to make just enough to ward off starvation. With "sighing tears and a hopeful heart," she urged the co-workers to take up the burden to reach the distressed and forgotten with the gospel.[339]

It is easy to see how Li may have become scandalized by Nee's sudden decision to engage in business. Ironically, both parties were probably moved by the same phenomenon, but simply had opposite reactions. Whereas Nee wanted to assuage the suffering of his co-workers, Li would have preferred to see him continue the path of a preacher living by faith, and perhaps taste more of their privations for himself.

In any case, the upshot of their disagreement was that at the end of 1942, the elders of the church in Shanghai asked Nee to stop his ministry in that

---

[338] Nee, NTSWJ 32, 106. The Chinese word "cold" here, *lengdan* (冷淡), does not refer to physical coldness but to sluggishness and indifference. Still, the choice of the headword, *leng*, is interesting, since the character does denote literal coldness.

[339] Nee, NTSWJ 32, 152–155.

city entirely. At least one of the elders, an ophthalmologist by the name of Yu Chenghua, may not have entirely agreed with the decision, since he also retired from preaching after the decision was made. Those responsible made no public announcement or explanation of their actions. For his part, as in the case of his excommunication from Fuzhou, Nee refused to defend or explain himself. Thus, many in the congregation were shocked and perplexed, and rumors swirled. For two years, none of the elders even approached Nee for a conversation.[340]

Nee appears to have thrown himself into the business, securing important contracts with the government and avoiding selling his products to the Japanese.[341] For over two years, he shuttled between Shanghai and Chongqing, the Nationalist Government's wartime capitol, occasionally preaching while he was at Chongqing. In the meantime, the Shanghai congregation floundered. It missed his leadership and even had to disband when the Japanese founded a "Religious Union" to exercise greater control over religious life in Shanghai. In order to avoid joining that body, the Shanghai members of the Little Flock ceased using their assembly hall until the end of the war and met only in the believers' homes when they met at all.

As the war came to an end in 1945, things began to change once more. Nee slowly divested himself of his business interests and arranged for his accumulated funds to be set aside for the future provision of his co-workers. Still unwilling to advocate on his own behalf, he stayed away from the Shanghai congregation. Nee's father had passed in 1941, and now, as the oldest son, he was the head of the household. He returned to the family home in Fuzhou with Charity and began making plans to restore it. At the time, he considered turning the property into a training center for his co-workers.[342]

Events would soon conspire to bring Nee back to Shanghai, however, and back into the center of events among the Christian Assemblies. In June 1946, after having gone six years without seeing one another face to face, Ruth Li invited Witness Lee to join her in Nanjing. Afterward, Lee was invited to Shanghai as well. The churches may have heard of Lee's successes during the war years. Besides his itinerating work in Suiyuan, Sha'anxi, and Shanxi, Lee had helped his home congregation in Shandong to grow by leaps and bounds. The church in Yantai had swelled in numbers and was energetically sending out groups of congregants to establish churches throughout northern China, a startling contrast to the scattered and demoralized Shanghai congregation.[343] Soon, the Nanjing and Shanghai congregations invited Lee to move his family to the south and work among them on a more permanent basis.

---

[340] Kinnear, *Against the Tide,* 213–214.
[341] Kinnear, *Against the Tide,* 217.
[342] Kinnear, *Against the Tide,* 219–220.
[343] Lee, *A Seer of the Divine Revelation,* 315. Kinnear, *Against the Tide,* 229–231.

When Lee arrived in the fall of 1946, he immediately went to look for Nee to ask his counsel. At that point, Nee had still not returned to public ministry, but he was happy to speak at length to Lee and Peace Wang, two co-workers who had supported him throughout all his troubles. Lee also challenged the elders who had excommunicated Nee, and they readily admitted that they regretted their decision.[344]

With Nee's blessing, Lee applied the methods he had learned in Yantai to Shanghai. This involved carefully organizing the members of the congregation into groups for practical and gospel services. As at Yantai, the combination of Lee's methods, bold personality, and fervent preaching produced dramatic results. The church in Shanghai began to see its numbers swell, even as Lee's repeated entreaties to Nee finally convinced the latter to speak in public again, beginning with a number of talks before a small audience in Fuzhou in September 1947.[345]

Nee had been virtually silent for about six years, but he had continued thinking deeply about his ministry and the Bible. A torrent of material would be produced in the coming years in multiple periodicals, addresses, and devoted "trainings." The topics Nee covered were broad, including a set of "Messages for Building Up New Believers," the character of a Christian worker, the nature of Christian ministry, how to study the Bible, spiritual judgment, and the principles of authority and submission.

The Little Flock's material circumstances also began to expand to fit the revival. The church in Shanghai finally purchased a second, larger property to accommodate its growing congregation, while Nee also made arrangements to develop a training center in Fujian. With the infrastructure and the audience in hand, Nee resumed his ministry. He did not know it at the time, but he had only a few years to sketch out his mature thought.

Self-Denial and Brokenness

Although Nee's mature ministry covered a breadth of topics, at its core, much of his new material drew from his experiences during his years "in the wilderness." Nee appears to have accepted his own excommunication and ban from ministry as God's personal arrangement, and there are no notes of self-vindication, self-pity, recriminations, or bitterness. Presumably, Nee would have been content to continue under God's judgment indefinitely, accepting what was basically the end of his public Christian work as the discipline of God.

---

[344] Kinnear, *Against the Tide*, 227.
[345] Kinnear, *Against the Tide*, 220–224. Lee, *A Seer of the Divine Revelation*, 317.

Nee's writings in these later years show that he had come to see brokenness and pliability as the signs of true advancement and growth in Christ. Of course, historically, many other Christians had picked up on these themes, mostly from an ascetic or monastic perspective. As befit one who learned these lessons while engaged in business, Nee did not teach Christians to withdraw into cells or deserts to confront the self, but rather to devote themselves to the actual messiness of ordinary, human experiences. There, God could use the difficulty and suffering of daily life to shine a piercing light on any pride, independence, and selfishness that remained in the soul.

It was a theology forged while China was engulfed in more than a decade of continual warfare, and it fit the grim situation. Nee did not pander to his audience, consoling them for their troubles. He did not promise better days to come. Instead, Nee described the way forward in terms that were alternately unsparing and transcendent, affirming that "When our outer person has been beaten, dealt with, and subjected to all kinds of difficulties, the wounds that are left on us, the scars that are left on us, these will allow the spirit within us to flow out."[346]

From his earliest experiences and writings, Nee's teachings had always emphasized self-denial as a means to access the spirit as opposed to the self.[347] Nee's early writings also frequently connected these aspects of personal spirituality to the practice of the church. Now, in his middle age, he continued his earlier trajectory, deepening and intensifying the language of sacrifice. At the same time, he linked these individual Christian experiences ever more tightly to the glory and victory of the church as a whole. The result was an intricately woven set of Christian teachings that distilled the entire Bible into a cohesive message with both eternal scope and immediate, practical consequences.

Nee spelled out vivid and compelling stakes for Christian lives that were deeply enmeshed in actual, local congregations. In Nee's mature understanding, every moment of a Christian's life could and should be spent in God's presence, free of base desires, selfish motives, and earthly entanglements. Such a life was best nurtured in the churches, where other Christians would become the ultimate test of spirituality. The friction present in all social relationships could teach true humility to every member of the body of Christ. Communally, Christians

---

[346] NTSWJ 34, 180. The phrase "outer person" is derived from Nee's original Chinese phrase *waimian de ren* (外面的人). Earlier translators have used the phrase "outer man." Since an actual man is not meant here, nor is gender relevant, I have chosen to translate the phrase into English with the more inclusive and general "person."

[347] Nee frequently uses the term 己(ji) or 自己(ziji) to discuss the "self" or the corrupted, independent aspect of the soul. English translations of Nee's work have generally translated these terms as "self," but because of extensive contemporary academic literature on notions of selfhood, identity, and the construction of the self, I will often translate as "ego" to give a general sense of what Nee meant—an inward aspect of human psychology and personhood that operates apart from God. This translation also has the benefit of connoting egotism, which corresponds to Nee's criticisms regarding self-interested motivations and interests.

could thus be perfected to live truly spiritual lives, lives that would give God the testimony he longed for: the glorious, victorious church.

It is hard not to read something of Nee's own experiences in the wilderness as reflecting on these conclusions. He had spent years separated from both active ministry and the leadership of the Shanghai church. He had been criticized and ostracized and now returned to a place of prominence among the churches he had personally led for so long. His message was that suffering at the hands of one's fellow Christians was an important step in spiritual maturity.

Nee's Rejection of Asceticism

As Nee spoke of the outer person being beaten and dealt with, he may have recognized that his words could be misinterpreted. In 1948, Nee also gave an extended message to his co-workers exegeting the Pauline metaphor of an athlete in the ninth chapter of First Corinthians.[348] Nee was quite familiar with the Greek New Testament and may well have chosen the passage deliberately.[349] Etymologically, the Greek word *askesis* (the root of the word "asceticism") was first used to refer to the strenuous exertions of athletes. Later, it was extended into religious contexts by Greco-Roman Christians and non-Christians alike. In the Corinthian passage, even though Paul does not use the term *askesis*, he clearly evokes its original semantic field by urging his audience to exercise self-control as a runner or a boxer would, even beating the body in order to make it one's slave.[350]

Nee may thus have chosen to engage the New Testament passage most likely to be referenced in support of Christian asceticism in order to explicitly deny it. After quoting the verse, Nee unequivocally declared, "Here, we must first make clear that when Paul speaks of 'buffeting my body, to make it obey me' he does not mean a kind of asceticism." Nee then clarified the distinction between what he saw to be the proper biblical teaching of self-control and the improper teaching of asceticism, arguing that ascetics believe "the body is the source of sin, and if people treat their bodies harshly, the problem of sin will be resolved." In contrast, "the Bible absolutely does not believe the body is a burden, even less does it believe that the body is the source of sin." Nee pointed out that the Bible called the body both the "temple of the Holy Spirit" and an object of redemption and eventual glorification.[351]

---

[348] Nee, NTSWJ 52, 50.

[349] *The Spiritual Person* begins with an exhaustive Chinese to Greek concordance compiled by Nee himself. At numerous other points in his writings, he refers to Greek words and their definitions.

[350] 1 Corinthians 9:23–27.

[351] Nee, NTSWJ 52, 50–51.

Because of the positive value that the scriptures assigned to the physical body, Nee encouraged his listeners not to exalt physical deprivation. Admitting that the Bible spoke of fasting, sleeplessness, and other privations, Nee still insisted that "Of course, all human needs are created by God and given by God, so the body is allowed its reasonable demands." For Nee, the way to balance the conflicting weights assigned to bodily rigor and the body's "reasonable demands" was to consider whether "there is anything there that may hinder your proper service to God."[352] In other words, Nee understood the Bible to be centrally concerned not with asceticism but with unimpeded service to God. For Nee, the Bible taught that "Human beings are under no compulsion to follow their bodies," either "in the matter of sexual desire, or in the matter of food," to give two examples. Other examples might include "rest, sleep, comfort, clothes, care during sickness, etc."[353] The crucial point was that the body should always be enslaved to the believer, rather than the believer being enslaved to the body's needs.

Such self-control could, theoretically, be cultivated or displayed in regimented or ritualized practices as had been true for so many Christians historically. Once again, however, Nee saw no biblical support for such programs or institutions. Instead, Nee felt that the Bible's descriptions of privations were occasional, arising only in response to specific needs, as in Jesus's specific demand for late-night wakefulness in the Garden of Gethsemane. Such prayer precluded sleep, but forgoing sleep was not a regular demand. It corresponded to Paul's exhortation to extraordinary feats of athleticism, as when running a race. Running races, Nee reasoned, was a matter of special exertion and was not a matter of daily, hourly practice. For most needs, walking sufficed. Likewise, Christians need not practice a regular discipline of sleeplessness, so long as they could respond when the Lord had special need.[354] Thus, refusing to institute any regular methods, Nee simply suggested that the extremes should be avoided, writing that "Of course, we do not agree that God's children would frequently spend the entire night in prayer, but we believe that if a person who is learning to serve God has never even once spent the night in prayer, that is also shameful."[355]

Since some form of ritual, physical self-deprivation is generally understood to be definitive of asceticism, it is difficult to assess Nee's late work, or indeed, any of his work as ascetic. Recent scholarship on asceticism has attempted to broaden older definitions that focus only on the control of the body. In an ambitious comparative study, religious studies scholar Gavin Flood has accepted the ritual, bodily dimensions of asceticism while also suggesting that asceticism highlights an inherent ambiguity wherein the practitioner attempts on the one hand to

[352] Nee, NTSWJ 52, 66.
[353] Nee, NTSWJ 52, 65, 56.
[354] Nee, NTSWJ 52, 57–60.
[355] Nee, NTSWJ 52, 59.

"eradicate the will or in some sense to erase the self," while paradoxically only being able to do so through "the affirmation of will in ascetic performance."[356]

The denial of the self is indeed central to Nee's spirituality. Furthermore, Nee's discussion of the tension between the "outer person" and the spirit may sound similar to the paradoxical subjectivity that Flood describes. Nevertheless, Nee explicitly rejected not only bodily self-discipline, but even programmatic *internal* self-discipline as well. Given this rejection and the fact that the term "asceticism" itself has been so heavily contested, it is more helpful simply to analyze what Nee says on its own terms.[357]

In place of asceticism, or indeed, any kind of ritual self-discipline, Nee suggested that the only requirement from the human side was "consecration" (*fengxian*), a simple "declaration of intention" or willingness, ideally "without qualification, without reservation, and without limit." Still, such a consecration could be completed "within five minutes, or even one minute."[358] After such a consecration, the actual dealing, or breaking, as harsh as it might seem, was to be initiated by God, not to be inflicted upon oneself. It was for this reason that both external and internal self-discipline had to be rejected.

Despite the severity of the language of "smiting" and "breaking," and the trauma of the recent war years, Nee did not have particularly terrifying referents in mind with regard to the Holy Spirit's discipline. If anything, Nee's images are striking for their ordinariness and attention to quotidian detail. God might see fit, for instance, to correct a person in "those most detailed matters of clothing, food, and drink." Nee marveled, "How fine the Holy Spirit is, he does not neglect even one thing." Thus, God might also deal with a hidden motive or cherished virtue, something so subtle that, at the outset, even the object of the dealing might not be conscious of its existence. Nevertheless, God would not relent, dealing with these inner points of pride or impurity in an "extremely fine" way, until "One day, these things are completely torn away, and you are released and you gain total freedom."[359]

Such dealings did not have to take the form of calamity or extreme privation. Rather, as Nee's invocation of "those most detailed matters of clothing, food, and drink" implied, they could be brought to light in the normal course of daily life. Nee did, however, seem to have considered one source of discipline to be particularly effective—one that was just as sundry as clothing, food, and drink, but one

---

[356] Gavin Flood, *The Ascetic Self: Subjectivity, Memory, and Tradition* (Cambridge: Cambridge University Press, 2004), ix.

[357] Oliver Freiberger has carefully delineated the ways in which asceticism is a tendentious term, rejected both by those within and without a tradition for a wide variety of reasons. Oliver Freiberger, *Asceticism and Its Critics: Historical Accounts and Comparative Perspectives* (Oxford: Oxford University Press, 2006), 16.

[358] Nee, NTSWJ 54, 239.

[359] Nee, NTSWJ 54, 247.

that could be much more adaptable and piercing. Nee believed that "Sometimes, God will use other people to deal with you, arranging for you to be dealt with by those who infuriate you, those who make you jealous, or those whom you despise. Frequently, he will also use those whom you love to deal with you."[360] Especially in the context of the church, Christians could be used by God to discipline other Christians. This social aspect of Nee's later spirituality requires some careful attention.

Denying the Self and Building the Church

Nee described the end result of human cooperation with God's dealing as a thorough brokenness, in which mature Christians had accepted God's discipline and now lived in God's presence continually. When he described this state of brokenness, he used an unexpected word to characterize the personality of a broken person: pliability. Truly spiritual Christians could take on a range of traits, depending on the variety of their natural dispositions and the paths God had taken to nurture and discipline them. Nevertheless, the overarching trait they all shared in common was not joy, glory, victory, or tranquility, as might be expected of ideal interior states. All of those virtues could conceivably be experienced alone, as an individual Christian hermit. Instead, Nee characterized his ideal spirituality with a decidedly social adjective, one that could only be understood in the context of relationships with others.

The Chinese word, *rouruan* (柔軟) literally means "soft," but Nee's descriptions suggest that it is not weakness, but a profound willingness to yield to others that comes from the very core of the being. Thus, "A pliable person is easy to speak with and easy to appeal to." An alternative translation could be "easily appeals to others"—the Chinese is somewhat ambiguous. Likewise, such a mature Christian is quick "to confess his sins." In context, Nee clearly means for this pliability to apply not so much to a Christian's confession of sins against God, but to admissions of fault with respect to other people.[361] In a similar fashion, Nee suggested that pliable persons "had feelings easily." This meant that they were sensitive to the feelings and reactions of their brothers and sisters in Christ and that they would not do "a foolish or insensitive thing and would not cause other's feelings to be offended."[362]

Nee's conception of pliability included notions of authority and submission. The pliable Christian was the true slave of all, one whose humility would be

---

[360] Nee NTSWJ, 54, 247.
[361] Nee, NTSWJ 54, 288.
[362] Nee, NTSWJ 54, 289.

proven by his ability to receive direction and correction from others. Nee taught that "The more help a person receives, the broader the range of help a person receives, the more that person is a broken one."[363] The most broken person, the most mature person, was one who was ready and willing to receive help from even the meanest member of the body of Christ. A broken Christian would see God's hand in every interaction with other human beings. Thus, even infuriating, petty, or despicable people could be beneficial. Eventually, all humans become the pliable Christian's teachers, rendering help and further spiritual insights.

Nee had learned to submit even to the leaders he himself had appointed in Shanghai. For if all social relationships could be thus sanctified, so much the more in the church and under church authority. Thus, Nee's mature ecclesiology was tied to his spirituality at the most practical, accessible level, that of local practice. Simultaneously, he began to teach that these local practices, as humble as they might seem, were the culmination of a long process of church history.

Just before his ministry was truncated by the Shanghai controversy, Nee had released a series of messages over three years, from 1939 to 1942, describing "the glorious church" as the goal of all of God's creation and eternal plan. According to Nee's understanding, God's creation of six days had culminated in the creation of humankind. Only with the establishment of "the authority of humanity" could God find his rest on the seventh day.[364]

Nee argued that the church, as the seat of God's authority, now stood at the brink of God's rest, able to fulfill God's plan for humanity. The church was to stand as the standard of God's rule over earth, representing a living rebuke to Satan's corruption of human authority. With Satan's work in humanity overthrown, God would finally have his ultimate rest. Thus, the building of the church represented the greatest of all God's actions in time. When the church was built, God could change the age for the last time, from the age of the church to the age of God's own kingdom. This final changing of the age, or dispensation, "removes man's power and the devil's power, and it brings in the kingdom." Nee concluded, "We live in the most privileged time; we can do the most for God."[365]

Similarly, in 1939, just after he returned to Shanghai from his trip abroad, Nee was sharing his expansive understanding of the church. The church was "produced from the life of Christ. After the death and resurrection of Christ, his life was released and imparted into his believers, and these believers compose the

---

[363] Nee, NTSWJ 54, 294.

[364] Nee, NTSWJ 34, 34, 28.

[365] Nee, CWWN 34, 157. CWWN, this appendix is only found in the English version of Nee's works—it may be taken from notes taken by Beth Rademacher, an English-speaking member of Nee's audience at the time. See Nee (CWWN 34, v). Nevertheless, similar sentiments highlighting the dispensational importance of the church are expressed frequently throughout Nee's works.

church." For this reason, the church was not only an earthly company of Jesus's followers but also an extension of the infinite Christ himself. Thus, 1 Corinthians 12:12 states that "Although there are many members, but one body, so also is Christ." Christ was not only the head, but even the members of the body, since the members were the result of Christ's imparting of his own life to his own body. Nee writes that "Because the church is composed of all the believers and Christ united as one, the church is the corporate Christ. The church is comprised of the Christ within all the saints, brought together. Since Christ is only one person, the church must also be one, so it cannot be separated and it must not be separated."[366]

The fact that the church was the unified, "corporate Christ" suggested an exacting standard by which to judge church history. And for Nee, the church's previous failings clarified the way forward. Thus, in 1945, while he was in Chongqing, during his exclusion from the Shanghai congregation, Nee gave a remarkable series of messages that were later compiled as *The Orthodoxy of the Church*. In *Orthodoxy*, Nee laid out his most comprehensive historiography or philosophy of history, focusing on understanding the church's place in history. Nee followed and developed an intricate and elaborate scheme of interpretation that had become something of a Plymouth Brethren tradition.

In his *Synopsis of the Books of the Bible*, John Nelson Darby had briefly sketched out the prophetic significance of the seven churches addressed in Chapters 2 and 3 of the Book of Revelation. For Darby, these seven churches—Ephesus, Smyrna, Pergamos, Thyatira, Sardis, Philadelphia, and Laodicea—pointed not only to seven churches in Asia Minor in the first centuries of the church but also charted the course of the church's development.

Thus, for Darby, Ephesus, Smyrna, and Pergamos generally suggested the early church. Thyatira foretold the development of the Roman Catholic Church, and Sardis pointed to Protestantism. Philadelphia signaled a return to some of the purity and humility God intended, while Laodicea warned of the "last state of the profession of the assembly," the church's final position of lukewarmness and misery at the end of the dispensation.[367] Darby's rough sketch was also adopted by a later Brethren historian, Andrew Miller. Miller's sizable history of the church included a foreword in which he gave the seven churches even more definite historical shape. Miller also weaved references to the seven prophetic churches throughout his lengthy monograph.[368]

Based on these works, Nee's *The Orthodoxy of the Church* was something of a combination of a Bible study and a work of church history. Phrase by phrase,

---

[366] Nee, NTSWJ 44, 64–65.

[367] John Nelson Darby, *Synopsis of the Books of the Bible, Volume 5* (Addison, IL: Bible Truth Publishers, 2004), 456–467.

[368] Andrew Miller, *Miller's Church History* (Glasgow: Pickering and Inglis, 1974).

Nee used the verses in Revelation 2 and 3 to spell out his distinct vision of God's work with the church in time. Agreeing with Darby and Miller, Nee saw the first three churches, Ephesus, Smyrna, and Pergamos, as representing historical churches that no longer existed, whereas the last four churches, Thyatira, Sardis, Philadelphia, and Laodicea, were contemporary churches that would continue to the end of the age. In each case, Nee specifically emphasized the impurities and failings of both historical and contemporary Christian practice and the ideal state to which God was now calling for "overcomers," those who would listen to God's speaking and remain faithful in God's church.

Thus, with regard to Ephesus, Nee posited that one of the virtues of the earliest church was its refusal to accept "a mediatorial class." Based on a literal translation of the Greek compound noun, *nikolaos*, Nee interpreted the "Nicolaitans" to be those who were "'conquering the common people,' 'climbing above the ordinary believers.'" In place of this, God would have all his people become "a kingdom of priests, and a holy nation," and the Ephesians had done well to hate the works of the Nicolaitans.[369]

When he came to Smyrna, Nee expounded on the biblical phrase "the slander from those who call themselves Jews." Nee suggested that Christians should distinguish themselves from Jews by rejecting the physical manifestations of the temple, law, priests, or promises. He understood the Christianity of his day to have been "Judaized" so that Christians looked to church buildings, outward regulations, priests and clerics, and physical blessings as promises, even though God's intention had been for the believers themselves to be the temple, to follow the Spirit directly as the inward law, enact a universal priesthood, and to accept every kind of suffering as joy in Jesus, rather than looking for outward blessings.[370]

On Pergamos, Nee turned to the various corruptions he saw as following from the Constantinian revolution. These ranged from the corrupting influence of money to the acceptance of hierarchy within the church, to compromise with secular standards and immorality in the name of convenience and political goals. In place of these compromises, Nee argued that "The holiness and distinction of the church must be upheld at any cost."[371] Those who maintained their faithfulness and purity in this regard would eternally savor the "hidden manna,"

---

[369] Nee, NTSWJ 47, 15.

[370] Nee, NTSWJ 47, 22–28. Nee's ideas on the Jews and Judaism were largely inherited from the Plymouth Brethren who influenced him in these analyses. Like them, he was often critical of Judaism as a religious system, while being philo-Semitic in regard to the Jews as a people. Thus, Darby spoke of the apostacy and carnality of Jewish religion, while still insisting that God's eyes, heart, and thoughts were continually fixed on the Jewish people. John Nelson Darby, *The Collected Writings of J. N. Darby*, vol. 32, 245 and David Yoon, "The Restored Jewish State and the Revived Roman Empire: The Transmutation of John Nelson Darby's Dispensationalism into Modern Christian Zionism," (PhD diss., University of California, Los Angeles, 2010), 156–160.

[371] Nee, NTSWJ 47, 41. "Holiness" (聖潔) here may also be translated as "purity."

recalling the sweet taste of God's personal consolation and comfort. Nee assured that for the overcomers in Pergamos, "All their experiences in the presence of God are valuable and will never be lost."[372]

When Nee turned to the churches that continued into the contemporary era, he was equally unsparing. He repeated the common Protestant critiques of Roman Catholicism for its idolatry, devotion to Mary, and persecution of other Christians.[373] Likewise, he took the Protestant churches to task for their improper understanding of the church—they "only caused the church of the world [Roman Catholicism] to become the church of the state," trading one political master for another.[374] In this, as in other things, the Protestant church had been incomplete and inconsistent. It had its revivals, but at the end of each revival, "The institution remains, but what is within [grace and blessing] is lost," leading to endless denominations and organizations that had lost the living water of the Spirit.[375]

Nee then came to Philadelphia, at which point the church finally returned to "the straight line" of "the orthodoxy of the apostles."[376] For this positive development, Nee gave significant credit to the Plymouth Brethren, appraising them as being "greater than the movement of the Reformation." Positively, the Brethren had set forth the gospel more clearly than at any previous moment in church history. They also initiated the vision of the church that Nee sought to continue, by showing that "the church cannot gain the whole world, that the church has a heavenly calling, [and] that the church has no hope in the world." The Brethren expounded prophecies and also some of the spiritual teachings of the inner life, teaching "what the law of sin is, what freedom [from sin] is, what being crucified with the Lord is, what being resurrected with the Lord is, how to be joined to the Lord through faith, and how to be transformed daily by looking to the Lord."[377]

Because the Brethren seemed to present such a prevailing and successful return to biblical teachings and practices, Nee focused with great attention on their eventual failure, writing that "We must be utterly careful and humble or else we will become caught up in the same failure." He suggested that the Brethren's concern for an "almost idealistic oneness of a spiritual church in heaven" was wrong, just like the Roman Catholic Church's emphasis on "the oneness of a united church on the earth" was also wrong. Once the church became so idealistic, love became a theory more than a practice. This theoretical love could be contrasted with the more concrete setting and recipients of Paul's own letters, which Nee

---

[372] Nee, NTSWJ 47, 42.
[373] Nee, NTSWJ 47, 46–52.
[374] Nee, NTSWJ 47, 58.
[375] Nee, NTSWJ 47, 60–61.
[376] Nee, NTSWJ 47, 65–66.
[377] Nee, NTSWJ 47, 75.

believed were clearly addressed to local churches. Thus, the Brethren "did not see, or did not see thoroughly enough, that the mutual love in the epistles is the mutual love of a church in a locality, that oneness is the oneness of a church in a locality."[378]

Nee offered his own ecclesiology, which focused on the unity of the church in a "locality" or city, as the only one that rigorously demanded that Christians actually love one another in a self-denying way. Although most of his other arguments in *The Orthodoxy of the Church* followed either Darby, Miller, or both, the emphasis on locality, or *difang* (地方, literally, "place"), was Nee's own. In fact, the theme of locality can be seen in some of Nee's earliest writings. Nee may not have been the first to notice that the New Testament generally spoke of each city as containing only a single church, but he was the first to explain this principle as a specific, biblical mandate. He argued that in God's eyes, there must only be one church in every city and that Christian church practice should therefore be restricted by the boundaries of the city. In other words, in every city, there should only be one Christian church.[379]

Nee now argued that when Christian groups like the Exclusive Brethren (and presumably Roman Catholics, various Orthodox bodies, Anglicans, Methodists, and other connexional, synodical, or episcopal churches) emphasized the "united Church" that "overstepped the boundary of locality," they allowed Christians to be "divided from brothers in their own locality," in the name of a nominal, universal oneness. In other words, spiritual, idealized unity became an abstraction and a pretext for practical, local egotism and infighting.[380]

Conversely, but equally problematically, Christian groups like the Open Brethren (and presumably the Congregationalists, Baptists, and various free groups) took "the meeting as a unit [of oneness]." This excessive narrowness also formed a pretext for division. Such Christians cared only for unity with others in their individual groups and were "not afraid to be divided from brothers in other meetings in the same locality." In fact, "With just one contrary word, they form another meeting, and with three to five in their group, they consider this to be oneness."[381] Both exceeding and coming short of the boundaries of locality would cause problems. In this case, super-local, congregational unity became a fig leaf for the ugly imposition of the ego, and an endless number of local churches could be formed to fracture Christian oneness.

Nee thus introduced a new critique of church history based on a novel hermeneutic. He took self-sacrificial spirituality in service to unity as his central interpretive principle. To him, this principle indicted both of the major

---

[378] Nee, NTSWJ 47, 85.
[379] Nee, NTSWJ 4, 59–61.
[380] Nee, NTSWJ 47, 86–87.
[381] Nee, NTSWJ 47, 87.

historical types of church government, episcopal and congregational. In either case, Nee pointed out how the cause of oneness could become little more than lip service. While paying homage to ostensible unity, the fallen self of the individual Christian was allowed to develop, promote its self-glory, and divide from other Christians when impinged upon, either by claiming unity with an ideal, universal whole or by schismatically starting an entirely new local congregation. Church history was thus significantly marked by failure with regard to unity and self-denial. Nevertheless, he believed that these mistakes now had a powerful antidote.

Nee's Contributions to Christian Ecclesiology

In his later writings, Nee saw his long-held concept of locality in a new light as a meaningful solution to the problem of Christian disunity and self-assertion. If all Christians were to practice unity within the boundaries of their city of residence, there would be definite limitations to their fractiousness and egoism. They could not simply find a "better" or "different" local church whenever they were offended by other Christians. Instead, they had to learn to make do with the one church in their city. The only option, in many cases, would be to practice the denial of the self—the application of Christ's crucifixion to personal superiority, opinions, and preferences, in order to pliably love and submit to the other members.

Furthermore, in Nee's mature writings, he made the case that such ecclesiology and spirituality were mutually supportive. Only by denying the self could the true church appear, and the properly constituted church was the best environment to learn the denial of the self. Nee explained that, strictly speaking, "The church is not me as an individual person added to you as an individual person," as far as the "me" and the "you" represented personal egos. Rather, "The church is the bit of Christ that is in you, the bit of Christ that is in him as well, and the portions of Christ from within all the believers around the world from ancient times until today." Nee was emphatic that "There is no relationship between our own natural element and the church."[382] In Nee's view, the church was composed only of Christ, and Christ was present only when the natural person, with all of its natural characteristics, tendencies, and elements, was denied. Thus, the existence of the church required the constant denial of the self.

In a complementary fashion, only in a properly constituted church could the self be adequately confronted. When Christians were forced to live together in local congregations, their opinions and hidden motives would eventually be

---

[382] Nee, NTSWJ 34, 34.

exposed and could then be dealt with. Such a church would encourage Christians to find oneness with all the other Christians in their city, without the easy escape clauses of simply joining or establishing "another church."

By arguing for Christ as the central, organizing factor of unity and the self as the basic factor of division, Nee was offering a way forward that relegated other controversial issues in biblical interpretation to subordinate importance. In this sense, it did not matter whether the church was understood to be a fluid association of local congregations following prophetic authority, a rigidly defined hierarchy built on obedience to official jurisdiction, or something else altogether. The outward practice of the church could never be sufficient in itself, no matter how faithful to the New Testament it tried to be. In addition to more formal factors, unity had to be maintained by the Holy Spirit, cultivating a willingness to yield in all of the members of the body of Christ. If everyone would obey the absolute restriction of the Spirit, all the controversies over church order would be spontaneously resolved.

Although Nee believed that "The light of 'locality' is becoming more and more clear," he warned that it would be up to God and history to validate this teaching. In the meantime, he urged that the churches continue in caution and with reserve, "If our consecration to the Lord is absolute and we are humble, perhaps we will receive mercy and receive protection to avoid error."[383] After all, in Nee's mind, the lesson of the seventh church was that "Laodicea's special characteristic is spiritual pride." Nee's contact with the Brethren had convinced him that at least some in the movement had "become proud and arrogant." The danger with success is that it bred complacency and self-satisfaction. Nee concluded, "How careful we must be so that we do not become Laodicea!"[384]

Through this exposition of the Bible, Nee's hearers could clearly see their position on the cosmic scale of God's history and economy of salvation. God had worked carefully throughout the ages, in church after church. Now, for the first time, the entire plan of Revelation was made clear, as well as a path to victory and fidelity until Jesus's return. As Nee exulted, "The Lord has placed us in Philadelphia that we may be Philadelphia . . . In all the history of the church, there has never been an opportunity better than our opportunity today."[385]

Nee's ecclesiology thus maintained a careful balance between the church's metaphysical and practical demands. Members of churches that held to the principle of "locality" shuttled between the transcendent vision of their spiritual testimony and their humble service toward one another in the local church in their city. Nee's principle of locality made the execution of his spiritual teachings

[383] Nee, NTSWJ 47, 87.
[384] Nee, NTSWJ 47, 93–94.
[385] Nee, NTSWJ 47, 112.

exceedingly concrete. Every local church had to struggle to maintain its own testimony, both in terms of love and unity. All the members collectively bore the burden of working to embody Philadelphia in each of their social interactions.

The very practicality of this arrangement is also one of Nee's contributions to Christian ecclesiology. Many of Nee's more mystical ideas regarding the church as the body of Christ were based on the writings of Theodore Austin-Sparks. Sparks seemed to conceive of his congregations as being rather abstract "Signs" or proofs to the wider world. He was not particularly concerned with the tangible organization or coordination of these "Signs."[386] Nee, however, was insistent that true spirituality required the actual contexts of local churches. For their part, these local churches helped to keep Nee's visions alive. They read his works and tried to follow them. They also become the concrete contexts in which individual Christians could learn the lessons of brokenness and pliability.

This was Nee's last significant contribution to the history of Christian theology. With the connection made between brokenness, the historic and prophetic timeline of the church, and the emphasis on locality, Nee constructed a throughline that could make all of his previous ideas more coherent and compelling. He had embarked on this long intellectual journey in Fuzhou, as a newly converted, teenage Christian, simply looking for a biblical way to constitute and practice the church. Now, well into his forties, he had propounded a complete set of teachings that was comprehensive, if not systematic, to address the question of both the church's constitution and its practice.

Nee's most dedicated followers would have aspired to become overcomers. Overcomers were spiritually mature Christians who knew the distinction between the self and the spirit, and constantly rejected the former in favor of the latter. As overcomers, they hoped to complete God's plan for the church, making Christ supreme, shaming Satan, and winning a personal reward for their faithfulness. The proof of their success would be Christ's second coming. In the meantime, the sign of their maturity was brokenness, that is, the ultimate standard of pro-social pliability. This spirituality was both forged and tested in local congregations through the practice of love and unity. The boundaries of locality helped to ensure that this process took place, neither allowing Christians to seek refuge in abstract, universal declarations of unity, nor to schismatically create their own local congregations. God willing, they would be Philadelphia, the church of brotherly love.

Nee's biblical, evangelical theology was built on Western traditions that were self-critical of the Western church's own shortcomings in holiness, love, and

---

[386] Rex G. Beck, *Shaped by Vision: A Biography of T. Austin-Sparks* (Cleveland Heights, OH: Greater Purpose, 2005), 56. Sparks wrote that he and his congregation had left the Baptist Union "in order to be made a Sign" to other Christians.

unity. And yet Nee had added significantly to his Western inheritance. His consistent emphasis on soul versus spirit, the notion of spiritual maturity as pliability, and the teaching of ecclesial locality were all significant. If Nee's most capable and thoughtful followers could revel in the nuances of his theology, even the simpler members of the Little Flock would understand, at least, that they were at the center stage of God's plan—that they were potentially more biblical and more spiritual than Christians anywhere else on earth.

Adjustments in Church Practice

As always, Nee's biblical teachings were not meant as academic theology, but as nourishment and guidance for actual congregations. Alongside his more abstract musings on the prophesies of Revelation and the ground of the locality, Nee continued to tinker with practical ecclesiology. From 1948 to 1950, Nee spoke extensively on the organization of the church and on the practice of total financial dependence, which he called "handing over (交出來)." Given the political situation of the times, it is possible that both of these changes were at least partially a reaction to the imminent victory of the Chinese Communist Party (CCP).

First, in 1948, Nee held a training consisting of twelve major topics, published as *Church Affairs*. Directed at the elders and co-workers he had invited to Mount Guling near Fuzhou, Nee carefully went over the offices, services, meetings, and finances of the church. He also reflected at length on the relationship between the local church and the extra-local "work." In other words, he wanted to clarify the relationship between the elders who held responsibility over the individual, local churches, and the itinerant co-workers who traveled among multiple locales.

Theologian Wing Hung Lam has suggested that *Church Affairs* indicated a major shift in Nee's thought. Lam points out that as late as 1939, with the book *Concerning Our Missions*, Nee was still arguing that local elders had the authority to receive or reject traveling apostles.[387] Now, in *Church Affairs*, Nee seemingly reversed himself, teaching that "the elders should learn to obey the apostles."[388] For Lam, this suggested that "The line of the church Nee proposed after the Sino-Japanese War was truly very different from that of his earlier period."[389]

It is important not to overstate the case. Earlier in the same chapter, Nee wrote that "In a local church, the elders are the highest authority" and that "apostles

---

[387] Wing Hung Lam, *Shuling Shenxue—Ni Tuosheng Sixiang de Yanjiu* (Hong Kong: China Alliance Press, 2003), 233.

[388] Nee, NTSWJ 51, 170.

[389] Lam, *Shuling Shenxue*, 257.

cannot deal directly with the affairs of a local church."[390] Nevertheless, *Church Affairs* does show Nee and the Christian Assemblies continuing down the path of greater coherence and coordination that had already been their direction for decades. As much as they held to the doctrine of local autonomy, there had been ample proof of a strengthening extra-local connection: letters, publications, conferences, co-workers, and, of course, the personal prestige of Nee himself, only enhanced with his return to public ministry after the repentance of the Shanghai elders.

This wider and more coordinated cooperation was also a source of order and strength in dealing with the rapidly changing political situation. Throughout 1948, CCP forces won victories over the Nationalists, and Nee was always a keen observer of current events. Witness Lee recounts that in the spring of 1948, Nee was speaking with thirty or forty co-workers, when "one day, the fellowship came up concerning the need to 'hand over.'"[391] Nee did not let the subject go. Over the next two years, he would speak repeatedly on the need for "handing over" all of one's property and finances, beginning with talks on "Money and Professions," "Dealing with Mammon and Serving God," "Being Delivered from Mammon," and "Voluntary Poverty."[392]

Nee himself set a tangible example by handing over *Shenghua*, the pharmaceutical company he had been managing.[393] He supplemented this lesson with repeated admonitions about the need for an "absolute consecration,"[394] arguing that "Handing over is not only of one's money to God, but also that one's time and one's future may all be for God."[395] Nee insisted that China had not been evangelized because his fellow Christians still spent too much of their time and energy on making a living and pursuing their own ends. Now, in preparation for the Lord's coming, they should entrust everything to the church, and in coordination, the church would work out what they should be doing, where they should live, and how they should be supported.

The response to Nee's exhortations and examples was strongly positive. For instance, during these years, the Little Flock churches gathered enough funds to begin building a much larger assembly hall in Shanghai on Nanyang Road. When complete, the Nanyang Road Assembly Hall would eventually seat five thousand. This response was due, at least in part, to the external forces that

---

[390] Nee, NTSWJ 51, 168–169. It is also possible that part of the switch from the Antioch to Jerusalem model was an attempt to emulate Witness Lee's success in Northern China. See Kinnear, *Against the Tide*, 229–233.

[391] Nee, NTSWJ 57, 1.

[392] Nee, NTSWJ 57, 175ff, 205ff, 263ff, 285ff. Mammon is a New Testament term for wealth.

[393] Kinnear, *Against the Tide*, 236–237. Nee also mentions this at NTSWJ 61, 180–181.

[394] Nee, NTSWJ 61, 27. Nee uses *chedi* (徹底) here instead of *juedui*. Whereas *juedui* emphasizes unconditionality, *chedi* literally means "to or from the bottom," with an implication of thoroughness.

[395] Nee, NTSWJ 61, 124.

pressed upon many Republican citizens in those years. Nee himself recounted at least two stories of Christians who had been reluctant to hand over valuable possessions, only to have their possessions confiscated by the Communists.[396] Nee also hinted at a more indirect way in which the Communists may have inspired the "handing over" movement, once again rooted in a sense of shame. Nee wrote:

> Communism proposes having all things in common. This proposal was derived by Marx from the book of Acts. If it becomes necessary one day for the Communist Party to teach Christians to have all things in common, to sell all and distribute to each according to their need, this will be a shame to Christians.[397]

Nee may have felt that he was simply guiding the church to better accommodate the coming regime, and he had reasons for cautious optimism. A natural corollary to "handing over" had been mission, as all the Little Flock members who had given up their professions and possessions now sought to serve the church in spreading the gospel. Nee's vision had always entailed local churches throughout China, and he had repeatedly urged the Assembly Hall Christians to evangelize inland China. Now, among so many who had given up their jobs, homes, and money, there were few barriers to missionary work. As these brothers and sisters spread into rural China, they encountered members of the new regime and found that, in many ways, they were working toward similar purposes.

Toward the end of 1948, the Xiaoshan region of Zhejiang Province was flooded. The local churches in that area were convinced that this was a sign from God that they should migrate for the gospel as Nee and Lee had been urging.[398] There were already three hundred local churches in the wealthy Zhejiang Province—possibly more than in the rest of China combined.[399] Now duly motivated, many of these Christians began to move out, having chosen nearby rural Yiyang County as the target of their mission. Over the next year or so, under the coordination of church elders and co-workers, hundreds of members left their home congregations in prominent cities such as Hangzhou and Shanghai and arrived in impoverished Yiyang.

The local CCP cadres were initially taken aback by the influx of outsiders and thoroughly examined them before welcoming them to the community. While the cadres were trying to enforce equality in Yiyang, the Christians willingly

---

[396] Nee, NTSWJ 61, 110–111, 186–187.
[397] Nee, NTSWJ 61, 66.
[398] Nee, NTSWJ 62, 238.
[399] Nee, NTSWJ 61, 183. Zhejiang has had a long history of Protestant success, and it seems this was reflected among the Assembly Hall churches by the mid-century.

practiced it, and indeed went so far in their egalitarianism that they were opposed by Communists, who feared that such a practice would "make people lazy."[400] Nonetheless, over time, the industry and skill of these Christian migrant missionaries appear to have impressed and inspired the local leadership, who were now "extremely satisfied" with what they saw, "sending down directives and putting out announcements to protect us." Nee added that "The cadres with a 2500 li [roughly 776 miles] circuit of oversight have told us, in about twelve years, we also will accomplish what you have done here."[401] And in fact, radio broadcasts from the provincial capital of Nanchang appear to have repeatedly mentioned Yiyang as a model county, worthy of emulation.[402]

Thus, as the Communist victories continued across China, Nee and the Little Flock Christians made their own practical changes and preparations. They formalized the links between their various congregations spread throughout China and Southeast Asia by granting apostles, or co-workers, more authority in relation to local elders. This made the Christian Assemblies function even more cohesively as a unified network, with greater coordination and ability to mobilize than many organized Christian denominations. Nee and his followers also mirrored Communist emphases, sending urban Christians to a rural county and practicing a radical form of financial equality that entailed giving up all of one's possessions. They had garnered the positive attention of at least one group of CCP cadres, and Nee continued to push for even more handing over and missionary migration.

Despite these arrangements, Nee maintained some reservations about the fate of the Chinese churches under the proudly atheistic Communist Party. Privately, he suggested to Witness Lee that the latter go to either Hong Kong or Taiwan, in case everything else on the mainland was "wiped out."[403] In their final conversations on the matter, one Hong Kong elder recalls that Nee explained his decision to return to the territories under Communist control with the analogy of a mother rushing into her burning house. "Although I know that my return is fraught with dangers, I know that many brothers and sisters are still inside. How can I not return?"[404] In the complicated years to come, both visions of the future would paradoxically play themselves out. On the one hand, both the Communist Party and the Christian Assemblies would flourish side by side, often finding themselves working toward similar ends. On the other hand, Nee and many of his most trusted co-workers soon found themselves rushing headlong into a chaotic conflagration.

[400] Nee, NTSWJ 61, 232.
[401] Nee, NTSWJ 61, 181.
[402] Nee, NTSWJ 62, 238–239.
[403] Lee, *Watchman Nee: A Seer*, 320.
[404] Lee, *Watchman Nee: A Seer*, 326–327.

6

Struggle and Surrender

During the early months of CCP rule, Nee and the Assembly Hall Christians found themselves in an unexpectedly fortuitous situation. In 1948, Nee still harbored misgivings that under the Communist regime, Christians would not even be allowed to meet, much less preach the gospel.[406] In July 1950, some months after the official establishment of the People's Republic of China, no restrictions had yet been placed on the Little Flock's activities. In fact, if anything, outward circumstances increasingly favored the growing, confident indigenous church. Nee was now speaking of a special opportunity for expansion.

"In the past," he declared, "we focused on gaining sinners from among those of different religions." As far as those who were already Christians, he continued, the preference was to "let them come to us as individuals" in order to avoid charges of "sheep-stealing," or robbing Christians from other flocks and denominations. But now, Nee was increasingly convinced that the temper of the times had changed. Instead of "gaining people who loved the Lord, one by one," the Christian Assemblies should focus on "gaining groups who loved the Lord, one by one." As Nee indicated, this was not due to any changes in principle, but rather circumstance.[407]

Intra-Christian politics in China, as elsewhere, could be touchy, with cross-proselytizing as one of the most sensitive topics. While some groups like the True Jesus Church boldly and defiantly tried to win others over to their cause as the true church of the true Jesus, we have seen that Nee was concerned when his co-workers used baptism, leaving denominations, and other outward practices as slogans to challenge other Christian groups. His subtle ecclesiology tried to maintain the fine balance between his belief that locality was the best and most biblical way to constitute the church and his insistence that the truth of locality included the fact that all God's children in any given locality were already part of the same church. This meant that Nee both felt that other Christians would do well to join the Christian Assemblies and that their feelings as fellow members of the body of Christ must be respected.

While none of these principles had changed, the environment of Christian China had shifted dramatically. Although disruptions to Christian activities

---

[406] Nee, NTSWJ 57, 335.
[407] Nee, NTSWJ 55, 236–237.

The Spiritual Person. Paul H B Chang, Oxford University Press. © Oxford University Press 2026.
DOI: 10.1093/9780197793664.003.0007

were minimal at this stage, July 1950 saw the completion of "The Christian Manifesto," which would be published on the front page of the *People's Daily* in September. The "Manifesto" clearly pointed to Christianity's complicity with imperialism as a major problem in the new China. The Manifesto also introduced the "three selves" of self-governance, self-support, and self-propagation, in contrast to governance, support, and propagation from overseas. Any Christian groups with international ties, including Roman Catholics, were increasingly apprehensive that these ties would be challenged. Many Protestant missionaries, who had been ostensibly touting the need for indigenization for decades, prepared to leave China while looking for the least disruptive ways of transferring their institutions and power structures into Chinese hands.

Nee had sensed the mood correctly, and in at least one notable instance, his admonition to win over groups rather than merely individuals bore significant fruit. The China Inland Mission (CIM), founded by James Hudson Taylor, had always been theologically and ideologically congenial to Nee and the Little Flock Christians. The CIM was non-denominational, theologically evangelical, and culturally sensitive. Now, recognizing the urgent need for a transition away from foreign control and influence, entire groups of CIM churches began to join the Christian Assemblies.[408]

On October 19, 1950, the People's Republic of China entered the Korean War, and there was another marked shift in both the political atmosphere and Nee's response. In keeping with his long-standing aversion to political entanglements, Nee had been hesitant to subscribe to the Christian Manifesto when it was published before China's entrance into the War. In 1951, however, in a startling about-face, members of the Christian Assemblies participated in a number of government-promoted marches and signed declarations as part of the larger "Resist American Aggression and Aid Korea Campaign." Furthermore, they participated not only as individuals, but in one march, carried a banner declaring themselves to be the "Church in Shanghai." The Shanghai Assembly also showed its relative financial strength, donating about one-twentieth of the total raised by Christians across the nation during a war fundraising effort.[409]

These changes were surprising enough on their own, but they were soon accompanied by further surprising decisions. The Little Flock was not only willing to be involved in politics strictly in regard to the war, but also Nee dramatically changed his mind regarding the Christian Manifesto. At one point, under Nee's direction, more than 17 percent of the signatories of the Manifesto were members of the Assembly Halls—a proportion probably larger than the

---

[408] Phyllis Thompson, *China: The Reluctant Exodus* (Littleton, CO: OMF International, 2000) and Fuk-Tsang Ying, *Fandi, Aiguo, Shuling Ren: Ni Tuosheng yu Jidutu Juhuichu Yanjiu* (Hong Kong: Christian Study Centre on Chinese Religion and Culture, 2005), 39.
[409] Ying, *Fandi*, 40–41.

Assembly Hall's share of Chinese Protestants in general. Nee even invited Wu Yaozong, the main author of the Manifesto, to come and lecture to almost one thousand Assembly Hall members at their newly constructed Nanyang Road building. Wu was a well-known proponent of theological modernism, equating the gospel with social reform, and was critical of those like Nee who continued to preach the importance of spiritual salvation and eternal life. Nevertheless, swallowing his pride and his theological preferences, Nee had come to realize that Wu enjoyed the CCP's confidence and would be a key figure in the struggles to come.[410]

At one level, Nee and the Christian Assemblies were simply responding out of necessity. China's participation in the Korean War gave the CCP a good reason to consolidate its dominance over the social and civil space of urban China, much as land reform had already begun to irrevocably change China's countryside. Historian Frederick Teiwes has shown how those changes trickled down from the very top, with CCP Chairman Mao Zedong explaining, just before the Korean intervention, that "It is imperative that we do not kill even a single [enemy] agent," and then, after the Chinese had entered the fight, neatly reversing his sentiments, concluding that "we must firmly kill all those reactionary elements who deserve to be killed."[411] Throughout the early 1950s, the demand for ideological conformity slowly increased as the CCP cemented its grip on power and sought to unify all of Chinese society under its totalizing and utopian Marxist vision.

To achieve that end, the CCP conducted various campaigns aimed at ideological reform. These campaigns could create significant psychological pressure as citizens were called upon to publicly confess their ideological errors and to denounce the ideological errors of others, including family members, friends, colleagues, and peers. If these campaigns did not achieve the desired results, official repression in the form of detention, incarceration, and execution all loomed as possible outcomes. The violent, sudden disintegration of social ties and personal relationships instigated a rash of suicides, possibly numbering in the hundreds of thousands.[412]

When faced with organized resistance, the general Communist strategy was to create a "united front" and to work with such members of the group as were willing to cooperate to whatever extent they were willing. Once this wedge was established, further concessions could be won with increased pressure. So, while

[410] Ying, *Fandi*, 43–45.

[411] Mao Zedong, "Comments on the Work of Suppressing and Liquidating Counterrevolutionaries" (1950–51), in *Miscellany*, 1.6, as quoted by Frederick Teiwes in "Establishment and Consolidation of the New Regime," *The Cambridge History of China*, vol. 14 (Cambridge: Cambridge University Press, 1987), 89.

[412] Teiwes, "Establishment and Consolidation," 88.

the local church in Shanghai held firm under Nee's direct leadership, the Church in Nanjing ended up as one of the first local assemblies to hold a relatively successful "denunciation meeting" in June 1951. There, some members confessed that religious organizations that had claimed to be "spiritual," "otherworldly," and "surpassing everything of this world" were in fact being utilized by imperialists and the Guomindang (GMD)—the Nationalist Party of Chiang Kai-shek—to oppose the CCP and the people.[413]

One month later, in July, the Church in Fuzhou followed suit as an elder, Zheng Zhengguang, declared in a denunciation meeting that American imperialists had used spiritual groups as a tool by "Emphasizing the ideology of being beyond politics and disseminating eschatology and demonology so that church members would not embrace the people's government." In other words, Zheng argued that the basic claim that religious beliefs could be "beyond politics" allowed for false neutrality during a time of war and mobilization. Furthermore, such supernatural teachings as the dramatic intervention of Christ at the end of the age or the existence of demons and other spiritual forces had deluded the simple Little Flock followers. In keeping with Marxist religious critique, Zheng protested that these false beliefs kept church members from trusting the CCP. Even Peace Wang, Nee's stalwart co-worker who stood with him throughout his excommunication and had helped Witness Lee restore his ministry, seemed to have turned, saying, "Admittedly, we must take responsibility for the fact that we have come to this point today. But Watchman Nee should bear even more responsibility."[414] Nee appeared to take Wang's words to heart. On August 20, Nee called a meeting of those leading the various services in the Church in Shanghai to Nanyang Hall, to share a long statement he had written beforehand, entitled "How I have changed."[415]

"How I Have Changed"

Written in the crucible of intense pressure, "How I have changed" is an important document for understanding Nee's thoughts in these final years of his ministry and leadership of the Christian Assemblies. In particular, "How I have changed" shows the extent to which Nee thought that compromise with politics was possible. He had spent years following both the Brethren and Keswick traditions

---

[413] Ying, *Fandi*, 61.

[414] Ying, *Fandi*, 63–64.

[415] The Chinese title, "我怎麼轉過來的," can also be translated, "How I have turned." Although this document has not been recorded in the NTSWJ, the style is clearly his and the script can be found in a number of places online, for instance, http://bbs.jonahome.net/thread-79458-1-1.html, accessed on June 28, 2023.

that stood aloof from politics, and he had criticized Western church traditions for their entanglement in earthly affairs. The GMD government, under which the Christian Assemblies had operated throughout most of the Republican period, had allowed the Assemblies significant freedom in the civil and religious spheres. The Japanese occupation represented a period of severe, but temporary repression. Now, under the CCP, extensive, continuous pressure had been applied to such an extent that even Nee's closest co-workers, like Peace Wang, were appealing to him for leadership. In her words, she bore responsibility for the situation, "But Watchman Nee should bear even more responsibility."

Wang may have felt stymied because some of the basic values she had learned from Nee had come into conflict. On the one hand, Nee taught that the church should be pure and should not allow itself to be used as a tool in politics, nor favor one faction above another. His prayer at the Keswick Convention had starkly demonstrated this ideal. Even as Japanese forces threatened the existence of the Chinese state, Nee prayed only for God's interests. On the other hand, Nee's notion of spiritual maturity emphasized sensitivity to others and a willingness to yield. Other elders and local churches now claimed that spirituality was being used as a pretext for imperialism. Any retreat into "spirituality" would seem to be begging the question and ignoring the suffering of other members of the body of Christ.

In "How I have changed," Nee discussed his unprecedented anguish in approaching this clash between spirituality and church responsibility. "In all these years, having passed through so many things, I have never prayed prayers of despair. But this time I prayed, asking the Lord to receive me back to him." Nee repeated this refrain several times, as if to remove any doubt, admitting that the difficulties were so distressing that he "hoped to leave the world early." Nevertheless, he had finally experienced a breakthrough, a solution to the contradiction. Nee wrote, "In the past, we felt that believers could be beyond politics. That night, I saw that a believer cannot be beyond politics. Whether you know it or not, whether you sense it or not, a person will naturally have a certain kind of political perspective."[416]

It seemed to be a stunning concession. Nee's teaching regarding the distinction between the human soul and the human spirit had been crucial because, from his perspective, it preserved the possibility for individual transcendence. The spirit was supposed to be the source for ultimate, moral purity, where actions and motives flowed only from Christ, free of personal, political, and selfish agendas. In addition, Nee's ecclesiology had insisted on an equivalent purity for the church. According to Nee, the church was a heavenly being that reflected the

---

[416] Nee, "How I have changed."

universal, unconditional love and unity of God. It should never be drawn into petty human squabbles. Was he now denying these possibilities entirely?

The rest of "How I have changed" was a careful exploration of the basic, shocking claim that "a believer cannot be beyond politics," and "a person will naturally have a certain kind of political perspective." Nee used three examples to illustrate his new understanding of the relationship between religion and politics. Based upon this new understanding, he offered a reassessment of the past and charted a way forward for himself and those Assembly Hall Christians who wanted to follow him.

Nee's first example considered a visit by a certain Western clergyman to Shanghai. This brother was sincere in his love for the Lord and his desire to preach the gospel. From the standpoint of religion, there was no problem between him and Nee. However, a few nights earlier, Nee had come to see this visit in a whole new light. Nee and the brother had strolled through the streets of Shanghai, passing by British police officers and British public offices. They had seen extraterritoriality and foreign soldiers, and a very strange thing had occurred, notable in its absence.[417] Nee wrote about the clergyman, "He had no sense regarding these things. It was as though he felt that there was no need to make a big deal of them, that they were natural, that there was no need to question them. Or, to say it a bit more strongly, he felt that these things were right and proper, that they were as they should be."[418]

At the time, Nee himself did not question this behavior, but according to his most recent understanding, this ideology was exactly the issue at hand: "religious belief is one thing, political position is another thing." To press the point home, Nee imagined the converse. He would certainly have found it exceedingly strange to be walking through the streets of London and watching Chinese people ignoring British police, doing as they wished, even to the point of carrying weapons.

Nee continued this example with a recollection of his visit to India, in which he had been asked by a British clergyman about the prospects for the gospel in India. Nee had responded frankly that there was no way forward as long as "the Indians cannot distinguish whether you are here as British or as Christians." A female missionary had stared at him, flabbergasted, asking pointedly, "Do you mean to say that it is wrong for the British to be in India?" Nee concluded that a person could be "pure in the faith," while "maintaining an imperialistic political position."[419]

---

[417] Extraterritoriality was the system imposed by the so-called Unequal Treaties as a result of the Opium Wars. The system designated that foreign nationals in China would not be subject to Chinese laws, but rather to the laws of their own home countries.

[418] Nee, "How I have changed."

[419] Nee, "How I have changed."

In his second example, Nee asked his audience to consider the analogy of a teacup and a saucer. The teacup represented religion, while the saucer represented one's political position. The government did not care about the shape or the contents of the teacup, but the teacup always came with a saucer and the saucer could only be imperialist or anti-imperialist, for the people or against the people. To say that one was a Christian was to miss the point. The government needed to know whether the individual was an imperialist Christian or an anti-imperialist Christian. Nee thus employed the logic of one of his own most important theological analogies. In defending his idea of locality as the proper ground of the church, he had argued that whatever the condition of the church, it should be located and built on the proper ground. A good church built on the wrong site would still be problematic, while even a bad church on the right ground was at least faithful to God's fundamental calling.[420] In "How I have changed," Nee seemed to imply that political position (the saucer) was in some ways more fundamental than any religious question (the teacup).[421]

For his final example, Nee again reversed the logic of a basic point of theology. In keeping with his evangelical tradition, Nee had taught that all human beings were either "in Adam" or "in Christ." No matter how well people might behave "in Adam," they could not earn their own salvation. Only being "in Christ" mattered. Nee argued that the government was now posing a similar challenge to the Little Flock Christians. It did not matter to the CCP that these Christians had opposed Western Christianity by being excommunicated, resigning from foreign schools, losing ministerial positions, and so on. From the political standpoint, all these actions had occurred in the religious sphere. None of these actions had merit in the political realm. They were all like good deeds done "in Adam" to try and earn salvation. Regardless of the religious actions taken in the past, the simple question remained: Would these Chinese Christians now stand with the people, or would they stand with the imperialists?

In light of these three examples, Nee felt that there were some clear lessons to be learned. "We must consider religion and politics separately, and we must separate them clearly." If they were kept separate in analysis, many perspectives would change. For instance, "From a religious perspective, we have truly practiced 'three-self' for thirty years, but from a political perspective, we have not even begun to implement 'three-self' for one day." The Christian Assemblies had always been religiously independent from foreign powers, but they had never actively supported "the three-self of political, anti-imperialistic patriotism."

Therefore, a new start was needed. Religion and politics should no longer be considered as two different, opposing perspectives. Rather, from the

---

[420] Nee, NTSWJ 22, 47–48.
[421] Nee, "How I have changed."

political perspective, religion was not an opponent, but rather, irrelevant. All that mattered was that the "saucer" of politics be firmly set. From that basis, it was "simple to be one of the people, and simple to be a Christian." If the politics were correct, religion could take whatever course it wanted. Thus, Nee ended his appeal with an exhortation for his listeners to rectify their politics, to be certain to firmly grasp the position of the people and the position of anti-imperialism.[422]

Nee's concessions in "How I have changed" were meaningful. Nee had spent significant time in the West, and he considered some Western Christians to be important mentors and peers in his Christian pursuits. To be sure, he always carefully grounded the authority for his teachings in the Bible alone, but even this attitude was, to an extent, an inheritance of an international, evangelical tradition. Nee now admitted, "I have changed, I think that perhaps it is very hard to find a foreigner who is not an imperialist."[423] From the perspective of the Communist ideology that the government now required all Chinese Christians to follow, even those Westerners who were most self-critical of the failings of the Western tradition had only ever acted in the religious sphere, "in Adam," as it were. None of Nee's interlocutors had ever taken up the politics of class solidarity or anti-imperialism. From a Communist political perspective, Nee had to admit that they, like he, were complicit. They had not actually acted "for the people."

Nee never had further opportunity to reflect publicly on the theological significance of these political failures. Nevertheless, throughout "How I have changed," he maintained an unresolved, paradoxical stance that recalled a basic hallmark of Christian theology: that is, the Chalcedonian claim that Christ was both fully divine and fully human. According to Nee's analysis, the teacup and the saucer were not replacements for one another. Instead, they were two distinct entities that always went together, that were, in fact, inseparable. Just as Jesus was both divine and human, Nee suggested that the Christian had both a religious and a political existence. The cup and its contents might be religiously orthodox or completely unbelieving. The plate and its position might be imperialist or anti-imperialist. The individual Christian was simultaneously a religious and a political entity.

And yet, without further elaboration along these lines, "How I have changed" also avoided dramatically revising Nee's theology. By removing the opposition of politics to religion and setting them on different planes, Nee was, in some ways, preserving a sphere for religious autonomy. If the government insisted on political action in service of anti-imperialism, this could be done without affecting his other religious beliefs and practices. In some ways, this was what the Little Flock had already begun to do by entering parades, fundraising, and signing

---

[422] Nee, "How I have changed."
[423] Nee, "How I have changed."

petitions. Nee seemed to be saying that from a political perspective, it was impossible to transcend politics, but, crucially, he made no theological claims from the *religious* perspective. He only repeatedly pointed out how irrelevant all such religious claims and actions were from the government's standpoint. Christian theology's irrelevance to politics did not preclude the fact that it could still hold relevance in itself, on its own terms. Significantly, Nee had only brought up theology as an analogy to illustrate the logic of the government's demands. He had made no direct revisions to his own Christian teachings.

Nee's logic in "How I have changed" may have been inspired by Jesus's political stance in the famous saying from the synoptic gospels about "rendering unto Caesar that which is Caesar's." The government had asked for full cooperation from the bodies and souls of the believers. Nee taught that they were owed this obedience, but he still reserved the human spirit for God alone. Nevertheless, according to Nee's own teachings, the human spirit and the human soul were deeply and problematically intertwined, like the joints and marrows of the human body.[424] Furthermore, the Roman Empire had never demanded as high a level of ideological adherence as the Maoist state.

For all that "How I have changed" clarified, it left multiple vagaries unaddressed. Crucially, as far as assessing Nee's own ideas and legacy, Nee never had a chance to revise, explain, or update his position. "How I have changed" stands as Nee's final explicit word on the subject. For that reason, a range of interpretations have surrounded this dramatic document, so different from the rest of Nee's oeuvre. One common interpretation is that "How I have changed" is a classic Communist confession. According to this view, like his co-workers who bowed to pressure and provoked Nee to write, Nee himself recognized the futility of continuing resistance in the face of the overpowering, intimidatory force of the Communist state. Nee capitulated and consigned the church to follow the CCP's pronouncements. Another interpretation is that "How I have changed" was a relatively meaningless tactical maneuver. Many of Nee's followers have never heard of the document or feel that it is not worth their notice. From this perspective, "How I have changed" was simply a minor concession in an ongoing set of negotiations with the CCP, the smallest change that could be made while still holding firm to fundamental principles. The subtlety and ambiguity of Nee's writing certainly allow for his "confession" to be interpreted anywhere within the wide scope between these two poles. For Nee and the rest of the members of the Christian Assemblies, the details would be worked out on the ground.

---

[424] Hebrews 4:12 describes the relationship between the soul and the spirit as being like that of the joints and marrow. The verse, which approvingly argues for the division between soul and spirit, was unsurprisingly a favorite touchstone of Nee's theology. He cites it in many places, for some examples, see NTSWJ 1, 48–50; NTSWJ 3, 59; NTSWJ 4, 219–220; NTSWJ 12, 224–228; NTSWJ 33, 217–222; and NTSWJ 54, 259–266.

Government Campaigns and Church Responses

The reaction of both the CCP and the Christian Assemblies to "How I have changed" seemed to suggest that Nee would not be able to lead his followers into the ideological conformity the government demanded. Although Nee was a Protestant leader of national importance, the state-sponsored Protestant newspaper, *Tian Feng*, declined to print or even report on his new position, suggesting that the authorities were not entirely convinced. They were looking for mass mobilization and the enthusiastic participation of the rank and file in a denunciation meeting. Nee and the Shanghai congregation had yet to successfully hold such a meeting.[425]

Nee's first presentation of "How I have changed" went relatively smoothly, but when the Shanghai elders attempted to carry out a denunciation meeting, they met with fractious opposition. One of the Little Flock members loudly declared his opposition to the whole project, claiming that the Denunciation Movement was not from God, but rather, that "'the People' were being taken as a god to be worshipped," adding that "A Christian who denounced others sinned and offended God." Although the elders quickly quieted the unruly speaker and asked for obedience to the leadership, the damage had been done.[426] The reaction was not altogether surprising. The Christian Assemblies prized spiritual maturity as pliability. They valorized the virtue of bearing loss without complaint and loving one another despite offensive behavior. They now found it hard to enthusiastically denounce one another, much less their respected leaders.

And yet the government representatives clearly understood that such a step was necessary to achieve the ideological conformity they sought. Representatives from the party continued to find disgruntled members and ex-members who individually denounced Nee and the practices of the Christian Assemblies as feudal, controlling, and imperialistic. At the same time, many other Little Flock members persisted in resisting the government edicts. It was clear that Nee would have to change even further if he wanted to convince the main body of the Christian Assemblies to participate in the Denunciation Movement. Instead of writing another confession, Nee eventually settled on two strategies: He would oppose the Denunciation Movement and he would try to drive a wedge between the CCP and the Three-Self Protestant organization they were beginning to form.[427]

In the longer term, the strategies Nee chose probably did not matter. The demands of ideological purity in Maoist China were endless and absolute.

[425] Ying, *Fandi*, 75.
[426] Ying, *Fandi*, 76.
[427] Ying, *Fandi*, 80–90.

During the Cultural Revolution, even the leaders of the eventual Three-Self Patriotic Movement were denounced and sent into forced labor or reeducation. In the immediate term, the Denunciation Movement gave way to the "Three-Anti" and "Five-Anti" campaigns, ostensibly waged to combat "corruption, waste, and bureaucratism" (Three-Anti) and "bribery, tax evasion, fraud, theft of government property, and leakage of state economic secrets" (Five-Anti).[428]

With these campaigns underway, it was simple for the government to find another angle from which to denounce Nee and remove him from his position of authority among the Christian Assemblies. Nee had operated *Shenghua*, the pharmaceutical business, during the final years of the famously corrupt GMD government. Some level of tax evasion was inevitably found, and Nee himself may have suffered some pangs of conscience with regard to the profits he made as one of the few legitimate businesses allowed to operate during the Sino-Japanese War. Rather than implicate the Christian Assemblies as a whole, Nee now asked the Shanghai co-workers and elders to remove his name from the church membership lists to insulate the larger body of believers from his own personal fall.

On April 10, 1952, Nee was taken into custody. Nothing more was heard from Nee or about his case until March the following year, when the Shanghai Municipal Court ordered Nee to pay the state 17.2 billion yuan in the old currency, equivalent to over ten million contemporary US dollars.[429] Unable to pay, he stayed in custody without formal charges being brought for another three years.

Although the interactions between Nee and the government during these years remain largely obscure, interesting parallels can be drawn with other figures. Elsewhere in Shanghai, a comparable struggle between ideological conformity and religious independence played out between the CCP and the Roman Catholic Church. One of the key figures in the Roman Catholic resistance was the Jesuit Beda Chang (*Zhang Boda*), who was quietly arrested in August 1951. Chang's biographer writes:

> It seems certain that he was offered the leadership of the Independent Church in Shanghai and that when he refused, every effort was made to break his will and to use him in spite of himself. Nights on nights of interrogation followed his refusal, when lack of sleep and continual tension combined to wear down the last resources of his bodily strength. Fellow prisoners heard him, exhausted and at the end of his strength,

[428] Joseph Tse-Hei Lee, "Watchman Nee and the Little Flock Movement in Maoist China," *Church History* 74, No. 1 (March 2005), 87.

[429] Ying, *Fandi*, 91–94.

repeating simply over and over again "Jesus, Mary and Joseph, help me."[430]

In the case of Chang, the interrogation went too far, and the priest slipped into a coma and died. Even if Nee was not subject to the same specific patterns of constant interrogation and sleep deprivation, the general purpose and means of the incarceration were likely similar. Both men were probably taken quietly in hopes that they could be induced to turn and lead their flocks into greater compliance. Ambiguous charges would allow for more flexibility, depending on whether the subject could be "exonerated" and turned. If the subject cooperated, charges could be minimized or dropped. If the subject refused to cooperate, the quiet arrest would allow the government time to build a more powerful case and attempt to more thoroughly tear down the religious leader's reputation. Either way, the faithful would be shaken and divided, and the government would strengthen its grip on power.

In the interim, since nothing was published, Nee apparently refused to cooperate with the government, and a quiet, uneasy truce characterized the relationship between the state and the Christian Assemblies. In service to their strategy of intentional ambiguity, the CCP declined to publicize news of either Nee's arrest or the charges of financial corruption that had been brought against him. At the same time, the leadership of the Christian Assemblies seems to have chosen to keep Nee's arrest a secret as well. It is possible that they felt that news of his arrest would be a blow to the Little Flock's morale. It is also possible that they did not want to publicize his arrest when they themselves were so uncertain both of the accusations against him and of the eventual outcome of his arrest.[431]

Instead, led by Ruth Li, Peace Wang, and Yu Chenghua, the ophthalmologist who had quietly supported Nee during his last excommunication, the Little Flock hardened its attitude toward government cooperation. Nee's leadership in this regard had been equivocal. On the one hand, he had led his followers to add their signatures to the Christian Manifesto and had seemed to indicate the need for joining the government's "three-self" project in "How I have changed." On the other hand, he later opposed both the Denunciation Movement and the "three-self" representatives by trying to argue that he could be patriotic without denouncing or joining another organization. The Little Flock leaders chose this latter line of resistance, and the Christian Assemblies across the country followed. Congregation after congregation began to formally withdraw from the

---

[430] Jean-Claude Coulet, *Father Beda Chang: Witness for Unity* (Hong Kong: Catholic Truth Society, 1953), 21, as cited in Paul Mariani, *Church Militant: Bishop Kung and Catholic Resistance in Communist Shanghai* (Cambridge, MA: Harvard University Press, 2011), 88.
[431] Ying, *Fandi*, 100.

Three-Self Reform Movement. The TSRM, for its part, saved face by continuing to list the names that had previously been submitted as members in its official *Tian Feng* periodical.[432]

In 1953, the government tested the waters again by inviting citizens to attend an exhibition put on by the Shanghai Public Security Office. The display was called the "Exhibition of Watchman Nee and Kung Pinmei's Anti-Revolutionary Crimes." Kung Pinmei was the Roman Catholic Bishop of Shanghai who defiantly refused to cooperate with the Catholic manifestos that were issued as analogues to the "Christian Manifesto." The juxtaposition of Nee and Kung was interesting. The government seemed to see a connection between these two men who were figureheads for Christian resistance in Shanghai, and indeed, across the nation. It also seemed to think that the people of Shanghai could benefit from a lesson in the reactionary nature of Christian religion, writ large.[433]

The CCP in Shanghai continued to deal with the Roman Catholic Church and Little Flock communities in similar ways, employing parallel strategies and even timelines in breaking down their resistance. After working through some of its own internal power struggles in 1954, the CCP eventually came to direct its attention to the persistent problem of recalcitrant religious groups with the newly empowered Religious Affairs Bureau (RAB).[434]

By 1955, cadres were remarkably descriptive regarding the tactics and purposes of their actions. In the Catholic case, they reported, "Then we used every kind of method to aim at each person's unique characteristics, and so win the psychological battle, destroying them one by one." With enough individuals won, the plan could proceed toward its goal: "A lot of them stopped their resistance and they confessed. This played a crucial role in dividing and destroying the entire foundation of the reactionaries of the Kung Pinmei clique among the masses."[435]

In order to divide and destroy the support of the masses, the RAB used large-scale meetings and rallies to show off the confessions and evidence that they had gathered. When it came to Catholics, pliable leaders who had changed their minds were encouraged to speak. Simultaneously, the masses were trained to shout revolutionary and denunciatory slogans and repeated them over and over again until the entire audience had learned the words by heart.[436] In the case of the Little Flock, the Nanyang Road Assembly Hall was the site of twelve days of

---

[432] Ying, *Fandi*, 103–109.

[433] *Shanghai Gongan Zhi* (Shanghai: *Shanghai Shehui Kexueyuan Chubanshe*, 1997) as quoted in Silas Wu, *Poke Feiteng: Ni Tuosheng de Beiqiu yu Tuibian* (Boston, MA: Pishon River Publishers, 2004), 11–12, 15, 68–69.

[434] Mariani, *Church Militant*, 140–141.

[435] Mariani, *Church Militant*, 154–155.

[436] Mariani, *Church Militant*, 151–156.

mandatory meetings where evidence of Nee's crimes was presented. He was accused of collaborating with imperialists and the GMD, lawless profiteering in business, harboring enemy agents, and gross sexual immorality.[437]

In September 1955, having gathered enough support, the CCP finally struck, swiftly arresting Bishop Kung and hundreds of other leading Catholics. Just a few months later, in January 1956, municipal police arrived at the Shanghai Assembly Hall on Wendeli Road after the church bread-breaking service. Officers arrested Ruth Li, Peace Wang, and at least four of the other elders who were present.[438] Other leaders, like Zuo Furu and Yu Chenghua, were not immediately arrested, but rather, were subjected to intense attempts to win them over. Zuo ended up participating and writing a confession that agreed with the government's position that it was not interfering with the faith, but merely clearing out anti-revolutionary elements. Yu, conversely, stubbornly refused to cooperate, despite being presented with evidence of others' confessions and denunciations. Finally, he too was arrested and subjected to continuous interrogation, at one point losing consciousness three times in a fifty-day span. He was finally released in mid-April, dying within a day of his release.[439]

In some sense, the fate of Nee and his fellow leaders in the Christian Assemblies was pre-determined. Observers like Gao Wangzhi have pointed out that "the most influential theologians and the charismatic evangelical leaders were the most vulnerable to denunciation." In the end, their cardinal sin was being "too influential or too popular."[440] The government's goal was to eradicate independent sources of authority, which would fracture the kind of ideological conformity it sought. Any strong, independent voices needed to be silenced or discredited, especially during this period of war and consolidation.

Comparing the cases of the Christian Assemblies and the Roman Catholic Church makes this conclusion even more obvious. The two institutions seemed to have little in common, but they suffered similar attacks with similar tactics along a similar timeline. To be certain, actual spies and imperialist agents among the populace would have been immediately arrested or executed in the name of national security. These Christian groups presented a much more abstract threat to the regime—a coherent, distinct ideology that did not follow the increasing demands of compliance with the party line.

---

[437] Kinnear, *Against the Tide*, 270–277. See also Lian, *Redeemed by Fire*, 177. Lian mentions grainy pictures of Nee, supposedly caught *in flagrante*, which date from this era (1955).

[438] Ying, *Fandi*, 129.

[439] Ying, *Fandi*, 131–132.

[440] Wuzhi Gao, "Y. T. Wu: A Christian Leader Under Communism," in *Christianity in China: From the Eighteenth Century to the Present*, Daniel Bays ed. (Stanford, CA: Stanford University Press, 1996), 349.

Watchman Nee Abroad: The Normal Christian Life

In Nee's case, this coherent, distinct ideology was just beginning to win acclaim from abroad. In 1952, Nee's speaking notes from his final trip to the West were compiled and published in German as *Das Normale Christenleben*.[441] This was not the first of Nee's works to be published in a language besides Chinese. While he was still in the United Kingdom, Nee had given a number of talks that were compiled as *Concerning Our Missions* and published by Austin-Sparks in 1939.[442] This book was the first of Nee's works to be published outside of China, but it was rather narrowly focused on Nee's conceptions of practical church organization, especially the role of apostles, their financing, and their relationship to local churches. The impact and circulation of the book were therefore somewhat limited.[443]

In contrast, *The Normal Christian Life* was written on broad, devotional themes, and throughout the 1950s, its publication and circulation rapidly increased. In 1957, the first English versions of the work were published by three different presses in Mumbai, London, and Fort Washington, Pennsylvania.[444] Subsequent editions of Nee's work quickly followed nearly every year thereafter throughout the 1960s and across the English-speaking world, predominantly in the United Kingdom and the United States, but also in India and Canada.[445]

The animating force behind this first set of English publications was Angus Kinnear, Nee's biographer and Austin-Sparks's son-in-law. Kinnear had spent

[441] Watchman Nee, *Das Normale Christenleben* (Wuppertal-Vohwinkel: Brockhaus, 1952), with further editions in 1953, 1960, 1963, 1964, 1965, 1966, 1967, 1968, 1969, and 1970. Another German publisher located in Stuttgart named Sayer had editions printed in 1957 and 1965.

[442] Watchman Nee, *Concerning Our Missions* (London: Witness and Testimony Publishers, 1939).

[443] Despite the general lack of interest in the book initially, it was translated into Finnish. See Watchman Nee, *Apostolinen lähetystyö: lähetystyömme tarkastelua uuden testamentin valossa* (Pietarsaari: Kaikille Luodille, 1940). There is also an interesting, early English publication of mysterious provenance published as Watchman Nee, *An Overall Discussion of the Spirit, the Body, and the Soul* (Shanghai: Bible Truth Depot, 1950).

[444] Watchman Nee, *The Normal Christian Life* (Mumbai: Gospel Literature Service, 1957); (London: Kingsway Press, 1957); and (Fort Washington, PA: Christian Literature Crusade, 1957). Angus Kinnear's preface to CWWN 33 (Anaheim, CA: Living Stream Ministry, 1993) makes clear that the version in Mumbai was the first to be printed.

[445] In the UK, Austin-Sparks's Witness and Testimony Publishers printed its own versions in 1958 and 1959. Kinnear's Kingsway Press reprinted the book in 1961 and 1969, while Victory Press printed its own editions in 1957, 1958, 1959, 1961, and 1963. In the United States, besides many printings undertaken by Witness Lee's various publishing houses, the book was also printed numerous times by the Christian Literature Crusade (1957, 1960, 1961, 1963, 1966, 1967, 1969, 1970, 1973, and 1974) and Tyndale House (1961, 1971, 1977, and 1985). Meanwhile, Nee's other early translated work, *Sit, Walk, Stand*, was published by Christian Literature Crusade in 1957, 1959, 1961, 1962, 1963, 1964, and 1966; by Witness and Testimony Publishers in 1958, 1959, and 1961; by Kingsway in 1958 and 1962; and by Victory Press in 1958, 1962, 1963, and 1965. It was also published in Canada by Welch Publishers in 1962 and in Mumbai by Gospel Literature Service in 1960 and 1967. *Love Not the World* and *What Shall This Man Do?* share similar extensive publication histories throughout the 1950s and 1960s.

some months with Nee in 1938, before setting off to India as a medical missionary. He came to see this time with Nee as a turning point in his own spiritual
pursuit, writing that "I found my whole outlook on Christian life and service
greatly enriched and given a fresh direction and purpose."[446] With his particular
access to some of Nee's European acquaintances, Kinnear compiled, edited, and
published not only the first English versions of *The Normal Christian Life* but
also *Sit, Walk, Stand; Love Not the World,* and *What Shall This Man Do?* All of
these books were primarily based on notes taken from Nee's various messages
and discourses during the time he spent in Europe from 1938 to 1939.[447]

Once available in European languages, the circulation and translations of
Nee's work intensified, building on the multilingual, transnational networks
of Holiness and Keswick circles. Since their founding, these amorphous
movements had crossed confessional boundaries and maintained a tradition of
ecumenism. They were well disposed, perhaps even intrigued, by a little-known
Chinese pastor. Furthermore, by the mid-nineteenth century, even the much
younger Keswick Convention had been operating for almost one hundred years.
There were, therefore, significant personnel and institutions who were interested
in and capable of translating and passing along helpful, effective works of devotional literature.

Thus, Nee's works were published in Danish, Finnish, and Dutch at around
the same time they were published in English. Both the translators and the
audiences were rooted in the significant evangelical and charismatic subcultures
that could be found in those countries. It was likely through the Netherlands
that Nee's work was then translated into Afrikaans, traveling to South Africa by
1961.[448]

The beginning of the 1960s also saw the near-simultaneous translation
of Nee's work into other European languages, including French, Italian, and
Swedish.[449] The earliest Spanish translation of Nee's work was *Sentaos, Andad,*

---

[446] Kinnear, *Against the Tide*, 9.

[447] *What Shall This Man Do?* is the slight exception here, since the preface indicates that it was
based on notes taken in China as well, going up to 1942. CWWN 40, 3. Kinnear also edited and
published two other books with slightly less extensive publication histories, *Song of Songs* and *Table
in the Wilderness*. The former appears in NTSWJ 23 in the original language and the latter was a devotional Kinnear constructed out of Nee's writings.

[448] Watchman Nee, *Det Normale Kristenliv* (Kbh, 1957); *Sidde, Vandre, Sta, En Hovedlinie i
Efserbrevet* (Kbh, 1957); *Kristityn normaali elama* (Helsinki: Kuva ja sana, 1958); *Zitten, Wandelen,
Standhouden* (Hoenderloo: Hoenderloo's Uitgeverij en Drukkerij, 1957); *Het Normale Christelijke
Leven* (Hoenderloo: Hoenderloo's Uitgeverij en Drukkerij, 1958); *Die Normale Christelike Lewe*
(Roodeport: Christelike, 1961).

[449] Watchman Nee, *Etre assis, Marcher, Tenir Firme* (Paris: Impr. Vieux-S. I. P. E., 1960); *La Vie
Chrétienne Normale* (Paris: Mme L. Ducommun, 1, rue Jacques-Offenbach, impr. Vieux Charles,
1961). Watchman Nee, *Non piu io ma Cristo* (Marchirolo (VA): EUN, 1961). "Not I but Christ" was
a common subtitle or alternative title used for *The Normal Christian Life*. Watchman Nee, *Ett Rikt
Kristenliv* (Orebro: OM, 1963), republished in 1970, and by the publisher Libris in 1967. *Segrande liv*
(Orebro: Libris, 1968) and *Trons liv* (Orebro: Libris, 1970).

Estad Firmes (or, *Sit, Walk, Stand*), first issued by an Argentinian publisher in 1960.[450] By the end of the 1960s, there would be more Spanish publishers of Nee in Spain, the United States, and Mexico as well, although Argentina still offered the most titles.[451]

At around the same time, Nee's work also began to be published in other Asian languages. It is unclear how a Japanese version of Nee's work came to be translated by 1961, but there were certainly Japanese evangelicals who knew of Nee's work and reputation. After all, during Nee's visit to the Keswick Convention in 1939, he had shared the stage with a Japanese Christian when he refused to pray for either Chinese or Japanese victory.[452] By 1966, the first Korean version of Nee's work was published.[453]

Melissa Inouye and theologian Michael Bergunder have provocatively suggested that Pentecostalism should be defined not so much by its doctrines and practices, but by the global network that sustained it.[454] The idea has much to recommend it. Rather than splitting hairs over the specific religious discourses and institutions that "count" as Pentecostal or Charismatic, historians should recognize that the transnational media itself is an inherent, constitutive part of the message. Nee's admirers saw the fact that *any* ideas and practices could travel so quickly as a mirror of the ubiquity and efficacy of the Holy Spirit.

Nee's call to a deeper Christian life, centered on the union between the Holy Spirit and the human spirit, flooded the channels of the international network of evangelical, Pentecostal, Charismatic media, becoming an important, constitutive part of the discourse going forward. It is especially suggestive that the sites of Nee's publishers and the languages of publication so closely mirrored the first Pentecostal media boom. Nee was published in the United Kingdom, India, South America, North America, Scandinavia, and Korea, while the first wave

[450] Watchman Nee, *Sentaos, Andad, Estad Firmes* (San Ignacio, Argentina: Fondo Evangelico Hebron, 1960). The Argentinian title probably uses Iberian Spanish since "sit, walk, stand" were phrases taken from the Epistle to the Ephesians, and the publisher was simply preserving the *vosotros* for Biblical citations, as has traditionally been the case for Spanish Bible translations.

[451] In 1968, three Spanish editions of *El Obrero Cristiano Normal* appeared. One was published in Argentina, by Ediciones Hebron, one in Barcelona Alturas, and one in Grand Rapids, MI, by the publisher Portavoz. The first Mexican printing of Nee's work is Watchman Nee, *La iglesia normal* (Cuernavaca, Mor.: TI, 1964). Nee's Argentinian publisher would reprint *Sentaos, Andad, Estad Firmes* in 1969, while also offering *Que Haré Senor?* (San Ignacio, Argentina: Ed. Hebron, 1965); *La Liberación del Espiritu* (Buenos Aires: Logos, 1965).

[452] Watchman Nee, *Kirisutosha no hyojun* (Tokyo: Inochi no Kotobasha, 1961) and *Kirisutosha no Kotei* (Tokyo: Inochi no Kotobasha, 1961). Inochi no Kotobasha appears to operate as World of Life Press Ministries, a "group of nondenominational evangelistic ministries, seeking to bring glory to God." https://www.wlpm.or.jp/en/wlpm-introduction/, accessed on July 12, 2023.

[453] Watchman Nee, *Chongsangjogin Kurisudo-in ui saenghwal* (Seoul: Saengmyong ui Malssumsa, 1966).

[454] Inouye, *China and the True Jesus*, 57–85; and Michael Bergunder, "Constructing Indian Pentecostalism: On Issues of Methodology and Representation," in *Asian and Pentecostal: The Charismatic Face of Christianity in Asia* (Eugene, OR: Wipf and Stock, 2011).

of Pentecostal revivals in the early twentieth century covered much of the same territory.

Into these channels, Kinnear's translations of Nee's works acted as concentrated, eloquent entrées into Nee's novel insights. Although Kinnear never made his notes and sources available to the public, his English publications were undoubtedly based on Nee's work, but with a slightly freer editorial hand than the NTSWJ or CWWN. When the NTSWJ is based on notes, it is conservative and literal in the liberties it takes to render those notes readable.[455] The CWWN also tends toward cautious fidelity in translating from the Chinese. In contrast, Kinnear's editorial style had the effect of rendering Nee's writing as more folksy and idiomatic, and therefore, somewhat more chatty and accessible than Nee's other works published in English.

As Nee's most internationally popular work by far, *The Normal Christian Life* merits attention, even though it was not particularly novel in the context of Nee's wider body of work. *The Normal Christian Life* was an exposition of Paul's epistle to the Romans, with special focus on Chapters 5 through 8. In the book, Nee described the path that led an individual Christian from being hopelessly mired in sin to becoming a fragrant testimony of Jesus's worthiness. Along the way, Nee passed a number of devotional touchstones, enriched with his particular theological perspective.

Thus, in reviewing the classic depiction of sin from the early chapters of Romans, Nee focused on the distinction in the original biblical text between "sins" in the plural and "sin" in the singular. On Nee's account, "sins" referred to the "question of the sins I have committed before God, which are many and can be enumerated," while "sin" referred to the "question of sin as a principle working in me."[456] While the blood of Christ wiped out the record of a person's sins, only the cross could offer deliverance from the sinful nature that persisted throughout a human lifetime.

The bulk of *The Normal Christian Life* then dedicated itself to the significance and application of that cross. First, Christians had to know that they were already crucified with Christ as a historic fact, then they had to reckon this fact to be true by faith.[457] This would allow them to walk in the newness of life in resurrection, in a spiritual union where their life and the life of Christ would be joined, as a lump of sugar melted into tea, or a grafted branch planted into a root stock.[458] In such a spiritual union, the victorious life was blissful and effortless. Nee wrote that "When the Holy Spirit takes things in hand, there is no need for strain on our part." Rather than "clenching our teeth and taking a grip

---

[455] See the Appendix to this work for a detailed example.

[456] Nee, CWWN 33, 6.

[457] Nee, CWWN 33, 31–56. Nee uses Romans 5 and 6 as his basis for these chapters.

[458] Nee, CWWN 33, 62–64. The example of grafting is found in Romans 11.

on ourselves," the Christian simply learned to let the "Christ in our hearts by the Spirit" do everything.[459]

The goal of such a life was not merely the individual's dependence on Christ, but the corporate interdependence of the body of Christ. Thus, Nee argued that Christ could only be fully revealed in the church and that the body was not simply a metaphor but a spiritual reality. Without further revelation, a Christian might seek "holiness and victory and fruitfulness for myself personally and apart, albeit from the purest motives." Yet, when the cross terminated "that old life of independence which I inherited from Adam," the Christian would be liberated from a deeper level of selfishness and egotism: "Jealousy will go. Competition will go. Private work will go. My interests, my ambitions, my preferences, all will go. It will no longer matter which of us does the work. All that will matter will be that the Body grows."[460]

This line of thinking led Nee to caution against the soul-life, which could seem honorable and pure. It could appear to be "perfectly innocent natural affection," such as the love Peter bore Jesus when he cautioned his master not to go to Jerusalem, where he would suffer or die.[461] In that case, Jesus rebuked Peter's good intentions as being from Satan. Nee similarly warned that Christian motives could be murky, rooted in the tricky entanglement of the soul and the spirit. Therefore, the Bible was needed as "the penetrating Scripture of truth, that settles our questions. It is that which discerns our motives and defines for us their true source in soul or spirit."[462]

Finally, Nee concluded *The Normal Christian Life* with the example of Mary Magdalene and her anointing of Jesus on the night before his crucifixion. Each of the four gospels recorded that the oil Mary used was exceedingly expensive, prompting Nee to launch into a passionate discussion on the concept of value. Nee wrote, "The whole question is: How precious is He to us now? If we do not think much of Him, then of course to give Him anything at all, however small, will seem to us a wicked waste. But when He is really precious to our souls, nothing will be too good, nothing too costly for Him; everything we have, our dearest, our most priceless treasure, we shall pour out upon Him, and we shall not count it a shame to have done so."[463]

Nee believed that Christians who evaluated Christ correctly would be willing to pay the ultimate sacrifice, the sacrifice of their soul-life. And just as the breaking of Mary's flask of oil had filled the house with fragrance, Nee suggested that Christians who had been broken by God exuded an attractive fragrance.

---

[459] Nee, CWWN 33, 123–124. The spiritual Christ found in the heart is a major theme of Romans 8.
[460] Nee, CWWN 33, 151. Paul's discussion of the body is found in Romans 12.
[461] Nee, CWWN 33, 175.
[462] Nee, CWWN 33, 164.
[463] Nee, CWWN 33, 193.

When such people were contacted, Nee wrote, "Immediately your spiritual senses detect a sweet savor of Christ." Nee claimed that such mature Christians lived a kind of life that "creates impressions, and impressions create hunger, and hunger provokes men to go on seeking until they are brought by divine revelation into the fullness of life in Christ."[464]

Nee himself obviously aspired to be this kind of a Christian, and *The Normal Christian Life* is a fitting summary both of his own aspirations and of his intellectual journey. Many of his major theological themes and novel contributions to the evangelical tradition were woven into the book. These included union with Christ, the difference between the soul and the spirit, the difficulty of distinguishing between good and evil, the importance of the body of Christ, and spiritual maturity as brokenness.

As a work of biblical exegesis and devotional literature, the work certainly seemed to stand apart from contemporary events in Chinese society. Nevertheless, Nee's ability to speak the evangelical idiom fluently, his refusal to indulge in Chinese chauvinism, and even his valorization of female piety were all hints at his own cultural background. It is certainly true, though, that these same effects only helped to make his work more legible to international audiences, especially those who had been exposed to the same, broadly Christian tradition. It was a poignant irony that these international audiences were only starting to learn about this theology as its original author and his closest followers slipped behind a veil of silence.

Imprisoned: Authority and Submission

One surprising voice eventually emerged to shed light on Nee's life in his final years. In 1960, a twenty-four-year-old Shanghainese teacher named Wu Youqi was sent to prison as a counter-revolutionary for criticizing the government in the aftermath of the spectacular failure of the second "Great Leap Forward." Wu and Nee were both sent to Shanghai Prison, better known as *Tilanqiao*, which was one of the largest prison complexes in the world at that time. Wu became Nee's cellmate on the fourth floor of Building 3 in 1963. Together with a disabled young man, the three men shared one of ninety cells on the prison floor. At first, Wu was suspicious of Nee because of the latter's position as a small group monitor (小组长, *Xiaozu Zhang*). As a monitor, Nee was required to lead and facilitate study sessions for thought reform and to make reports to the cadres.[465]

---

[464] Nee, CWWN 33, 195.
[465] Wu Youqi Interview, April 21, 2021, and Wu, *Poke Feiteng*, 67.

After a few months, during a designated prison visit, Wu's wife shared the distressing news that she had lost her job because she had refused to divorce Youqi, despite his being a condemned counter-revolutionary. In great distress, Wu returned to his cell and leaned against the wall to cry. Even though crying was against the rules, Nee quietly approached from behind and put his arm around the younger man and said, "Youqi, Youqi, you can cry, you can cry. You will feel better." Afterward, Nee handed Youqi his own towel to wipe his face, and the two became friends.[466]

In general, prison conditions at *Tilanqiao* were harsh. Although prisoners were supposed to receive a diet that met a certain nutritional standard set by doctors, the food was almost always below standard in quality and never enough to stave off hunger. During the ten years of the Cultural Revolution (from 1966 to 1976), the only food that was served was wheat bran and rice porridge.[467] In the winter, the inmates were each allowed only one quilt to be supplied by their families. The three cellmates decided to sleep on the cold concrete, sharing one quilt beneath them and two above them, while the walls were as cold as ice.[468] In 1962, two Christian Assembly elders were released from prison, and they reported that Nee, who was over six feet tall, now weighed less than one hundred pounds.[469]

Wu also recalled that in 1965, Nee was summoned out of the cell for an exceptionally long interrogation lasting almost six hours. At the end of it, Nee returned with a solemn face. Soon, a general announcement was made over the loudspeakers, denouncing Nee for his obstinacy. Apparently, Nee and two Roman Catholic leaders had been offered their freedom in return for rejecting their faith. Although the Catholics had renounced their church affiliation and been pardoned, Nee had turned down the offer. In awe, Wu, who had been raised as a Buddhist, immediately declared, "Watchman Nee, from today I follow you. I believe in Jesus Christ."[470]

Nee's behavior in jail bears analysis. Nee appeared to be a model prisoner, having already become a respected small group monitor by the time of Wu's arrival. Furthermore, it seemed that Nee followed the government's prohibition of proselytizing and Christian practice.[471] It is notable that it was Wu who initiated his own Christian conversion and that Nee himself said nothing to encourage it. Nee's refusal to leave the prison showed clearly that his personal faith was intact, but his opposition to government campaigns and institutions seemed to have

---

[466] Wu Youqi Interview.
[467] Wu, *Poke Feiteng*, 38.
[468] Wu Youqi Interview.
[469] Kinnear, *Against the Tide*, 294.
[470] Kinnear, *Against the Tide*, 294.
[471] Prayers and saying grace before a meal were counted as "opposing reform," that is, old, counter-revolutionary behavior according to Wu, *Poke Feiteng*, 44.

vanished. One final piece of Nee's Christian writings may help to explain this behavior.

In 1949, Nee gave a series of messages later published as *Authority and Submission*. In these writings, Nee did not break new ground in the history of Christian thought. Obedience was a central theme of Christian morality with a long history. Nevertheless, Nee's arrangement of his ideas was interesting and certainly offered significant insight into his own perspective on the topic. *Authority and Submission* also illuminates Nee's attitude toward the government in general, including the CCP. The book was Nee's most dedicated treatment on the question of authority and the role of Christian obedience. From this perspective, it explained both Nee's behavior in prison and the general principles by which he led the Christian Assemblies. Furthermore, these teachings also shaped the culture of the Christian Assemblies, especially their attitude toward power struggles and challenges to authority.

Authority and Submission was composed of two main sections. The first section was comprised of twelve chapters in which Nee described the general principles of both authority and submission. As was typical in Nee's thought, he began with the cosmic perspective—that God's throne was the center of the universe, and all authority was centered on God's throne. Therefore, "Authority is the greatest thing in the universe, and nothing can overcome authority."[472] Nee depicted Satan's origin as a rebellion against authority and claimed that all the conflict in the universe was, at a fundamental level, a struggle against authority. Nee even used Jesus's prayer in the garden of Gethsemane to prove his belief that submission to God's will was a matter of higher importance than the cross of Christ. Nee pointed out that before choosing the cross, Jesus sought God's will and would have followed it, regardless of the consequences.[473]

Nee then elaborated on this central conflict of the highest importance, walking through the importance of submission in the Old and New Testaments, while illustrating the main point of his book: namely, that God's authority was not primarily known directly, but indirectly. Nee conceded that Jesus submitted to the Father directly and that submission was an integral part of the mystery of the Trinity. However, Nee explained that the point of his writing was to show that God generally governed most Christians through the means of human representatives or deputy authorities. The very first human authority Nee described was that of worldly government.

On this subject, Nee's fundamentally submissive attitude toward all human governments was given full expression. Nee wrote, "We cannot choose between two options: God's direct authority and God's deputy authority. We must not

---

[472] Nee, NTSWJ 47, 119.
[473] Nee, NTSWJ 47, 123–124.

only submit to God's direct authority; we must also submit to God's deputy authority because there is no authority except from God."[474] Nee's attitude toward politics has been called "passive" or "quietist," but there was something more active being imagined here.

Traditionally, political passivity or quietism has been used to describe Christian groups like Anabaptists and Mennonites, who have avoided swearing oaths of loyalty and wanted only to avoid involvement with government policies and institutions. Nee, however, outlined governmental authority as a positive good, one that Christians should do their utmost to seek out and comply with, as such authority bore the marks of the divine itself. Nee continued, "People who reject the authority of God's deputy reject the authority of God himself. In the Bible, authority has only one nature. There is no authority that does not come from God, to resist power is to resist God. God will not relent. The ones who resist must surely bring punishment upon themselves."[475]

Nee recognized some common objections to these categorical statements, and he refused to give them much leeway. "All the nations of the earth have a ruler. Even if they do not believe in God, even if the whole nation is Satan's nation, still, the principle of authority is established by God."[476] Nee explained that this was because even the worst of human governments reflected God's law by enforcing the basic principle of "upholding good, punishing evil." Even in the most twisted cases, where governments uplifted evil officers and punished righteous subjects, they still did so under the explanation that evil was good and good was evil. Even in these worst cases, the authorities still would not promote evil as evil or punish good as good.[477]

Therefore, the righteous Christian had to pay attention to the deeper divine principle and submit to God, who was the hidden, guiding principle of all authority established by any human beings anywhere. Christians should go out of their way to submit, not only to the authorities of their "own nation and own people," but, when visiting or living abroad, to local authorities as well. In all places, Christians should actively look to comply with the requirements listed by Paul in Romans 13: "revenue to whom revenue is due, tax to whom tax is due, fear to whom fear is due, respect to whom respect is due."[478]

Authority and Submission thus helped to explain Nee's attitude and actions both before and during his imprisonment. As long as he was free, and the government's demands were ambiguous, Nee felt that he had space to negotiate and to try to convince Party authorities that the Denunciation and Three-Self

[474] Nee, NTSWJ 47, 170.
[475] Nee, NTSWJ 47, 70.
[476] Nee, NTSWJ 47, 71.
[477] Nee, NTSWJ 47, 72.
[478] Nee, NTSWJ 47, 71–72, quoting Romans 13:6–7.

Movements were not necessary for the Christian Assemblies, which were already patriotic and indigenous. Nee hoped that the government would agree with his own understanding of "good" and "evil." After his incarceration, however, Nee seemed to conclude that he was now under the deputy authority of God. He would do everything in his power to be a model inmate, except, of course, forsake the God whose authority was represented by the prison officials.

Authority and Submission reveals why Nee was in such anguish when writing "How I have changed." Nee's core values of spiritual transcendence and holiness were clashing not only with his sense of responsibility to the church, but, even more fundamentally, with his understanding of total obedience to God, through the intermediary of the Communist state. He may have viewed his experience akin to the experience of Jesus at Gethsemane, where personal stakes and motivations were weighed against the simple demand for submission. The irony, of course, is that very few governments before or since have demanded such rigorous and absolute fidelity to state ideology and direction. The CCP could hardly have found a more pliable Christian ideology to work with, but in the end, even Nee was pushed beyond his limits.

It may be helpful to note here that *Authority and Submission* also set limits on the boundaries of Christian obedience. For one thing, Nee distinguished between submission, which he defined as an attitude, and obedience, which he defined as a behavior. Therefore, while the demand for submission was absolute, and Christians should always bear an attitude of unlimited respect and honor for human authorities, "Obedience is not absolute. There are authorities that must be obeyed and there are authorities that cannot be obeyed."[479]

Furthermore, except in a few places, *Authority and Submission* was concerned mainly within the boundaries of the church and the Christian life. While secular governments seemed to be ordained by God simply by virtue of their coming to power, Nee felt that God's requirements on the church were far more stringent. The entire second half of *Authority and Submission* was devoted to the requirements for being a proper, *Christian* deputy authority. In Nee's view, "There is nothing more terrible and more serious than misrepresenting authority."[480] One who was invested with such authority was subject to much higher standards and faced with much greater consequences.

In brief, Nee argued that proper deputy authorities were themselves servants of others, and were keenly, intensely subject to God's authority in their lives, whether God spoke to them directly, through other humans, or in the environment. In keeping with the other aspects of Nee's spirituality, authority was also

[479] NTSWJ 47, 221.
[480] NTSWJ 47, 286.

understood as a total yielding, a welcoming acceptance of God's arrangement. Thus, he wrote,

> We should not do anything to defend ourselves, we should not say anything on our own behalf. We should not do anything according to ourselves, not even move a little finger to prove that I am chosen by God. We must be able to believe, to wait, to be humble. We must wait for God's time, for what God wants to do, he surely will do. The more you submit, the more you know authority. The more you can be prostrate before God, the more God will vindicate you. But if you try to speak for yourself, make known your injustices, complain, you will ruin all that God is doing. You must learn to humble yourself under the mighty hand of God. The more you try to make yourself an authority, the more you are wrong. This way is most clear.[481]

Nee may well have felt that, as a deputy authority among the Christian Assemblies, his behavior must show exceptional quiescence, even an eager acceptance of the sufferings that afflicted him. Nee may have seen the years in prison as a quiet test. His own bearing and attitude would tell whether or not the spirituality he had taught while he was free had really found a place in his soul.

Of course, Nee's personal application of his own theology is not the only possible interpretation of events. To some extent, Nee's compliance was a foregone conclusion. He had no choice but to comply. In this sense, one might argue that his theology was not liberating, but deeply oppressive. According to this reading, if Nee had simply compromised his inflexible theological tenets, there is every chance that at multiple points he could have written a moving confession that exhorted his followers to unstintingly obey the Chairman and follow the CCP ideology. As a compliant tool, Nee would have had more value as a free man than as a prisoner.

Other church leaders, like the outspoken, independent pastor, Wang Mingdao (1900–1991), had recanted and been released from their incarceration. Thus, one way of reading the final years of Nee's life is to account for his confession, arrest, and imprisonment as the tragic story of ever-tightening pressure applied to civic independence, as embodied in a single conscience, set against the unyielding, coercive power of a totalizing state. As in the case of "How I have changed," the silence of the evidence allows for an abundance of narratives.

Still, Nee's silence itself, that is, his refusal to recant is, in fact, a kind of tangible evidence of its own. This evidence can be joined to the other scant pieces of evidence that remain: Wu's accounts of Nee's placid temperament as a prisoner, Nee's promotion to small group monitor, and Nee's assiduous care in conducting

---

[481] NTSWJ 47, 307–308.

the duties of a prison monitor. Furthermore, as will become apparent, Nee seems to have earnestly studied Communist writings, attempting to make himself useful in a way that went beyond the direct mandates of the prison authorities. All of these suggest that Nee's behavior was not begrudging, nor did he see himself as a tragic figure or a part of a resistance. Instead, the best possible explanation for all of this fragmentary evidence is that Nee saw the conditions of his imprisonment, and potentially his denouncement, confession, and arrest as well, primarily through the lens of his own theology.

Coda: Final Days and Death

In 1967, Wu's sentence was technically complete, but due to the exigencies of the Cultural Revolution, instead of being freed, he was sent to a labor camp in rural Baimaoling in the Anhui province. Two years later, Wu was surprised to find that Nee had also been transferred to the same labor camp, and so the two men spent the next three years together in adjoining bunks in the same dormitory.[482] Together, they were considered "partially rehabilitated" and forced to work eight hours a day, six days a week.[483]

Nee was noticeably weaker, as his congenital heart condition, angina pectoris, had deteriorated with age and the harsh conditions of his life. Although most of the inmates at the camp worked in the fields, provision was made for Nee due to his physical limitations. He primarily worked with four or five other older or disabled inmates cleaning the crops that the others had harvested. Occasionally, they were instructed to pull weeds around the campground, clean the communal toilet, or do other household chores.[484]

Still, Nee's health continued to decline. Eventually, he could no longer climb the slight slope leading up to the cafeteria, and Wu had to get him his three meals a day. Still, Nee's characteristic intelligence and humor seem to have remained. Wu recalled Nee saying, "If someone asks me which page a certain saying of Chairman Mao's might be found on, I know them all." Nee then poked fun at his own diminished abilities by saying, "I cannot serve the people in other ways, but at least in this one way I can serve them."[485] Finally, in 1972, Nee was transferred alone to Shan Xia Pu, an even more remote labor camp, ostensibly designated for the old and infirm. He died, probably of his heart condition, a few days later, either on May 30th or 31st of 1972.

---

[482] Wu Youqi Interview.
[483] Wu, *Poke Feiteng*, 96–97.
[484] Wu, *Poke Feiteng*, 115–116.
[485] Wu, *Poke Feiteng*, 116–117.

Toward the end of his imprisonment, Nee was allowed to write a few letters to his family. As expected, they touched on his desire to see his relatives, his practical needs for food and medicine, and his feelings for Charity. In 1971, Charity had fallen and broken two ribs, which, exacerbated by her chronic high blood pressure, had led to her death. In one of the rare glimpses into their very private relationship, Nee wrote poignantly to his sister-in-law, "Tomorrow (May 7th) it will be half a year since Sister Hui [Charity's] passing. The changes over this last half year have been too great. In thinking over the past and turning over the things she left behind, I cannot stop feeling grief in my heart. Over these last twenty years, the fact that I could not serve her even once will always be the regret of my whole life. In everything I let her down and caused her hardship."[486] Little is known about the relationship between Watchman and Charity, but it is clear that she was a source of comfort to him. Their loyalty and devotion during his two decades in prison are the best hints that remain as to the nature of their marriage.

At the time of Charity's death, China was still in the midst of the Cultural Revolution and all religious services and activities had been forbidden for years. As with his behavior in general, Nee's letters carefully avoided any mention of God or theological topics, but a sensitive reader can find at least two meaningful references, small glimpses into Nee's mindset during his final years and days in prison. In one letter, Nee wrote that "In my sickness, I really miss my own family and want to be with them. But I submit to the arrangement of my environment."[487] Finally, in his last letter, possibly written on the very day of his death, Nee wrote, "In my sickness, my heart still rejoices, please do not worry. I continue to do my best to not be upset over my illness."[488]

These understated expressions befit a life and theology based around seeing and embracing all environments, especially human interactions, as being arranged by God. Nee taught consistently that the purpose of such arrangements was for Christians to learn to deny the self, and that in this way, the spirit would be released, and the soul transformed. During twenty years in the Communist prison and labor camp system, Nee applied the lessons he taught over a lifetime. He refused to resist and even positively submitted to authority, seeing God even in difficult and apparently unjust situations. And in the very end, he faced terminal illness and expressed his painful regrets regarding his marriage while still trying to comfort his sister-in-law, asking her not to worry. Nee's last words affirmed the duality of his condition: the struggle with human physical and psychological frailty, and the transcendence of maintaining joy in the heart.

---

[486] Translated from Letter 2 as reprinted in Witness Lee, *Seer*, 337.
[487] Translated from Letter 2 as reprinted in Witness Lee, *Seer*, 337.
[488] Translated from Letter 8 as reprinted in Witness Lee, *Seer*, 343.

One final note may serve as an epitaph. Nee's nephew, Wu Qing, made the long journey to Shan Xia Pu to collect Nee's belongings and ashes. When he arrived, the work group leader surprised him with the remark, "It seems like he [Nee] killed himself. There's a suicide note as proof." Wu Qing was quite surprised, since the phone call to the family had indicated sickness as the cause of death.

Because of his poor health, Nee's effects had included various medicines, which may have caused some misunderstanding by suggesting the possibility of intentional overdose. Furthermore, Christianity had always been a small minority religion and was almost completely invisible to most Chinese during the Cultural Revolution. The work group leader thus ended up misreading a triumphant declaration of faith as an explanation of motive for suicide.

In any case, the official showed Wu Qing the small scrap of paper that Nee had left under his pillow. Recognizing its significance, Wu Qing quickly memorized the contents of the note and wrote them down as soon as he had the opportunity. The paper stated: "Christ is the Son of God. He died to redeem humanity. He rose after three days. This is the greatest truth in the universe. I die believing in Christ."[489]

---

[489] Wu Qing's note is reproduced in Wu, *Poke Feiteng*, 143. The final phrase, 我信基督而死, contains some ambiguity. Its natural force is to indicate causality, ergo, "I die *because* I believe in Christ." The work group leader was likely ignorant of Christian discourse and culture and seems to have understood something along the lines of "I die so that I can be with Christ." Preserving the causal force in another sense indicates that Nee understood himself to be a martyr, especially since he was offered freedom at least once for denying his faith.

Legacies

Nee's death did not mark the end of his influence. This chapter offers a few brief forays into some of Nee's posthumous legacies to trace the broad shapes of his continuing influence on the world. In particular, these legacies will focus on theological appraisals of Nee's thought and give an example of the lived experiences of one of Nee's Chinese followers. Finally, Nee's influences on global Christianities outside the Sinosphere will be explored in three different cases, as well as the institutions that have come to embody his heritage of teachings and practices.

Theology

The reception of Nee's teachings continues to provoke lively theological conversation and debate. This work has traced the development of Nee's ideas in the context of his life and has adopted Nee's own perspective to explain the formation of his teachings. Accordingly, the presentation of Nee's writings up to this point is one that is broadly acceptable to most of his followers. Nevertheless, Nee's legacy includes important critics and detractors as well. Although significant engagement with theological debates lies outside the scope of this book, some general comments and observations can sketch the contours of Nee's theological legacy.

Many of the more detailed theological critiques of Nee come from his fellow evangelicals, whose differences with Nee often turn on some of the finer points of evangelical theology. Nee is one of the more famous representatives of Keswick theology, with its unique emphasis on sanctification. The Keswick position lies in the contested space between Reformed theologies that emphasize the persistence of sin and holiness spiritualities that focus on the possibilities of holiness, perfection, and transcendence. Like other Keswick teachers, Nee argued both for the continuing effects of sin during human life and for the need for Christians to experience progress in living holiness.[490]

---

[490] A recent example of this kind of critique is Stephen Williams, "The Contribution of Ni Tuosheng (Watchman Nee)," in *Shaping Christianity in Greater China: Indigenous Christians in Focus*, Paul Woods ed. (Minneapolis, MN: Fortress Press, 2017). For a more general overview of the intra-evangelical theological issues involved, see Dieter et al., *Five Views on Sanctification* (Grand Rapids, MI: Zondervan, 1987).

The Spiritual Person. Paul H B Chang, Oxford University Press. © Oxford University Press 2026.
DOI: 10.1093/9780197793664.003.0008

Nee's ecclesiological claims have also attracted some critical attention. Because of the diverse nature of Christian ecclesiology, such criticisms are difficult to summarize. In general, it can be said that Nee's most striking contribution to Christian ecclesiology was his principle of the local church or one church in each city. Nee emphasized the local church as a concrete way to practice and maintain the unity of the one universal church. As contemporary Christianity appears more fractured than ever, the vast majority of Christians have obviously ignored or rejected such appeals. Those who have been convinced by Nee's core ecclesiological claims have tended to become his followers, while many other Christians have remained unconvinced, preferring their own ecclesiological justifications ranging from apostolic tradition to personal preference or convenience.

Finally, it is worth spending some time to consider a recurring critique of Nee's work that seems to cut to the heart of his theology, in particular, his foundational claims about the distinction between the soul and the spirit. One of the first to raise this objection was theologian Wing Hung Lam, whose early, thoughtful engagement with the whole of Nee's oeuvre helped guide the theological conversation to follow. Lam characterizes Nee's thought as "spiritual theology" because "Nee believed that the essence of Christianity was not creeds, traditions, rituals, or institutions, but rather, a kind of spiritual reality. If this reality were present, so was Christianity, if it were missing, so was Christianity."[491] Lam accurately portrays Nee's understanding of this spiritual reality as being rooted in his theological anthropology. For Nee, Christians could participate in this spiritual essence of Christianity because they were endowed with a human spirit, distinct from the soul and able to contact the spiritual realm.

Lam criticizes Nee's perspective, however, for over-emphasizing the distinction between the soul and the spirit as two different facets of the human being. In Lam's view, "The Bible is not a book of psychology, and does not engage in any analysis of the structure of humanity, but only uses various phrases such as 'spirit,' 'soul,' and 'body' to describe the different activities of human beings in their lives." Thus, Lam suggests that the most accurate biblical perspective on the human being would be an integrative anthropology, in which the spirit, soul, and body, rather than being understood as three separate parts of the human, would be better understood as three aspects of human activity, and that "each aspect represents the whole person."[492]

There are two responses to Lam's argument. The first, more straightforward response is to simply point out the texts in which the Bible, in the Pauline writings especially, *does* seem to engage in something like psychology. For instance, in the second chapter of First Corinthians, Paul conducts an extended discourse

---

[491] Lam, *Shuling Shenxue*, 278.
[492] Lam, *Shuling Shenxue*, 279–280.

about the difference between the spiritual Christian and the soulish Christian. The writer of Hebrews, meanwhile, seems to approvingly mark the scriptures as a tool for dividing the soul from the spirit. Without entering a definite judgment, it is probably fair to say that the extent to which the Bible is concerned with making psychological claims is open to debate. Thus, Lam's summary conclusion that the Bible "does not engage in any analysis of the structure of humanity" is oversimplified.

At another level, Lam's concern for a more integrative anthropology appropriately highlights a basic concern about Nee's teachings. At the crux of the issue is the balance between two possible depictions of the human being. Is the individual human being a whole, integral unit, or are individual humans conflicted and divided within themselves? To give Nee's theological critics their due, certain passages of Nee's writings seem to be describing a deep, ontological chasm between the spiritual and the soulish, as if God is only active in the spirit, while leaving the psychological and material realms outside of God's purview.

In the larger context of his work, of course, this is a matter of emphasis. Nee does not actually deny that human beings are integral wholes. In fact, his teaching about salvation reunifying the spirit, soul, and body under the singular will of God seems to presuppose not only the possibility but even the desirability of integrity and wholeness. Nee also approvingly notes the positive functions of the soul when it works in tandem with the spirit.[493] Conversely, even though Lam supports an integrative anthropology, he also feels the need to distinguish between the "essential nature" of the human, as good and created by God, and the "existential nature" of the human, in which the person is "completely separated from God."[494] Most Christian theologies thus recognize that the Bible, the Christian tradition, and human experience all encompass a range of possibilities for the human person, from seamless, integrated wholeness to complexity and internal division.

A final note of clarification may offer a helpful heuristic to theological appraisals of Nee in general. Many theological discussions of Nee's writings have engaged with perceived inconsistencies in his thought, such as the switch from the Antioch to the Jerusalem model of church organization or the ramifications of a rigid insistence on separating the soul from the spirit. Such "inconsistencies" have less to do with Nee's own concerns than they have to do with the values placed on terminological precision and systematic metaphysics found in much of Western academic theology. Like many other non-Western Christians, Nee's personal priorities were otherwise.

---

[493] For one such instance, in *NTSWJ* 62, 151–154, Nee speaks at length about the necessity of the "functions of the mind."

[494] Lam, *Shuling Shenxue*, 281.

Almost all of Nee's work was crafted in response to the pressing demands of actual congregations, individual Christians, and society at large. Probably the most notable exception to this rule was *The Spiritual Person*, which was an attempt to summarize Nee's ideas during what he presumed was the end of his life. Even in this regard, later in his life, Nee repudiated *The Spiritual Person* for being "too analytical."[495] Thus, Nee should be understood to be much more of a contextual or occasional theologian. Apparent "contradictions" in his ideas or terminology can usually be explained by thinking about the wider context or specific occasion to which he tried to respond.

Lived Experiences

This book has also recorded some of the developments between Nee and the congregations that supported him throughout his life. Although Nee's imprisonment and death ended their direct interactions, Nee's loyal followers continued his legacy forward posthumously. A brief institutional history will be offered at the end of this chapter, but it is also possible to seek more granular insight into the lived experiences of Assembly Hall members. Since Nee's story necessarily focused more on his interactions with urban, educated followers, one example may serve as a point of reference for those in the Assemblies from more rural, humble backgrounds.

In 1921, Zhang Lijiao (章立姣) was born in Dongan Village (东安) in Taishun County (泰顺), part of Wenzhou Prefecture in Zhejiang Province. She was raised in a Christian family associated with the China Inland Mission. Her family had become Christian when her grandmother was seriously ill. Christians came and cared for her and preached the gospel to her. Upon her recovery, the entire family converted. As was the custom in rural China, when Lijiao was eighteen, she was sent to nearby Dongxi Village (东溪) in an arranged marriage to another Christian, two years her junior.

Her new family, the Zhangs (章) belonged to the local Assembly Hall and quickly brought her into its customs. She was baptized within the year. The vicissitudes of rural life soon followed. Within the next two years, her father-in-law passed, she conceived and bore a son, and then her young husband died, leaving Zhang a young widow and mother at the age of twenty. She would never remarry, dedicating herself instead to serving her family and the church.

During her childhood with the China Inland Mission, she had learned a number of hymns but never really understood her faith. After some time with

---

[495] Lee, *Collected Works of Witness Lee* 1958, vol. 1 (Anaheim, CA: Living Stream Ministry, 2021), 205.

the Little Flock, Zhang came to understand that they were "different from the denominations" and should be kept separate from them. She also came to feel assured of her own salvation, knowing that she had eternal life. Zhang felt empowered to spread this good news, going out with members of the Dongxi congregation into neighboring villages.

Each evangelistic team had about five or six members. As in the apostolic commission, they would go door to door, moving on when they were rejected and entering the home when they found a willing audience.[496] News of the out-of-town visitors would spread quickly. If they spoke at the north gate of the town on their first day, by the second day, when they visited the south gate, they would find people on the street and in the stores and tea shops waiting to hear their message. Publicly, the brothers preached the gospel, while the sisters listened. In private, she and the other sisters on the team would minister to the women, praying, singing hymns, and teaching them to read and understand the revelation of the Bible.

Although Dongxi Village was geographically isolated, located in the narrow valleys of southwestern Wenzhou, the local church remained connected to the larger movement. Dongxi maintained subscriptions to Nee's periodicals and publications, and the individual members of the congregation would read and borrow the new writings as they arrived from the Gospel Bookroom. Thus, when Watchman Nee announced that he would be holding a training in Mount Guling in 1948, the Dongxi Assembly felt that it should send at least two representatives. Since the chosen representatives were an older man and woman who were not married to each other, however, it was felt that another person should accompany them on their trip, which would be a journey of at least three days. Sister Zhang was chosen, and her experience at Guling became a highlight of her Christian life.

Zhang would later recall many details of their time at Guling—how the Dongxi contingent arrived late because of a typhoon, the practical services they engaged in (brothers clearing brush, sisters raising silkworms), and even how they were taught to pay attention to their clothing—that is, to dress neatly and cleanly. Nee himself impressed her with his caring oversight—she mentioned that he was loving and that he prayed for each of the participants. He also left a lasting impression of his spiritual insight. Zhang mentioned a number of cases in which Nee's diagnoses of certain attendees' spiritual conditions proved prescient. Nee claimed that one seemingly eloquent brother had "no ministry" and, in the years to come, the brother proved "unable to stand." Another sister was warned to "expand her capacity" and ended up enduring great suffering. Zhang concluded that "When we came to Brother Nee, it seemed like he knew

---

[496] Some of the relevant passages can be found in Matthew 10, Mark 6, Luke 9–10, and John 10.

everything about us—your situation is one way, yours is another way. Everyone was scared when it was their turn to be judged."

When Zhang returned from Guling, she continued to itinerate. Her stature may have been boosted by her growing experience and her training by Nee at Guling. Throughout the 1950s, she walked through all of neighboring Pingyang County, sometimes in mixed-gender groups, and sometimes leading groups of women to visit and teach their younger sisters in so-called perfecting meetings. Having been trained by Nee, she was now learning to train others. Her message was simple: "You must know our God. You must know his overcoming. He is the more-than-overcoming God. Our God is strong and capable. We Christians must not fear, but rather believe. Don't look at the environment, don't look at yourself, and don't look at the people around you. The Lord has given us a mind that can bear suffering. It is all God's grace, there is nothing good in us at all."

Zhang's citation of a "mind to suffer" was one of the few times she discussed a theological matter that bore the marks of Nee's distinct teachings.[497] Such a "mind to suffer" was repeatedly tested during times of intense political movements. The Zhang family owned some land and were therefore classified as petty landowners. Zhang's own personal, material circumstances were always humble. When Nee had called on his followers to "hand over" their possessions, she had nothing more than a few articles of clothing to "hand over," which she promptly donated. Nevertheless, her status as both a nominal landowner and an outspoken Christian could put her in a tenuous position.

In our interview, Zhang repeatedly emphasized the fact that she held no grudges or even criticisms; she just wanted to let go and forgive as the Bible commanded. Nevertheless, she admitted that over the years, she had suffered quite a lot, being forced to wear denunciatory placards and march on many occasions while people shamed her and shouted. On one memorable occasion, around the time of the Cultural Revolution, she was forced to sit on a stool next to a fishpond in the winter. Her interrogators asked her to renounce Christianity, and when she refused, she was thrown into the pond. This happened over and over, while her son stood nearby and shouted encouragement to stand firm in the faith. Zhang believes she would have died had the local police not arrived to stop the demonstration.[498]

---

[497] Nee discusses the importance of a "mind to suffer" in NTSWJ 52. Another interesting evocation of Nee's unique theology came in Zhang's nickname for her son, Songling. The Chinese characters of his official name (松灵) mean "Pine" and "Spirit," but Zhang said that "We always call him 'Congling (从灵)' instead," using the characters for "Follow" and "Spirit."

[498] Interview with Zhang Lijiao, March 13, 2013.

Global Christianities

As important as Nee has been to Chinese Christians, one of the distinguishing legacies of his work has been its translation and flourishing in non-Chinese Christian cultures. Three examples, both historical and contemporary, follow. One special edition of *The Normal Christian Life* published in 1973 had a back cover entirely devoted to an endorsement from "Dr. Jerry Falwell." Falwell wrote:

> Shortly after God led me to establish the Thomas Road Baptist Church in Lynchburg, Virginia, in June, 1965, someone gave me a copy of **The Normal Christian Life** [*sic*]. At that time, I was searching for a deeper understanding of what the Christian life is all about. I can sincerely say this book has been used of God more effectively in my life than any book outside the Bible itself. Watchman Nee has put into words the true simplicity of the victorious Christian life. His emphasis is "Christ in you."
>
> Every new convert ought to read this book immediately after his conversion. If I had known of this book after my conversion in 1952, I could have avoided wasting many, many years struggling to please God through Christian service. Down through the years, I have distributed hundreds of copies of this book to my friends. The best description of this book is "revelation." There is no question in my mind but what God has given to Watchman Nee special wisdom in defining the dynamic of the Christian life as no other man has. You will probably read the book several times. Each time, the Holy Spirit will make the indwelling of Christ a more blessed reality to you.[499]

It is important to note that this endorsement predated Falwell's public involvement in national politics. Instead, in 1973, his congregation was becoming "notably more middle class" with the college he founded drawing "more highly educated students, faculty, and their families," to his congregation. He had also begun his explicit shift away from supporting racial segregation.[500] In this transitional context, he found *The Normal Christian Life* more helpful "than any book outside the Bible itself," certainly the highest praise possible for a conservative, Christian ministry. Falwell quite accurately summarizes Nee's message as "Christ in you"—a simple way to describe the spiritual union that Nee emphasized. Falwell also regretted the fact that he had not read the book earlier,

---

[499] Watchman Nee, *Normal Christian Life,* The Old-Time Gospel Hour Special Edition—Not For Sale (Fort Washington, PA: Christian Literature Crusade, 1973).

[500] Susan Friend Harding, *The Book of Jerry Falwell: Fundamentalist Language and Politics* (Princeton: Princeton University Press, 2000), 16, 22. Harding also notes that by the 1980s, Falwell employed about a thousand people, including ghostwriters. Since, by 1973, his congregation already had over ten thousand members, it is possible that this endorsement was only written in Falwell's name. (Harding, *The Book of Jerry Falwell,* 15).

else he could have "avoided wasting many, many years struggling to please God through Christian service."

Because Nee so carefully distinguished the hard labor of the soul from the effortless victory in the spirit, his work had a special appeal for struggling but earnest Christians. By accurately "defining the dynamic of the Christian life," Falwell saw the possibility of escape from the frustrating, repetitive cycle of failure and self-effort in the Christian life. As a result, he distributed Nee's book widely.

A very different example of the reach of Nee's ministry could be found in Dublin, Ireland, in 1976. At that time, four high school students in Mount Temple Comprehensive School came together to form a rock band. The school was Dublin's first non-sectarian school, and the boys came from different religious backgrounds: two were Protestant, one Roman Catholic, and one was the product of a mixed marriage. The band they formed would eventually become famous as U2, one of the best-selling musical acts in history, and well known for the spiritual imagery in their lyrics.

While the four boys were still together at school, Mount Temple appears to have undergone a powerful revival, reminiscent of Nee's own school experience. Paul Hewson, also known as Bono, recalled those days, "Charismatic things started happening. That was when we became involved in the Shalom group. We were studying scriptures and it was amazing. When everyone was learning how to get served and how to score, we were all completely wrapped up in this."[501]

As part of the involvement in this charismatic revival, three of the band members joined the Shalom Group, beginning an intense personal affiliation with Christianity that has continued through the decades of the band's success. That engagement with Christianity was so strong that at one point, in 1982, the three briefly decided they would refuse to tour to support the release of their second album. In a later interview, Bono explained:

> We were just being pulled in two different directions. A lot of it was based on the idea of the ego. We'd been reading a lot of Watchman Nee, a Chinese Christian mystic. His idea was: "Unless the seed shall die and be crushed into the earth, it cannot bear fruit."
>
> Rock 'n' roll had this idea: "It's *me!*" You know, "Look at me, 'cause I'm looking at you, motherfucker!" Like, "Out of my way, looking out for number one, "I Can't Get No Satisfaction!" Watchman Nee's attitude to that would be: "So what? What's so important about you anyway?" (*laughs*)
>
> So it was like we were being torn in two. We felt almost subconscious pressure being applied to us by a lot of people we looked up to within that spiritual

---

[501] Steve Beard, "Bono: The Gospel of Heaven and Hell," in *Spiritual Journeys: How Faith has Influenced Twelve Music Icons* (Lake Mary, FL: Relevant Media Group, 2003), 243.

community that we were in and out of. In the end, I realized it was bullshit, that what these people were getting close to with this idea was denial, rather than willful surrender. It was denial, which is the next-door neighbor to self-flagellation, and that awful idea that "through pain is gain." Yes, there is pain. Yes, you may gain from it. But you don't get into your car looking for a traffic jam. (*laughs*)[502]

Bono understood Nee to be a Chinese mystic and quite accurately summarized another key aspect of Nee's ministry—the opposition to the self or the ego and the release of life that results from that obedience to God. Popular music was obviously an industry built on promoting large personalities and egos, and Nee's spirituality was focused on the liberation that came from selflessness. Interestingly, Bono did not seem to disagree with Nee's basic claims, only the application of those claims as interpreted by members of the Shalom Group. In fact, Bono's description of denial as opposed to willful surrender was very close to Nee's own arguments against asceticism. For Nee, as for Bono, true broken-ness came from accepting what happened in one's life naturally, rather than from seeking out discipline or suffering.

Later, in an introduction to a set of excerpts from the Psalms published in 1999, Bono wrote suggestively of his search for "the way into my spirit" as well as his understanding of his own beliefs: "My religion could not be fiction but it had to transcend facts. I could be mystical, but not mythical and definitely not ritual."[503] It seemed that Nee's mystical teachings concerning the transcendent realities encountered in the human spirit continued to rouse the Irish musician who had encountered them as a young man.

From Falwell to Bono, very different audiences found aspects of Nee's writings to be revelatory and life changing. Earnest fundamentalist Christians might find in Nee's work an escape from the endless cycle of failure and the inability to meet God's standards for holiness. For them, Nee presented the possibility of spontaneous, effortless service that flowed out of recognizing the crucifixion of the self and the unity with Christ in the spirit. Desperate spiritual seekers might also see deliverance in Nee's message. For them, understanding the human spirit offered a basis for the rejection of the ego, while holding out hope for mystical transcendence. Across the spectrum of Western religion and spirituality, Nee's message found its audiences. But as the larger discourse of evangelical and charismatic Christianity spilled over the boundaries of the West, so too did Nee's particular message within that conversation.

---

[502] https://www.motherjones.com/media/1989/05/bono-bites-back-0/, accessed on July 15, 2023.
[503] Bono, Introduction to Pocket Canons Psalms (Edinburgh: Canongate Books, 1999), ix, as quoted in Steve Beard, "Bono," 254.

Eventually, the pace of the publication of Nee's work slowed, especially in Europe and North America, where its peak crested around the 1960s and 1970s. Nevertheless, Nee's work is now printed in more languages than ever, and it continues to find audiences in unexpected places. A final example illustrates this latest generation of Nee's followers.

During the late 1990s, a group of students regularly gathered as the Christian Students Fellowship (CSF) in what was then the Faculty of Natural Sciences at Ethiopia's premier institute of tertiary education, Addis Ababa University. The Fellowship was composed of over one hundred students who had largely come from a Protestant background, against the backdrop of the successful spread of evangelical and Pentecostal groups among the traditionally Ethiopian Orthodox people.

In 1998, some of these students began finding Watchman Nee's English books on their parents' bookshelves and circulated these works among themselves. They started with *The Spiritual Man* and continued with *The Normal Christian Life, The Breaking of the Outer Man and the Release of the Spirit,* and *The Glorious Church*, among others. Nee's works quickly changed the young Fellowship's outlook on Christianity, answering some of their basic questions and reorienting their perspectives on key Christian doctrines.[504]

One leader of the Christian Student Fellowship in those days was Jegnaw Zeggeye. He had grown up in an Ethiopian Orthodox family with a mother who believed that she had suffered for years from demonic possession. She would fall seriously ill whenever she went to large events like weddings, funerals, or celebrations of new births. Similarly, the demon would strike her with sickness if it was not appeased with specific daily rituals and yearly sacrifices. Zeggeye's father had taken her to various healers and witches to no avail. Then, around 1992, when Jegnaw was fourteen, local Pentecostal Christians had visited the family and cast out the demon. The family joyfully held a burning to destroy all the implements and household goods that had been related to the demon and began to attend the Pentecostal congregation.[505]

Throughout high school, Zeggeye read his Bible daily and attended church services regularly. Still, he recalled that he was not clear as to the fundamental question of whether he could lose his salvation. When he read Nee's work on the "Assurance, Security, and Joy of Salvation," at university, he experienced a rush of relief and happiness, "the return of my joy of salvation." But Nee's influence went further still. Like many of the other members of the Fellowship, Zeggeye recalls, "I was trying to improve myself, trying to be better, to be a good person

---

[504] https://newsletters.lsm.org/having-this-ministry/issues/Jun2023-021/lords-move-ethiopia. html, accessed on July 16, 2023. Interview with Jegnaw Zeggeye, July 16, 2023.
[505] Interview with Jegnaw Zeggeye.

and a good Christian. That was our struggle." In the midst of this struggle, Nee's words seemed to offer the key to transcendence: "We saw the light that we didn't need to be a good Christian, we just needed to die. The cross was the solution for dealing with the soul-life. And we were already crucified with Christ! That was really a relief and a joy for all of us."[506]

Armed with this new perspective on the fundamental principles of the Christian life, the young group of students no longer invited other Christian ministers to come speak to them, finding that traditional Christian exhortations to morality and better behavior now seemed counter-productive. Instead, Zeggeye and other leaders within the group took over, preaching and leading Bible studies based on their understanding of Nee's work. As their engagement with Nee's teachings deepened, they became convinced by *The Orthodoxy of the Church* that God was not satisfied that they would simply maintain a student fellowship but rather that "The Lord's desire is the church, and this church needs to be on the ground of oneness, with the reality of the Spirit, and that the boundary of the church should be the city."[507]

The group now began to preach regularly on this theme. Unsurprisingly, the students found that other Protestant groups that had previously welcomed them now began to shut their doors. Nevertheless, they were undeterred. "Our impression was that Brother Watchman Nee got into prison and he spent twenty years in prison and that everyone had forgotten about him and his ministry. Yet somehow, the Lord had brought this ministry to us, so now we had to spread this ministry to the rest of the world." They legally registered themselves as the "Church in Addis Ababa," and around fifty of them began to meet as what they believed to be possibly the only Christian Assembly in the world.

Nee's works had inspired them to such dedication that many of them chose not to pursue romantic relationships, further education, or more serious careers in order to better devote themselves to their mission. Zeggeye said, "We had a sense of absoluteness, of speaking the truth at any cost—whether it would make people happy or not, whether we were accepted or not, we just had this impression: 'If someone wants to continue with us, let him continue, if not, we will still go this way.' We had this absoluteness and impression from Watchman Nee."[508]

Eventually, the group's extensive search for more materials written by Nee led them to Witness Lee's press, Living Stream Ministry, the publisher of the most extensive collection of Nee's works. Through Living Stream Ministry, they also came to be welcomed into the global network of Christian Assemblies with visits from contemporary co-workers, who encouraged them to marry and pursue

[506] Interview with Jegnaw Zeggeye.
[507] Interview with Jegnaw Zeggeye.
[508] Interview with Jegnaw Zeggeye.

normal, professional development to help sustain their local congregations for the longer term.

The interventions seem to have been successful, as well as the native leadership, because the Christian Assembly spread rapidly throughout the country. Today, there are over fifteen hundred adult members in dozens of cities throughout the country, with more than two hundred fifty children in the Church in Addis Ababa alone. This success has enabled them to employ full-time Christian ministers, one of whose highest priorities has been to translate the works of Watchman Nee into the major local languages, Amharic and Afan Oromo.[509]

Institutional Legacies

How had Nee's theology spread so quickly around the globe? Between Nee's arrest in 1952 and the arrest of the other national leaders of the Little Flock in 1956, the Little Flock assemblies continued to grow. Historian Joseph Lee has shown how the remaining leaders of the Little Flock still managed to pursue three simultaneous and relatively successful strategies to preserve their congregations in the aftermath of Nee's arrest: They consolidated their internal unity, challenged the government-sponsored Three-Self movements, and worked "to proselytize and recruit members from all social sectors across the country." This even included people in important positions in the lower levels of the government bureaucracy, in a kind of reverse infiltration.[510]

Nee's constant addresses to his co-workers throughout his ministry attested to the fact that he had trained many able followers and trusted them to make their own decisions. There was already a well-developed tradition of local leadership, and the Little Flock congregations did not need Nee's personal guidance to continue, even in adverse circumstances. As they had done for decades, local leaders sensed and reacted to the changing opportunities on the ground. Many congregations began to absorb large numbers from the newly undesirable classes of capitalists, businessmen, landowners, and former Nationalist or GMD officials.[511] This provided an interesting contrast with other Christian groups. For instance, during the same period, the True Jesus Church avoided baptizing "Nationalist agents, corrupt persons, local tyrants, and counterrevolutionaries" to avoid being tarnished by association.[512]

---

[509] Interview with Jegnaw Zeggeye; "Lord's Move to Africa," (April 2022), accessed on July 16, 2023, at https://www.lmafrica.org/images/LMAfrica_Newsletter_April_2022_English.pdf

[510] Lee, "Watchman Nee and the Little Flock," 88–99.

[511] Lee, "Watchman Nee and the Little Flock," 90.

[512] Inouye, *China and the True Jesus*, 206.

Little Flock members continued their traditional focus on retaining their own children in the faith and growing the ranks of the next generation through campus evangelism at high schools and universities. They also managed to spread in regions where official organs of supervision and control were relatively weak—in rural areas and among ethnic minorities along China's vast borders. In 1956, however, government opposition to the Little Flock's independence ramped up significantly. The senior Little Flock leaders who resisted cooperation with the party were arrested *en masse*, and the serious allegations made against Nee were publicly aired in front of large numbers of people in the CCP's public exhibitions.[513]

Much of the rank and file were unconvinced and unshaken. Certainly, many of Nee's followers assumed that the evidence was forged or politically motivated.[514] Still, with the hardline leaders all arrested, only more compromising figures remained. Furthermore, they had the authority of Nee's own words in "How I have changed" to support their position. Many of the Christian Assemblies began to join the government-sponsored umbrella organization for organizing Chinese Protestantism, the Three-Self Patriotic Movement (TSPM). Until the Cultural Revolution in the late 1960s, they maintained their independent self-identity as Christian Assemblies under Nee's teachings while practicing formal compliance with TSPM-sponsored ideology.[515]

During the worst upheavals of the Cultural Revolution, the TSPM, public security offices, and religious affairs bureaus were all shut down, along with many of the basic functions of government. After the terror of the early years of the Cultural Revolution subsided, the relative vacuum in civil society allowed some religious groups to operate more freely without the strict oversight of the early Maoist years. At least one Little Flock leader remembered the later years of the Cultural Revolution as a time of unprecedented growth in his region of Henan and suggested that many other local congregations had had similar experiences. He explained that because the Cultural Revolution had crippled much of China's medical infrastructure, people came to Christians for prayers and healing. Many of those who were miraculously healed ended up converting, along with their families.[516] If true on a larger scale, these facts would suggest that China followed what may be one of the most significant patterns of global Christianity: that is, conversion following divine healing.[517]

---

[513] Ying, *Fandi*, 132–133. Ying suggests that thousands of Christians from across Shanghai may have seen the evidence against Nee in the multiple exhibitions held in the early part of 1956. He also indicates that at least two hundred representatives of the Christian Assemblies were brought in from other parts of China to view the evidence.

[514] Interview with Zhu Rukai, March 16, 2013.

[515] Lee, "Watchman Nee and the Little Flock," 90–92.

[516] Interview with Bai Shuqian and Bai Xinlai, January 2014.

[517] Candy Gunther Brown, *Global Pentecostal and Charismatic Healing* (Oxford: Oxford University Press, 2011).

Unfortunately, much of the history of the period can be reconstructed only with speculation. Historian Melissa Inouye has pointed out that, especially for Christian groups, the Maoist period is characterized by a "dearth of sources" and an "abundance of judgment." The documentary history has been impoverished by the destruction of the Cultural Revolution, while the heightened political stakes of the period have incited significant criticism.[518]

But it is clear that Nee's co-workers flourished outside of China. Nee's connections to the diasporic community reached back into at least the early 1920s, when he visited Malaysia with his mother. Especially during the 1950s, the growing Chinese diaspora proved to be a receptive audience for Nee's co-workers who worked outside of CCP control. Simon Meek in the Philippines, Faithful Luke in Singapore and Malaysia, and Wei Guangxi (K. H. Weigh) in Hong Kong all continued to find success and grow their local congregations. Probably the most significant concentration of Chinese people outside the mainland, however, was in Taiwan, where much of the GMD government and its armed forces had fled after their defeat.

There Nee had sent his most trusted co-worker, Witness Lee. Lee had been a catalyst of revival everywhere he went, and it was no different in a place and time that were primed for revival. Just as ex-GMD members on the mainland were joining the Christian Assemblies in large numbers, many of the refugees on the Taiwanese island were primed to reconsider Christianity in the face of their enormous losses. While membership in all of Taiwan's major Christian churches grew during the 1950s, the Christian Assemblies grew the fastest.

When Lee first began working there in 1949, there were only about thirty members in the Taipei assembly, the largest on the island. Within a year, there were nine hundred members in various localities throughout Taiwan, and by the mid-1950s, they numbered twenty-five thousand.[519] By 1970, there were forty-seven thousand Christians who counted themselves to be members of the Christian Assemblies on the Taiwanese island.[520] They had become the third largest Christian group in Taiwan, after the Roman Catholic Church and the Presbyterian Church in Taiwan, both of which had gotten a considerable head start, having operated continuously on the island since the mid-nineteenth century.

As the number of Christian Assemblies in Taiwan continued to grow, the island began to act as a hub for the movement, which was rapidly becoming international. Lee frequently sent co-workers to Southeast Asian countries, and

---

[518] Inouye, *China and the True Jesus*, 188–189.

[519] Witness Lee, *Life-study of 1 & 2 Timothy, Titus, Philemon* (Anaheim, CA: Living Stream Ministry, 2001), 14–15.

[520] Zhu Zunhong and Zhou Xiuhuan, *Li Changshou Xiansheng Xingyi* (Taipei: Guo shi guan, 2010), 38.

from 1950 to 1961, he himself spent three to four months in Manila each year. Furthermore, in 1958, 1960, and 1961, Lee made short trips to the United States, where Chinese immigrants had founded local congregations on the West Coast and in New York City. In 1962, Lee decided to immigrate to the United States himself, becoming a naturalized citizen and spending much of his time visiting congregations where Nee's reputation and writings had prepared significant audiences for his message.[521]

Lee's decision to immigrate was partially prompted by his recognition that Nee was garnering a significant reputation in the American evangelical and Pentecostal subcultures. During the Cold War, the fact that Nee was a Christian who was imprisoned by Communists lent him considerable credit among more conservative Christians. At the same time, his Chinese heritage, principled objection to denominations, and devotional embrace of highly mystical themes meant that he could also be read against mainstream Christianity, an intriguing proposition in an age marked by searches for religious alternatives to traditional Western religions. And indeed, in the late 1960s and throughout the 1970s, both evangelical religion and resistance to traditional Christian formality coalesced in the form of the Jesus People movement, one of the formative events of twentieth-century American religion.

Within this large and growing youth subculture, Lee quickly gained a significant audience, drawing thousands of followers from across the United States. As was true of the Little Flock tradition, Lee focused much of his evangelistic attention on young people and college campuses. Nee's and Lee's extensive production of literature proved especially attractive to literate, thoughtful Christians.

Meanwhile, Southern California in general and Orange County in particular were developing into a base for American and international evangelicalism.[522] Lee made his own headquarters in Anaheim in 1974. There, he continued to develop his ideas, adding new teachings and practices to the tradition he had inherited from Nee. Lee also directed the international spread of the local churches and their printed publications. Largely due to Lee's influence, Christian Assemblies with indigenous leadership can now be found in all fifty states of the United States and on all six continents of the world. Leaders have translated and promulgated Nee and Lee's writings in dozens of languages.[523]

In the meantime, during the waning years of the Cultural Revolution, religious actors within China gained increased space for operation. Lee's writings

---

[521] Zhu and Zhou, *Li Changshou*, 40.

[522] Larry Eskridge, *God's Forever Family: The Jesus People Movement in America* (Oxford: Oxford University Press, 2013), see especially pp. 54ff. See also Lisa McGirr, *Suburban Warriors: The Origins of the New American Right* (Princeton: Princeton University Press, 2015).

[523] Yi Liu, "Globalization of Chinese Christianity: A Study of Watchman Nee and Witness Lee's Ministry," *Asia Journal of Theology*, April, 30 (1): 109–110.

and audio tapes were smuggled back into China. In that religious vacuum, his articulate preaching and accessible teachings were like fire on dry tinder. They sparked powerful and unexpected currents of indigenous religion.

The resurgent Little Flock movement splintered, with the majority, now called the "Old Assembly Hall," rejecting Lee's developments of Nee's doctrine. A significant minority, however, now called the "New Assembly Hall" or the "Shouters," enthusiastically adopted Lee's teachings. As their derogatory nickname suggested, some of Lee's followers were especially taken with his teaching concerning "calling on the name of the Lord." They took to exuberantly and repetitively proclaiming Jesus's name, which shocked more settled sensibilities and occasionally led to bitter squabbles. Both the Old and New Assembly Hall forged links with amenable congregations of the Christian Assemblies overseas.

At the same time, more creative religious leaders also adapted Lee's ideas. They leveraged the popularity and the dynamism of Lee's teachings to support their own visions and started their own sects. Many of the most popular, so-called evil cults or *xiejiao* in China today have genealogies that lead through either Old or New Assembly Hall congregations. The founders of the Established King (*Beiliwang*), Lord God Sect (*Zhushenjiao*), Disciples' Society (*Mentuhui*) or Narrow Gate in the Wilderness (*Kuangye Zhaimen*), and Eastern Lightning (*Dongfang Shandian*) or Almighty God (*Quanneng Shen*), all spent time in or around Little Flock congregations.[524] Their colorful teachings included intricate new celestial pantheons, strict institutional hierarchies, and even the claims of charismatic leaders to be Christ reincarnated. Most of them no longer recognize either Nee or Lee as their founders, and Lee himself strongly denounced their deviations from Christian orthodoxy.[525]

Today, Nee's institutional legacy is vibrant and diverse. There are growing, dynamic congregations throughout the world that directly pay Nee homage and try to follow his teachings while printing, translating, and promoting his writings. There are other groups with genealogies that reach into the Christian Assemblies, but whose debt to the movement is only tangential. With these groups, Nee's inheritance may simply be a general orientation toward Christian discourse, a practice of close-knit congregational life, apocalyptic expectations, or the hope of spiritual transcendence.

Prospects for the future indicate continuous growth and proliferation because of two larger trends. First, the Chinese state is unlikely to return to the levels of social control and the monopoly over the civic sphere that characterized Maoist

---

[524] Lian, *Redeemed by Fire*, 220–230.
[525] Beiliwang (Established King), Zhushenjiao (Lord God), Kuangye Zhaimen (Narrow Gate in the Wilderness), Sanbanpuren (Three Grades of Servants), and Dongfang Shandian/Quanneng Shen (Eastern Lightning/Almighty God) can all be traced to founders who had some interaction with the New Assembly Hall in China.

China. Instead, the contested civic space of contemporary China has proven especially amenable to religion in general and to Protestant Christianity in particular. Second, as the demographic balance of Christianity shifts from Europe and North America to the other continents of the world, Nee's voice and his concern for creating a Christian message without illicit Western interventions and imperialism have grown increasingly relevant and resonant.

About one hundred years ago, a young man in China was captivated by a vision of local churches—an ideal Christian society in an imperfect world. He was never formally trained, but somehow, between his Bible, his Christian mentors, and his own spiritual resources, he crafted a theology that began to captivate scattered audiences in China. Throughout his lifetime, the largest group of followers he ever gathered in one place may not have topped two thousand. Fifty years after his death, there are certainly thousands if not tens of thousands of congregations around the world that are inspired by his teachings. Nee himself would probably have found a certain satisfaction with his simultaneous obscurity and popularity—nearly his first Christian lesson was that the way of the cross leads to spiritual life. It has been in death, even more than in life, that Nee has attained his spiritual aspiration, to be the buried seed that bears much fruit.

On Sources

This dissertation relies heavily on the materials printed in Nee's name, particularly the Chinese *Ni Tuosheng Wenji* (NTSWJ) and the English version of the same, the *Collected Works of Watchman Nee* (CWWN). Both the NTSWJ and the CWWN were published by Nee's followers as a central repository for all of Nee's writings and materials that had previously been published in a piecemeal fashion through various publishers. Each new set of materials within the two series is also prefaced by helpful introductory material explaining the sources and context of that particular volume.

Although the NTSWJ and the CWWN represent the most complete and most carefully edited versions of Nee's works, they are marked by several limitations. During his lifetime, Nee published a number of periodicals. Although the NTSWJ and CWWN reproduce those articles that were written and sometimes translated by Nee himself, they do not reprint the issues as a whole. As a result, the NTSWJ and CWWN are missing some translated articles and almost all of the essays written by Nee's ministerial colleagues or "co-workers" (*tonggong*), as he preferred to call them. Other contextual materials may also be missing.

For those who are seeking an exact representation of Nee's original thoughts and words, one of the most significant challenges is posed by the portions of the NTSWJ and CWWN that are taken from handwritten notes of Nee's oral preaching. Most of this source material has not been made accessible to the public. Although my own references are by no means exhaustive, I can offer some analysis on the editing of the NTSWJ and the CWWN by giving an extended example. I will first reproduce two Chinese passages and then give their translations in English.

The following is a transcription of notes in the hand of Lin Yitian (Weigh Lin Yi-tian), the wife of one of Nee's co-workers:

1949   29/8 拜一晚

八時

1. 周康耀:

問: 勝不过在講台之感覺

Nee: 棄絕所有 feeling 的生活. F 有時雖是對, 但他也 lie. 所以也要拒絕. 不要從 lie 去找 truth. Satan 有時亦說真理. 但凡從他來的一概拒絕. 因他乃撒謊著. F 要完全 cool down. Outer man 要拆毀.

　　　　灵套魂上. 如手套手套上. 手套必須空. 才能聯起來. 灵要使用魂, 思想, 而他的不空叫灵沒法出來.

The following is the same passage as reproduced in the NTSWJ:

講時：一九四九年八月二十九日晚上(週一)
講地：廣州
關於感覺
學習棄絕過度的感覺
周康耀弟兄問：我自己常常覺得勝不過在講臺上的感覺。
倪弟兄答：你要學習棄絕所有感覺的生活。感覺有時雖然是對的，但基
本上牠乃是虛謊。你不要從虛謊去找真理，因為你不能從虛謊找到真理。
撒但雖然有時也說真理，但凡從他來的都要一概拒絕，因為他乃是撒謊
者；即使他說真理，也是為了要欺騙。你的感覺要完全冷靜下來，這需要
你外面的人被拆毀。
　　靈是套在魂裏，就如手是套在手套裏一樣。手套必須空了，纔能與手聯
起來。手套裏面如果已經有東西，如何叫牠來套手？同樣的，若是靈要使
用魂的思想、情感、意志，而牠們卻不空，裝滿了各種感覺、思想、判
斷，那麼靈就無法出來，你也就很難有正確的判斷。

Now, my own English translation of the handwritten note is as follows. Words and letters written in English in the original notes are reproduced in bold.

1949	29/8 Monday PM
	8 o'clock

1.   Zhou Kangyao

Q: Can't overcome consciousness[, or feelings] on the speaking platform

Nee: Abandon all living by **feeling**. Although F[eelings] are sometimes correct, they also **lie**. Thus, they must be rejected. Do not look for the **truth** from a **lie**. **Satan** sometimes also speaks the truth. But whatever comes from him must be categorically rejected. Because he is a liar. F[eelings] must be totally **cool down. Outer man** must be demolished.

The spirit encases the soul. Like a hand encases a glove. The glove must be empty. Thus [the hand] can connect to it. The spirit wants to use the soul, mind, but its lack of emptiness causes the spirit to have no way to come out.

The editors of the CWWN offer the following:

A TALK WITH CO-WORKERS
FROM HONG KONG AND CANTON
(1)

Date: Monday evening, August 29, 1949
Place: Canton

CONCERNING FEELINGS
Learning Not to Go Along with
Too Many Feelings

Chou Kang-Yao: I am very conscious of myself when I stand on the platform, and I am not able to overcome this feeling.

Watchman Nee: We have to learn to deny living according to feelings. Our feelings may be right some of the time, but in essence they are deceptive. We should not look for truth among deceptions, because we can never find it. Satan can speak some truths, but we have to reject everything that comes from his mouth because in essence he is a liar. Even when he speaks the truth, he speaks it for the purpose of deceiving others. We have to calm down our feelings completely. This requires the breaking of the outer man.

The spirit is surrounded by the soul, just as a hand is surrounded by a glove. A glove must be empty before a hand can get into it. If a glove has something in it, how can it receive a hand? Similarly, if our mind, emotion, and will are filled with thoughts, feelings, and opinions instead of being empty and available, when the spirit needs to use them, it will find itself bound. Under such circumstances, it is hard to have right judgments.

A few apparent discrepancies immediately emerge. Front matter, a title, and section headings have been added. Like many handwritten notes, the source material contains a number of fragmentary, incomplete phrases, which have been combined and polished in the edited material. Generally, this has been done with the help of punctuation, transitions, and additional phrases. Sometimes, entirely new phrases have been added, such as "Even if he speaks the truth, he speaks it for the purpose of deceiving others." Especially at the end of the last paragraph, a substantial number of new terms and clauses have been filled in—a reference to the soul has been redacted and the words "emotions" and "will" have been added. A simple reference to a "lack of emptiness" has been fleshed out with a reference to "thoughts, feelings, decisions" and a final note on the difficulty of making "right judgments."

Upon closer examination, however, these problems are less significant. The front matter only presents information that is already in the note, leaving off only the exact time of day. Likewise, the title and section headings are carefully chosen to organize the material. If the reader is aware that they are editorial emendations, there is little chance of confusion. The addition of such titles and headings is a common practice in scholarly publications of similar material. Edited volumes of the church fathers or the *Classics of Western Spirituality* series adopt similar standards.

In terms of the main text itself, many of the editorial changes correct grammatical errors or make sentence fragments into full thoughts in a straightforward manner. It is true that the phrases "Do not look for the truth from a lie" and "We should not look for truth among deceptions, because we can never find it" are not equivalent. The first phrase is a simple command, aphoristic and vague. The second offers a reason for the aphorism and suggests a more categorical rejection, namely, that it is impossible to find truth from lies. Still, even if the phrases are not equivalent, they are not opposed, and the second may be understood as an earnest attempt to elucidate the former. These additions may also trace back to other source materials. Lin's husband, Wei Guangxi (Weigh Kwang-Hsi), also took notes during some of these meetings, and Witness Lee, who was personally involved in the CWWN's editorial process, may also have been present.[526]

The carefulness of the editors' efforts can also be seen in the two most significant departures from the original text. The original notes suggest that the spirit "encases" or surrounds the soul like a hand "encases" or surrounds a glove. Even if one were not familiar with Nee's theology, which emphatically places the human spirit *within* the human soul, the error in the original notes seems obvious. The confusion may be partially explained by a subsequent passage in which Nee talks about the relationship between the

---

[526] CWWN, Vol. 61, v.

spirit and the soul in similar terms. There, in an analogy similar to that of the glove, Nee suggests that the foot must wear the shoe rather than the shoe wearing the foot. Whether Nee misspoke with regard to the hand and the glove or Lin's notes were mistaken, there can be no doubt that the NTSWJ and CWWN more accurately represent Nee's original intent.

Further context also helps to explain the apparent digression on having right judgments at the end of the passage. Lin's notes, the NTSWJ, and the CWWN all unanimously record that the next section of Nee's talk had to do with making right judgments. In the notes, this transition is rather abrupt. Thus, it appears that the editors of the NTSWJ and CWWN attempted to smooth over this larger transition, just as much of their editorial work smooths over smaller transitions between sentences and phrases throughout the passage. The editors removed the general and somewhat inconsistent phrase "soul, mind" and replaced it with a reference to the mind, emotion, and will, which, for Nee, were the three component parts of the human soul. Since for Nee, the will was the soulish faculty involved in making decisions, the whole passage now leads more naturally to Nee's next point.

I chose this passage as it presents something of a worst-case scenario for the NTSWJ and CWWN. The text was composed from fragmented, handwritten notes. The editors converted these notes that were composed of Chinese with scattered English phrases into one entirely Chinese document and then one entirely English one. The editors had to do considerable work smoothing out transitions and making the passage readable and coherent. In the end, however, the reader of the edited passage may have a better sense of Nee's original speaking and intention than can be derived from the choppy notes, which contain at least one major error.

The additional phrases and clauses may not be exact representations of Nee's original utterances, but they embody a good-faith attempt at recreating them, even at the cost of being repetitive. It should be noted that Nee himself had a stylistic tendency to explain concepts repetitively, working in much the same way as the editors of the NTSWJ and CWWN. In the works that Nee himself wrote and edited, he tended to present a concept, repeat it, consider it from slightly different perspectives, and then slowly transition to his next, closely related topic, as we can see him doing here.

Fortunately, only a portion of the NTSWJ and CWWN were based on handwritten notes, which were then subjected to the editorial process established here. In addition, most of those other handwritten notes were more complete and thorough than this instance of Lin's notes. Much of the remainder of the NTSWJ and CWWN were based on Nee's published and written materials. Those were much more straightforward reprints of the originals, with very minor editing required, and can be considered, for all intents and purposes, primary documents from Nee's own hand.

Having reviewed a number of archival photocopies of handwritten notes such as the one reproduced here, I concluded that the editorial changes of the NTSWJ and CWWN had been made with the meticulous care that one would expect of Nee's devoted followers, who have significant interests in maintaining fidelity to his ideas and intentions. Since the original source materials are inaccessible and difficult to work with, the NTSWJ and CWWN can stand in as valuable resources for scholars interested in Nee's thought. Especially in terms of Nee's continuing influence and the reception history of his teachings, the NTSWJ and CWWN may be more valuable than the original notes themselves, since contemporary followers of Nee know him entirely through his published works.

For the purposes of this book, I decided between the NTSWJ and the CWWN based on the original language of Nee's speaking and publication. Thus, this book overwhelmingly uses the NTSWJ and only occasionally cites the CWWN. The translations from the NTSWJ into English are my own.

Bibliography

Alford, Henry. *The New Testament for English Readers*. Cambridge: Deighton, Bell, 1868.

Austin-Sparks, Theodore. "Editorial." *A Witness and a Testimony*, January–February, 1933.

Bai Shuqian and Bai Xinlai, in discussion with author, January 2014.

Bebbington, David. *Evangelicalism in Modern Britain: A History from the 1730s to the 1980s*. New York: Routledge, 2004.

Barthélémy, Marc. "De l'anthropologie à l'éthique: la pensée de Watchman Nee." Master's thesis, Faculté Autonome de Théologie Protestante, 1999.

Bassett, William Clyde. "The Formulation of a Basis for Counseling from a Christian Theory of Personality as Represented by C. S. Lewis and Watchman Nee." EdD diss., University of Arkansas, 1976.

Baudraz, Olivier. "De la Sanctification selon Watchman Nee: Une analyse de son anthropologie et de sa soteriologie." Master's thesis, La Faculté Libre de Théologie Réformée d'Aix-en-Provence, 1984.

Bays, Daniel H. *A New History of Christianity in China*. Malden, MA: Wiley-Blackwell, 2012.

Beard, Steve. "Bono: The Gospel of Heaven and Hell," in *Spiritual Journeys: How Faith has Influenced Twelve Music Icons*. Chad Bonham ed. Lake Mary, FL: Relevant Media Group, 2003.

Beck, Rex G. *Shaped by Vision: A Biography of T. Austin-Sparks*. Cleveland Heights, OH: Greater Purpose Publishers, 2005.

Benedict, Ruth. *The Chrysanthemum and the Sword*. Boston, MA: Houghton Mifflin, 1946.

Bennett, James. *History of Dissenters, During the Last Thirty Years (from 1808–1838)*. London: Hamilton, Adams, 1839.

Bergrunder, Michael. "Constructing Indian Pentecostalism: On Issues of Methodology and Representation," in *Asian and Pentecostal: The Charismatic Face of Christianity in Asia*. Allan Anderson ed. Eugene, OR: Wipf and Stock, 2011.

Bitton, W. Nelson. "Report of the Proceedings of the World Missionary Conference in Edinburgh from June 13th to 23rd." *Chinese Recorder* 41 (August 1910). Quoted in Lian Xi, *Redeemed by Fire*, 35.

Borlase, Henry. "Separation from Apostasy Not Schism." *Christian Witness* 1 (1834).

Boyer, Paul. *When Time Shall Be No More: Prophecy Belief in Modern American Culture*. Cambridge, MA: The Belknap Press of Harvard University Press, 1994.

Broadbent, Edmund. *The Pilgrim Church*. Oxford: Oxford City Press, 2019.

Brown, Candy Gunther. *Global Pentecostal and Charismatic Healing*. Oxford: Oxford University Press, 2011.

Callahan, James. *Primitivist Piety: The Ecclesiology of the Early Plymouth Brethren*. Lanham, MD: Scarecrow Press, 1996.

Carlson, Ellsworth C. *The Foochow Missionaries, 1847–1880*. Cambridge, MA: Harvard University Press, 1973.

Carter, Grayson. *Anglican Evangelicals: Protestant Secessions from the Via Media, c. 1800–1850*. Oxford: Oxford University Press, 2001.

Case, Jay Riley. *An Unpredictable Gospel: American Evangelicals and World Christianity, 1812–1920*. Oxford: Oxford University Press, 2012.

Chao, Jonathan T'ien-en. "The Chinese Indigenous Church Movement, 1919–1927: A Protestant Response to the Anti-Christian Movements in Modern China." PhD diss., University of Pennsylvania, 1986.

Chen, James. *Meet Brother Nee.* Hong Kong: The Christian Publishers, 1976.

Cheung, James Mo-Oi. "The Ecclesiology of the 'Little Flock' of China Founded by Watchman Nee." Master's thesis, Trinity Evangelical Divinity School, 1966.

Chow, Alexander. *Theosis, Sino-Christian Theology and the Second Chinese Enlightenment: Heaven and Humanity in Unity.* London: Palgrave Macmillan, 2013.

Cliff, Norman Howard. "The Life and Theology of Watchman Nee, Including a Study of the Little Flock Movement Which He Founded." Master's thesis, Open University, 1983.

Confucius. "Analects." US-China Institute. Accessed on December 8, 2016. http://china.usc.edu/confucius-analects-2

Coulet, Jean-Claude. *Father Beda Chang: Witness for Unity.* Hong Kong: Catholic Truth Society, 1953.

Cox, Harvey. *Fire from Heaven: The Rise of Pentecostal Spirituality and the Reshaping of Religion in the Twenty-First Century.* Reading, MA: Addison-Wesley Publishing, 1995.

Darby, John Nelson. *The Collected Writings of John Nelson Darby.* Edited by William Kelly. Vol. 1. London: George Morrish, n.d.

Darby, John Nelson. *Synopsis of the Books of the Bible.* London: George Morrish, 1820.

Darby, John Nelson. *Synopsis of the Books of the Bible.* Addison, IL: Bible Truth Publishers, 2004.

Dieter, Melvin, Anthony Hoekema, Stanley M. Horton, J. Robertson McQuilkin, and John F. Walvoord. *Five Views on Sanctification.* Grand Rapids, MI: Zondervan Academic, 2011.

Dikötter, Frank. *The Age of Openness.* Berkeley: University of California Press, 2008.

Duara, Prasenjit. *Sovereignty and Authenticity: Manchukuo and the East Asian Modern.* Lanham, MD: Rowman and Littlefield Publishers, 2003.

Dunch, Ryan. *Fuzhou Protestants and the Making of a Modern China, 1857–1927.* New Haven: Yale University Press, 2001.

Eskridge, Larry. *God's Forever Family: The Jesus People Movement in America.* Oxford: Oxford University Press, 2013.

Flood, Gavin. *The Ascetic Self: Subjectivity, Memory, and Tradition.* Cambridge: Cambridge University Press, 2004.

Freiberger, Oliver. *Asceticism and Its Critics: Historical Accounts and Comparative Perspectives.* Oxford, Oxford University Press, 2006.

Fu, Poshek. *Passivity, Resistance, and Collaboration: Intellectual Choices in Occupied Shanghai, 1937–1945.* Stanford, CA: Stanford University Press, 1993.

Gao, Wuzhi. "Y. T. Wu: A Christian Leader Under Communism," in *Christianity in China: From the Eighteenth Century to the Present.* Daniel Bays ed. Stanford, CA: Stanford University Press, 1996.

Gardiner, A. J. *The Recovery and Maintenance of the Truth.* London: Stow Hill Bible and Tract Depot, 1951.

Goosaert, Vincent and David Palmer. *The Religious Question in Modern China.* Chicago: University of Chicago Press, 2011.

Govett, Robert. *Entrance into the Kingdom or Reward According to Works.* Miami Springs, FL: Conley & Schoettle Publishing, 1978.

Gunson, Niel. *Messengers of Grace: Evangelical Missionaries in the South Seas, 1797–1860.* Melbourne; New York: Oxford University Press, 1978.

Gwynn, R. M., E. M. Norton, and B. W. Simpson. *"T. C. D." in China: A History of the Dublin University Fukien Mission, 1885–1935. Compiled for the Mission's Jubilee.* Dublin: Church of Ireland Printing and Publishing, [1935?].

Harding, Susan Friend. *The Book of Jerry Falwell: Fundamentalist Language and Politics.* Princeton: Princeton University Press, 2000.

Hartwell, Charles. *Jubilee Notes.* Fuzhou, China: Foochow College Press, ABCFM, 1904.

Harvey, Peter. *An Introduction to Buddhism: Teachings, History and Practices.* Cambridge: Cambridge University Press, 2013.

Howes, John. *Japan's Modern Prophet: Uchimura Kanzo, 1861–1930.* Toronto: UBC Press, 2005.

Hung, Chiang-tai. *War and Popular Culture: Resistance in Modern China, 1937–1945.* Berkeley: University of California Press, 1994.

Inouye, Melissa Wei-Tsing. *China and the True Jesus: Charisma and Organization in a Chinese Christian Church.* Oxford: Oxford University Press, 2018.

Inouye, Melissa Wei-Tsing. "Miraculous Mundane: The True Jesus Church and Chinese Christianity in the Twentieth Century." PhD diss., Harvard University, 2011.

Ip, Hung-yok. *Intellectuals in Revolutionary China, 1921–1949: Leaders, Heroes and Sophisticates.* London: RoutledgeCurzon, 2005.

The Keswick Convention, Pickering and Inglis, 1938.

Kilcourse, Carl S. *Taiping Theology: The Localization of Christianity in China, 1843–64.* New York: Palgrave Macmillan, 2016.

Kinnear, Angus. *Against the Tide: The Unforgettable Story of Watchman Nee.* Wheaton, IL: Tyndale House Publishers, 1978.

Kushner, Barak. *The Thought War: Japanese Imperial Propaganda.* Honolulu, HI: University of Hawai'i Press, 2006.

Lam, Wing Hung [林榮洪]. *Shuling Shenxue: Ni Tuosheng Sixiang de Yanjiu* [Spiritual Theology: A Study of Watchman Nee's Thought]. Hong Kong: China Alliance Press, 1985.

Lan, Hua R. and Vanessa L. Fong, eds. Women in Republican China: A Sourcebook. Armonk, NY: M. E. Sharpe, 1999.

Lan, Pan-chiu and So Yuen-tai. "Mahayana Interpretation of Christianity: A Case Study of Zhang Chunyi (1871–1955)." *Buddhist-Christian Studies* 27 (2007): 67–87.

Lee, Joseph Tse-Hei. "Watchman Nee and the Little Flock Movement in Maoist China." *Church History* 74, No. 1 (March 2005): 68–96.

Lee, Witness. *Collected Works of Witness Lee.* 139 vols. Anaheim, CA: Living Stream Ministry, 2021.

Lee, Witness. *Elder's Training, Book 10, The Eldership and the God-ordained Way.* Anaheim, CA: Living Stream Ministry, 1992.

Lee, Witness. *The Genuine Ground of Oneness.* Anaheim, CA: Living Stream Ministry, 1979.

Lee, Witness. *The History of the Church and the Local Churches.* Anaheim, CA: Living Stream Ministry, 1999.

Lee, Witness. *Life-Study of Proverbs, Ecclesiastes, Song of Songs.* Anaheim, CA: Living Stream Ministry, 1995.

Lee, Witness. *Life-study of 1 & 2 Timothy, Titus, Philemon.* Anaheim, CA: Living Stream Ministry, 2001.

Lee, Witness. *Watchman Nee: A Seer of the Divine Revelation in the Present Age.* Anaheim, CA: Living Stream Ministry, 1991.

Lian, Xi. *Redeemed by Fire: The Rise of Popular Christianity in Modern China.* New Haven: Yale University Press, 2010.

Liao, Yuan-wei. "Watchman Nee's Theology of Victory: An Examination and Critique from a Lutheran Perspective." PhD diss., Luther Seminary, 1997.

Lin, Heping. *Enai Biaoben.* Accessed on October 10, 2015 at http://found-treasure.org/cht/94/page94.htm.

Lin, Jennifer. "The Secret Flock of Watchman Nee: Curiosity About a Famous Relative Becomes an Unexpected Voyage of Discovery." *The Philadelphia Inquirer Magazine,* March 12, 2000.

Link, Perry. *Mandarin Ducks and Butterflies.* Oakland, CA: University of California Press, 1981.

Liu, Yi. "Globalization of Chinese Christianity: A Study of Watchman Nee and Witness Lee's Ministry." *Asia Journal of Theology,* April, 30 (1) (2016): 96–114.

Living Stream Ministry. "Lord's Move to Africa." Accessed on July 16, 2023, at https://www.lmafrica.org/images/LMAfrica_Newsletter_April_2022_English.pdf

Living Stream Ministry. "The Ministry and the Lord's Move in Ethiopia." Accessed on July 16, 2023, at https://newsletters.lsm.org/having-this-ministry/issues/Jun2023-021/lords-move-ethiopia.html

MacCulloch, Diarmaid. *The Reformation*. New York: Penguin Books, 2003.

Mariani, Paul. *Church Militant: Bishop Kung and Catholic Resistance in Communist Shanghai.* Cambridge, MA: Harvard University Press, 2011.

Marsden, George M. *Fundamentalism and American Culture.* 2nd ed. New York: Oxford University Press, 2006.

May, Grace Ying. "Watchman Nee and the Breaking of Bread: The Missiological and Spiritual Forces That Contributed to an Indigenous Chinese Ecclesiology." ThD diss., Boston University School of Theology, 2000.

McGirr, Lisa. *Suburban Warriors: The Origins of the New American Right.* Princeton: Princeton University Press: 2015.

Miller, Andrew. *Miller's Church History.* London: Pickering and Inglis, 1974.

Mother Jones. "Bono Bites Back." Accessed on July 15, 2023, at https://www.motherjones.com/media/1989/05/bono-bites-back-0/

Nee, Watchman. *Apostolinen lähetystyö: lähetystyömme tarkastelua uuden testamentin valossa.* Pietersaari: Kaikille Luodille, 1940.

Nee, Watchman. *Chongsangjogin Kurisudo-in ui saenghwal.* Seoul: Saengmyong ui Malssumsa, 1966.

Nee, Watchman. *The Collected Works of Watchman Nee.* 62 vols. Anaheim, CA: Living Stream Ministry, 1991–1996.

Nee, Watchman. *Concerning Our Missions.* London, Witness and Testimony Publishers, 1939.

Nee, Watchman. *Etre assis, Marcher, Tenir Firme.* Paris: Impr. Vieux-S. I. P. E., 1960.

Nee, Watchman. "How I Have Changed." Accessed June 28, 2023, at http://bbs.jonahome.net/thread-79458-1-1.html

Nee, Watchman. *La iglesia normal.* Cuernavaca, Mor., TI, 1964.

Nee, Watchman. *La Liberación del Espiritu.* Buenos Aires: Logos, 1965.

Nee, Watchman. *Kirisutosha no hyojun.* Tokyo: Inochi no Kotobasha, 1961.

Nee, Watchman. *Kirisutosha no Kotei.* Tokyo: Inochi no Kotobasha, 1961.

Nee, Watchman. *Kristityn normaali elama.* Helsinki: Kuva ja sana, 1958.

Nee, Watchman. *Ni Tuosheng Wenji.* 62 vols. Taipei: Taiwan Gospel Book Room, 1993–1996.

Nee, Watchman. *Non piu io ma Cristo.* Marchirolo (VA): EUN, 1961.

Nee, Watchman. *The Normal Christian Life.* Fort Washington, PA: Christian Literature Crusade, 1957, 1960, 1961, 1963, 1966, 1967, 1969, 1970, 1973, and 1974.

Nee, Watchman. *The Normal Christian Life.* The Old-Time Gospel Hour Special Edition—Not For Sale. Fort Washington, PA: Christian Literature Crusade, 1973.

Nee, Watchman. *The Normal Christian Life.* London: Kingsway Press, 1957, 1961, 1969.

Nee, Watchman. *The Normal Christian Life.* London: Witness and Testimony Publishers, 1958, 1959.

Nee, Watchman. *The Normal Christian Life.* Mumbai: Gospel Literature Service, 1957.

Nee, Watchman. *Het Normale Christelijke Leven.* Hoenderloo: Hoenderloo's Uitgeverij en Drukkerij, 1958.

Nee, Watchman. *Das Normale Christenleben.* Wuppertal-Vohwinkel: Brockhaus, 1952.

Nee, Watchman. *Die Normale Christelike Lewe.* Roodeport: Christelike, 1961.

Nee, Watchman. *Det Normale Kristenliv.* Kbh, 1957.

Nee, Watchman. *El Obrero Cristiano Normal.* San Ignacio, Argentina: Ediciones Hebron, 1968.

Nee, Watchman. *El Obrero Cristiano Normal.* Grand Rapids, MI: Portavoz, 1968.

Nee, Watchman. *An Overall Discussion of the Spirit, the Body, and the Soul.* Shanghai: Bible Truth Depot, 1950.

Nee, Watchman. *Que Haré Senor?* San Ignacio, Argentina: Ed. Hebron, 1965.

Nee, Watchman. *Ett Rikt Kristenliv.* Orebro: OM, 1963.

Nee, Watchman. *Sentaos, Andad, Estad Firmes.* San Ignacio, Argentina: Fondo Evangelico Hebron, 1960.

Nee, Watchman. *Segrande liv.* Orebro: Libris, 1968.

Nee, Watchman. *Sidde, Vandre, Sta, En Hovedlinie i Efserbrevet.* Kbh, 1957.

Nee, Watchman. *Sit, Walk, Stand.* Fort Washington, PA: Christian Literature Crusade, 1957, 1959, 1961, 1962, 1963, 1964, 1966.

Nee, Watchman. *Sit, Walk, Stand.* London: Witness and Testimony Publishers, 1958, 1959, 1961.

Nee, Watchman. *Trons liv.* Orebro: Libris, 1970.

Nee, Watchman. *La Vie Chrétienne Normale.* Paris: Mme L. Ducommun, 1, rue Jacques-Offenbach, impr. Vieux Charles, 1961.

Nee, Watchman. *Zitten, Wandelen, Standhouden.* Hoenderloo: Hoenderloo's Uitgeverij en Drukkerij, 1957.

Nedostup, Rebecca. *Superstitious Regimes: Religion and the Politics of Modernity.* Cambridge, MA: Harvard University Asia Center, 2010.

Newton, Benjamin and Henry Borlase. *Answers to Questions Lately Considered at a Meeting, Held in Plymouth.* Plymouth: J. B. Rowe, 1834.

Ni Furen, in discussion with author, June, 2013.

Ownby, David. *Falun Gong and the Future of China.* Oxford: Oxford University Press, 2008.

Pan Qindao, in discussion with author, March 13, 2013.

Pember, George Hawkins. *Earth's Earliest Ages; and Their Connection with Modern Spiritualism and Theosophy.* London: Hodder and Stoughton, 1889.

Penn-Lewis, Jessie. *Soul and Spirit: A Glimpse into Bible Psychology.* Fort Washington, PA: The Christian Literature Crusade, n.d.

Rainbow, Gordon. "The China Episode, 1932-1935." Accessed on September 5, 2025, at www.mybrethren.org/history/hy29chin.htm.

Reetzke, James. *M. E. Barber: A Seed Sown in China.* Chicago: Chicago Bibles and Books, 2007.

Reilly, Thomas H. *The Taiping Heavenly Kingdom: Rebellion and the Blasphemy of Empire.* Seattle: University of Washington Press, 2004.

"Report of the Foreign Band 1930." 1930. Norwich Records Office (NRO) 76/82 and 76/85.

Sanneh, Lamin. *Disciples of All Nations: Pillars of World Christianity.* New York: Oxford University Press, 2008.

Schwartz, Benjamin. *The World of Thought in Ancient China.* Cambridge, MA: The Belknap Press of Harvard University Press, 1985.

Seitz, Jonathan, ed. *Liang A-Fa: China's First Preacher, 1789–1855.* Eugene, OR: Pickwick Publications, 2013.

Sell, Phillip W. "A Theological Critique of the Spiritual Life Teaching of Watchman Nee." Master's Thesis, Dallas Theological Seminary, 1979.

Spence, Jonathan D. *God's Chinese Son: The Taiping Heavenly Kingdom of Hong Xiuquan.* Princeton, NJ: Princeton University Press, 1996.

Spence, Jonathan D. *The Search for Modern China.* New York: W. W. Norton & Company, 1990.

Spicer, William Ambrose. *Our Day in the Light of Prophecy.* Washington, DC: Review and Herald Publishing Association, 1918.

Starr, Chloë. *Chinese Theology: Text and Context.* New Haven, CT: Yale University Press, 2016.

Sutton, Matthew Avery. *American Apocalypse: A History of Modern Evangelicalism.* Cambridge, MA: Harvard University Press, 2014.

Teiwes, Frederick. "Establishment and Consolidation of the New Regime." *The Cambridge History of China,* vol. 14. Cambridge: Cambridge University Press, 1987.

Thompson, Phyllis. *China: The Reluctant Exodus.* Littleton, CO: OMF International, 2000.

Triandis, H. C., R. Bontempo, M. J. Villareal, M. Asai, and N. Lucca. "Individualism and Collectivism: Cross-Cultural Perspectives on Self-Ingroup Relationships." *Journal of Personality and Social Psychology* 54 (1988): 323–338.

Wacker, Grant. *Heaven Below: Early Pentecostals and American Culture.* Cambridge, MA: Harvard University Press, 2001.

Wacker, Grant. "Travail of a Broken Family: Radical Evangelical Responses to the Emergence of Pentecostalism in America, 1906-1916," in *Pentecostal Currents in American Protestantism,* Edith L. Blumhofer, Russell P. Spittler, and Grant A. Wacker eds. Urbana, IL: University of Illinois Press, 1999.

Walls, Andrew F. *The Missionary Movement in Christian History: Studies in the Transmission of Faith.* Maryknoll, NY: Orbis Books, 2007.

Wang, Leland. "Testimony." Accessed on November 1, 2016, at http://www.joyfulheart.com/maturity/no-bible-no-breakfast.htm

Williams, Stephen. "The Contribution of Ni Tuosheng (Watchman Nee)," in *Shaping Christianity in Greater China: Indigenous Christians in Focus*, Paul Woods ed. Minneapolis, MN: Fortress Press, 2017.

Wu, Silas. *Poke Feiteng: Ni Tuosheng de Beiqiu yu Tuibian.* Boston, MA: Pishon River Publishers, 2004.

Wu, Youqi. "Interview." April 21, 2021.

Ying, Fuk-Tsang. *Fandi, Aiguo, Shuling Ren: Ni Tuosheng yu Jidutu Juhuichu Yanjiu.* Hong Kong: Christian Study Centre on Chinese Religion and Culture, 2005.

Yoon, David. "The Restored Jewish State and the Revived Roman Empire: The Transmutation of John Nelson Darby's Dispensationalism into Modern Christian Zionism." PhD diss., University of California, Los Angeles, 2010.

Zarrow, Peter. *After Empire: The Conceptual Transformation of the Chinese State, 1885–1924.* Stanford, CA: Stanford University Press, 2012

Zeggeye, Jegnaw, in discussion with author, July 16, 2023.

Ziporyn, Brook. *Evil and/or/as The Good: Omnicentrism, Intersubjectivity, and Value Paradox in Tiantai Buddhist Thought.* Cambridge, MA: Harvard University Asia Center for Harvard University Press, 2000.

Zhang, Hanbang, Zhou Fuchu, and Li Junhui. *Busi jiu busheng.* Taipei: Olive CCLM Press, 2011.

Zhang Lijiao, in discussion with author, March 13, 2013.

Zhu Rukai, in discussion with author, March 16, 2013.

Zhu Zunhong and Zhou Xiuhuan, *Li Changshou Xiansheng Xingyi.* Taipei: Guo shi guan, 2010.

Index